Theology and Scientific Knowledge

Theology and Scientific Knowledge

CHANGING MODELS OF GOD'S PRESENCE
IN THE WORLD

CHRISTOPHER F. MOONEY, S. J.

Foreword by
John E. Thiel

Afterword by
Margaret A. Farley

University of Notre Dame Press
Notre Dame and London

Grateful acknowledgment is made to the following journals for permission to reprint articles which first appeared in their pages:

Theological Studies for "Theology and Science: A New Commitment to Dialogue" in vol. 52 (1991), pp. 289–329, and for "Cybernation, Responsibility, and Providential Design," in vol. 51 (1990), pp. 286–309.

Horizons for "The Anthropic Principle in Cosmology and Theology" in vol. 21 (1994), pp. 105–29.

The Heythrop Journal for "Theology and the Heisenberg Uncertainty Principle" in vol. 34 (1993), pp. 247–73, 373–86.

Library of Congress Cataloging-in-Publication Data

Mooney, Christopher F.
    Theology and scientific knowledge : changing models of God's
presence in the world / by Christopher F. Mooney ; foreword by
John E. Thiel ; afterword by Margaret A. Farley.
        p.   cm.
    Includes bibliographical references.
    ISBN 0-268-01892-8 (alk. paper)
    1. Religion and science.   2. Providence and government of God.
3. Heisenberg uncertainity principle.   I. Title.
BL240.2.M625   1995
261.5'5—dc20   95-16517
                                                              CIP

To
Francis M. O'Connor, S.J.,
wise counselor, true friend

CONTENTS

FOREWORD

Five years before his death on September 25, 1993, after a sudden and brief illness, Christopher Mooney began to devote his reading and writing to the issues at stake in the contemporary dialogue between theology and science. Those who knew him through his published work were hardly surprised by this commitment of his extraordinary intellectual energy. His interest in the relationship between theology and science was at least implicit in his award-winning first book, *Teilhard de Chardin and the Mystery of Christ* (1964), which explored the Jesuit paleontologist's efforts to reconcile evolution on a grand scale with the Christian doctrine of sanctification. Teilhard's hopeful vision of Christ's presence to the vicissitudes of a developing universe was one to which Christopher Mooney continued to subscribe throughout his life, even if Teilhard's broad, cosmic strokes were given finer, disciplinary detail in the seven books Mooney penned subsequently.

However much Mooney's abiding interest in Teilhard appears in this, his last book, it would be a mistake to account for the concerns of *Theology and Scientific Knowledge* only by reference to the content of his first book. The simple and yet telling fact that these two Jesuits devoted their lives to the religious ideals of Ignatius Loyola offers a wider framework in which to place their particular intellectual efforts toward, in the words of Ignatius, "finding God in all things." The spirituality suggested by the Ignatian direction to the Christian life, at once mystical and practical, is reflected in the lifework of both Teilhard and Mooney. While Teilhard's cosmic scope and explicitly mystical orientation made it easier for him to address the totality of the Ignatian "all," Mooney's more nuanced and directed studies of theological anthropology, American culture, film, law, and now, here in these pages, discrete topics in scientific theory and culture, allowed him to attend to the "all" more particularly and practically through the "things" of God's creation. Even though scholars from all sorts of backgrounds address the same topics Mooney does, there is a profound sense in which his scholarship, even amid its remarkably various concerns, remains Ignatian.

And yet, whatever help its placement in Teilhardian and Ignatian contexts might lend to its fuller understanding, Christopher Mooney's work cannot be reduced to the intellectual and religious influences upon it, however important these might be. Those who knew Christopher Mooney personally, as well as through his published work, know well that it was the cast of his own person that accounted in his writings for his choice of subject matter, the perceptiveness of his analysis, the direction of his argument, and the sparkle to his prose.

In Mooney's own judgment, the single focus of his intellectual life was the religious significance of secular experience. His theological interpretation of the secular was charged with optimism and hope—an optimism and hope generated not only by the message of the Christian gospel but also by his own confidence in humanity, his commitment to the values of free choice and personal responsibility, and his willingness to see truth wherever it appeared. Years from now, scholars who could never have known him might interpret his work by concluding too quickly that this or that influence, or a constellation of them, accounted for his persistently expressed expectation that reconciliation was woven into the order of things. A truer explanation would not overlook the extent to which Christopher Mooney's own character and temperament, his confidence in and openness to the future, account for his abiding interest in Teilhard, the home he found in the Society of Jesus, and his own lifetime pursuit of the religious meaning of the secular.

All these qualities that have shaped Christopher Mooney's scholarship for the past thirty years and have led both academicians and nonacademicians to value his work so highly are present in this last book. From its opening irenic chapter on the possibilities for mutual disciplinary understanding in the new dialogue between theology and science, through its careful studies of the anthropic principle, the Heisenberg uncertainty principle, and biological evolution, to its closing chapter on divine providence in a cybernetic world, *Theology and Scientific Knowledge* offers the reader generous entry to these challenging topics and rich insight into their religious and theological dimensions. In the last lines of this book's final chapter, Christopher Mooney reflects on the relationship between God's providence and human responsibility by observing:

> This divine initiative proceeding from love, far from hurting the delicate functioning of human freedom, necessarily fosters the growth of human personality and, gradually in the course of time, the interrelationships of human community. But this meshing is as delicate as gossamer. It cannot be reduced to a mere intellectual problem. Ultimately it is an object not of probing curiosity but of reverence and adoration.

These words speak as much to their author's treatment of God's providential workings in nature in the book's middle chapters as they do to its closing discussion of God's effective presence to the human will. One cannot but agree that divine providence *ultimately* is not an object of probing curiosity. And yet, the mystery of God's providence is penultimately explored in the pages of *Theology and Scientific Knowledge* with a probing intellectual curiosity tempered by reverence at every step of the way. Such is the task of theology. May there always be theologians who accomplish it as well as Christopher Mooney.

JOHN E. THIEL
Fairfield University

ACKNOWLEDGMENTS

Had Christopher Mooney been able to bring this book to press, he would have thanked colleagues and friends who read and commented on earlier versions of the manuscript: Margaret Farley, R.S.M., Richard Mooney, John Thiel, Paul Lakeland, Evangelos Hadjimichael, and David Winn. The manuscript was typed by Teresa Delco and Edith Meyer with their usual accuracy and was carefully proofread by Helen Zeccola. The Fairfield Jesuit Community (particularly through the efforts of its rector Michael Boughton, S.J.) and the Department of Religious Studies at Fairfield University together provided an enriching atmosphere in which Christopher Mooney lived and worked. As he did in the acknowledgments to his other books, Fr. Mooney would have thanked his family, especially Cecilia and Richard Mooney, for all of their support over the years. Finally, he would have expressed his gratitude to his longtime friend Francis O'Connor, S.J., to whom he dedicated this book.

1. Theology and Science:
A New Commitment to Dialogue

In June 1988 Pope John Paul II made a remarkable statement to participants in an international conference held at the Vatican on the contemporary dialogue between theology and science. He asserted that these two large spheres of human experience and inquiry are interdependent, and that collaborative interaction ought to characterize their present relationship rather than the misunderstandings and conflict so prevalent in their past. "We need each other to be what we must be," the Pope said. "Science can purify religion from error and superstition; religion can purify science from idolatry and false absolutism. Each can draw the other into a wider world, a world in which both can flourish." He envisaged a "relational unity between science and religion," which would result not in identity or assimilation but in dynamic interchange, with each "radically open to the discoveries and insights of the other."

If such intense dialogue does not take place, he warned, then these two institutions will contribute not to the future integration of our common culture but to its fragmentation. Initiative for such dialogue, moreover, must come from the theologians, because historically they have as a group made such little effort to understand the findings of science. Now, however, they must recognize that the

> vitality and significance of theology for humanity will in a profound way be reflected in its ability to incorporate these findings. . . . The matter is urgent. Contemporary developments in science challenge theology far more deeply than did the introduction of Aristotle into Western Europe in the thirteenth century. . . . Christians will inevitably assimilate the prevailing ideas about the world, and today these are deeply shaped by science. The only question is whether they will do this critically or unreflectively, with depth and nuance or with a shallowness that debases the Gospel and leaves us ashamed before history.[1]

In spite of appeals such as this, there is general recognition today that it will not be easy to bring about this dialogue. For a number of reasons, theologians do not yet know how to deal theologically with the findings of science. On the other hand, as we shall see, scientists have been having their own problems in recent years regarding collaboration with theologians. In what follows, then, I would like to examine the functioning of these two enterprises, first the professional commitment of scientists, second that of theologians. It will then be easier for us, thirdly, to understand their mutual reluctance today to converse seriously with each other. This understanding will enable us, finally, to evaluate the dialogue itself, such as it is at present, and to ask what opportunities now exist for a more fruitful rapprochement in the future.

It is important to emphasize at the outset that my chief concern in exploring these four large areas is to understand the present possibilities for dialogue. I thus see a need to begin with some historical perspective and then to develop some sense of the obstacles to conversation. What I do not see as necessary at this point is to prescribe some theoretical framework within which to overcome these obstacles. This would take us far too deeply into the philosophy of science, a field that still interests very few scientists and theologians, even though in principle its analyses may be essential as connecting links between scientific and theological data. While mutual agreement on fundamental issues may well be what the dialogue should ultimately aim at, this cannot be its point of departure. For the initial question that puzzles the generality of scientists and theologians, in so far as they are curious about the subject at all, is whether what one group is doing can possibly have any relevance for the pursuits of the other.

Nevertheless, exploring such relevance must inevitably reveal the unspoken assumptions of both parties. Their dialogue cannot, in other words, avoid touching upon many of the theoretical concepts that have long been the province of philosophers of science. Indeed, the two groups may be in a better position to dialogue more effectively today precisely because they have already developed such implicit assumptions. I shall try to point these out as they arise in the course of our discussion, but the particular approach I take to the dialogue, as well as limitations of space, preclude elaboration of these mainly philosophical issues.

───── The Commitment of Science ─────

Let us begin by recognizing certain common misconceptions about the scientific enterprise. Three very common ones are that science starts with no presuppositions in its research, that it is based on hard and unimpeachable factual evidence, and that its findings are unalterable and will eventually explain all areas of human experience. In other words, says this stereotype, the hidden explanatory mechanisms of the world can be discovered through observation by scientists standing apart from the world and theorizing about it objectively. The problem with these misconceptions is not that they are totally false but that they are only partially true. They have been fostered almost unconsciously in the popular mind because all around us we see the extraordinary achievements of science's progeny, technology, achievements that provide for most of our physical needs and for much of our need for entertainment. Hence it is not surprising that scientific attitudes and methods should have become integral to the thinking of most contemporary men and women, many of whom conclude, not unreasonably, that these attitudes and methods are so all-encompassing and reliable as to constitute a sufficient foundation upon which to build their lives.

This conclusion is fostered today by not a few scientists who, sometimes unconsciously, inject its implications into the scientific enterprise as such. A closer examination, however, reveals these convictions to be actually outside the domain of science itself and not required by it at all. They really constitute certain ways of thinking *about* science, an ideology that has come to be known as "scientism," which demotes to the purely subjective all forms of knowledge that fail to deliver prediction and control of what is tangible and concrete. Langdon Gilkey has neatly summarized the two major suppositions of this ideology: first that science represents the *sole* cognitive entrance into reality, and second that scientific knowledge of nature exhaustively defines reality itself, so that what cannot be known by science is simply not there.[2] Jacob Bronowski's story of the "Ascent of Man" is one example of this scientific triumphalism; Carl Sagan's "Cosmos" is another. Sagan puts it bluntly: "The cosmos—as known by science—is all there is, all there was, and all there will be."[3]

It is important for us to be clear about the full implications of these ideological assumptions. In their most extreme form they deny to the knowable cosmos all subjectivity, all qualities in any way connected with human emotions and personal experience or with which the human spirit could feel some sense of kinship. All downward causation from the personal to the impersonal is thus eliminated, and everything is explained in terms of the most elementary physical processes. Because the human plays no role in the natural world, no role consequently exists for purposes, values, ideals, or freedom. Hence physicist Gerald Feinberg can refer to life simply as "a disease of matter,"[4] and psychologist B. F. Skinner can state flatly: "We cannot apply the methods of science to subject matter that is assumed to move about capriciously. . . . The hypothesis that man is not free is essential to the application of scientific method to the study of human behavior."[5]

The saddest implication of all, however, is that if all human activity, precisely as human, is devoid of any meaning, then the discoveries of science, as one of the activities of the human, must share in this meaninglessness. Nobel Prize physicist Steven Weinberg does not shrink from this conclusion: "The more the universe seems comprehensible, the more it also seems pointless. . . . The effort to understand the universe is one of the very few things that lifts human life above the level of farce, and gives it some of the grace of tragedy."[6] In scientism, then, we have the ultimate manifestation of that imperialistic tendency of science to present itself as the only genuine and exhaustive description of the real. Geneticist Jacques Monod draws the logical conclusion for humankind: "The ancient covenant is in pieces; man at last knows that he is alone in the unfeeling immensity of the universe out of which he emerged only by chance."[7]

In recent years historians of science have begun to question whether this ideology of scientism is really what undergirds the scientific enterprise. Is science as such really so value-free? Is what scientists do really so totally focused on objects, so uninfluenced by personal beliefs and subjectivity? Consider, for example, the massive resistance of the scientific community a few decades ago to the discovery that the universe is expanding at enormous speeds of millions of miles an hour, and that this and other confirmatory evidence indicate that billions of years ago there has to have been some gigantic cosmic explosion that marked the birth of the universe. One physicist trivialized this theory by calling it "the big bang," as if the cosmos were a gigantic firecracker. Einstein was upset simply because the theory implied that the world had a beginning. "The circumstance of an expanding universe is irritating," he wrote in a letter to a fellow physicist. "To admit such possibilities seems senseless to me."[8] The great British astrophysicist Sir Arthur Eddington complained that "the notion of a beginning is repugnant to me. . . . The expanding universe is preposterous."[9]

The reactions of many astronomers at the time, wrote one astronomer recently, "provide an interesting demonstration of the response of the scientific mind—supposedly a very objective mind—when evidence uncovered by science itself leads to a conflict with the articles of faith in our profession. It turns out that the scientist behaves the way the rest of us do when our beliefs are in conflict with the evidence."[10] The root problem here is that the majority of scientists find it extremely difficult to deal with a natural phenomenon whose causes apparently cannot be explained. Hence the initially strong resistance of many to the discovery that the cosmos very likely did have a beginning, under conditions in which the present laws of physics are not valid and as a product of forces which are as yet unknown. This quasi religious faith in the power to understand is well illustrated by the following assertion of Nobel Prize physicist Sheldon Glashow:

> We believe that the world is knowable, that there are simple rules governing the behavior of matter and the evolution of the universe. We affirm that there are external, objective, extrahistorical, socially neutral, external and universal truths and that the assemblage of these truths is what we call physical science. Natural laws can be discovered that are universal, invariable, inviolate, genderless and verifiable. . . . This statement I cannot prove, this statement I cannot justify. This is my faith.[11]

Beyond these candid remarks of scientists themselves, we should note that philosophers of science have long distinguished between the instrumental success of science (whereby it provides correct expectations about the workings of the natural world) and scientific theories (whereby scientists claim to describe this natural world comprehensively and realistically). The former deals with the value-neutral grounds for nature's control and for successful predictions regarding our natural environment. The latter, in contrast, often tend to conflict with each other, and are frequently undermined by further empirical investigation. The norm for truth of instrumental science would thus seem to be whether or not it corresponds to the physical world of nature. The norm for the truth of a scientific theory, on the other hand, cannot be such empirical correspondence (since multiple theoretical interpretations may fit any given set of accepted facts), but rather whether or not it coheres with the total relevant context and achieves consensus among scientists themselves, a process characterized by judgments of value as well as of fact.[12]

This distinction has been the source of a number of contemporary challenges to the presumed impersonal "objectivity" of scientific theories, insofar as these lay claim to the prestige of empirical science. Studies have revealed in striking ways the extent to which seemingly objective theories are both culture-dependent and subject-dependent. Science as a whole is now coming to be seen as a far more relativistic project, influenced to a considerable extent by social ideologies and attitudes. Its imperialistic claim to be the single road to certain knowledge has thus been largely eroded, and it is increasingly being viewed as just one of the ways in which humans have sought to make sense of their world. Scientific theories seek answers to practical questions in particular historical circumstances, just like theories in all other areas of human knowing. Often this is done for purposes that are not exclusively scientific, but are also social, moral, political, and economic as well.

In his influential 1962 study, *The Structure of Scientific Revolutions*,[13] Thomas Kuhn, a theoretical physicist turned historian of science, focused on those rare moments when major changes occur in the world views of scientists. These world views he calls "paradigms," clusters of broad suppositions, both conceptual and methodological, which constitute the "received tradition" of a given scientific community and dictate the norms for good science and the direction of research at any particular historical period. Through paradigms, scientific communities define and limit the types of question that can be asked as well as the types of solution that are acceptable. During long periods of "normal science" knowledge advances by the application of these key concepts and large methodological assumptions to observed phenomena. But unexpected findings can produce sudden shifts in prevailing paradigms, and these intellectual upheavals have such far-reaching effects that they constitute a scientific revolution. Obvious examples would be the shift from a Ptolemaic model of the universe to a Copernican model, and the displacement of Newton's mechanistic model of the interaction of matter and energy by those of relativity and quantum theory.

Kuhn's major point, however, is that there is really very little logical connection between any two paradigms; the choice between them is not dictated by any objective rules. A new paradigm is produced not by data but by intuition, and it then so transforms the imagination of the scientific community that old data come to be seen in a completely new light. Even the meaning of terms changes as in the switch from Newtonian physics to relativity, in which terms like "time," "mass," and "velocity" came to be understood quite differently. Paradigm shifts are therefore really conversion experiences on the part of scientists. This conversion must occur at once or not at all, says Kuhn, for the simple reason that the paradigms themselves are basically incommensurable and even contradictory.

New paradigms explain dimensions of reality that old paradigms do not. Adherence to these new insights is so problematic precisely because their acceptance cannot be forced by logical proofs or neutral experience. Young scientists generally embrace the new paradigm and perpetuate it within their community; the older generation lose the struggle for dominance of the original paradigm, but continue to follow it nonetheless until they eventually die off. For Kuhn, then, paradigm shifts are like political revolutions: they clash with vested interests and they take place outside normal methods of change. In many ways they are, as one critic calls them, the equivalent of "scientific mob rule."[14]

Understandably scientists have been reluctant to follow Kuhn in equating science as a social system (within which scientists function under community pressures) with science as a cognitive system (in which data ought to be value-free and governed by logic and experiment).[15] Nevertheless, it is widely accepted today that the two systems cannot be completely separated. The way the scientific community thinks at the time of a paradigm shift, its social goals, and other historical circumstances are not simply superficial manifestations of the change that is taking place but to some limited extent also its cause. This is not to say, however, as Kuhn seems to imply, that the causes of paradigm shifts are neither rational nor objective. Unfortunately it is not always clear, in his critique of these shifts, whether he is referring to the sociology of scientific communities or to the epistemology of scientific discovery. Continuities and overlap are clearly evident between certain paradigms: physicists agree, for example, that Newton's mechanics are the slow-moving equivalent of Einstein's mechanics, and that they still remain valid for systems whose velocities are tiny compared to the velocity of light. Moreover, to hold that all observations are theory-laden, and so subject to social distortion, is not to say that they exert no control at all over theories. For theories themselves are also fact-laden. They must therefore submit to the correctives that come through the continuous testing of objective data in different social contexts over many years, procedures which have always characterized scientific method.[16]

Nevertheless, scientists as subjects can no longer be thought of as somehow separated from the objects they study. Their observations, as well as the concepts and models they develop to understand these observations, are interrelated in much more subtle ways than the popular image of science allows. It is therefore not the case that unquestionable experimental facts lead to exact predictions and then to theories that objectively and comprehensively describe the material world. For science is before all else personal knowledge, something going on in persons. The skill of the knower is always present along with the object known. The scientist thus assesses evidence and formulates theories in the same way that a doctor makes a difficult diagnosis, or a judge weighs ambiguous evidence, or a wine taster blends a good sherry. Intellectual beauty, symmetry and simplicity are as operative in these choices as are empirical data. "But just as the sherry blender has to submit the result of his labors to the judgment of the discerning public, so the scientist has to persuade his colleagues of the soundness of his judgment. This necessity saves personal knowledge from degenerating into mere idiosyncrasy."[17]

This socially contextualized and personalistic coefficient in scientific knowledge has prompted many scientists to reconsider how accurately they can know reality, and even whether they have any right to speak about knowing reality at all. The chief catalyst for both reconsiderations has clearly been the discovery of the subatomic world. Long a puzzle to physicists, this world of elusive entities has now become the dominant focus of their thought and experiment. Early in the century Werner Heisenberg formulated his famous uncertainty principle: the more accurately we know about one half of this world (the location of particles) the less we know about the other half (what these particles are doing). While the source of this mysterious indeterminism is not yet known (it could be instrumental, epistemological, or ontological), the knowledge-limitation itself is experimentally certain and its consequence clear: no absolute predictions can be made about the total behavior of anything in the microworld.

Picturability has therefore been lost, and rigid mechanistic causality is now recognized as impossible at this level. None of the entities can be known in itself but only in its relation to the observer. All such observations are thus radically observer-dependent. Niels Bohr once remarked, when a student of his in Copenhagen complained that quantum mechanics made him giddy, "If anybody says he can think about quantum problems *without* getting giddy, that only shows he has not understood the first thing about them."[18] Years later Nobel laureate Richard Feynman made the same admission: "I think it safe to say that no one understands quantum mechanics. Do not keep saying to yourself, if you can possibly avoid it, 'But how can it be like that?' because you will go 'down the drain' into a blind alley from which nobody has yet escaped. Nobody knows how it can be like that."[19]

Many scientific positivists would go one step further than Feynman and say that all this talking about entities not accessible to experience is just a conceptual tool to facilitate prediction of phenomena. Such theories are neither true nor false, they say, but simply convenient ways to summarize and harmonize the experimental data available to everyone. What scientists actually see, in other words, are just numbers on computer screens or marks on photographic plates. Besides, how can theories developed from these data possibly represent existing realities, when it is clear that science has changed its mind so often in the past about the basic structure of the universe? When scientists construct models for the subatomic world (i.e., analogies between the behavior of entities on the macrolevel and the behavior of quantum particles), no one doubts the value of the model for purposes of theory. But why must we presume that the theory represents actual existing particles?[20] Here the positivist is not far from the idealist: a theory is simply a mental construct that the scientist imposes upon the chaos of experimental data in order to achieve some modicum of understanding.

These discussions of the relationship of scientific theories to truth and reality have over the last generation moved the scientific community as a whole very far from that naive realism that celebrated a mechanistic view of the world. Today most scientists are more modest in their truth claims about the physical world. Their goal is no longer certain knowledge but only verisimilitude, a slow but progressively more accurate understanding, a gradual tightening of their grip on a reality that they have come to realize will always elude them in its totality. They still seek the truth about nature, but now they are fully aware that what they seek is often selected to accord with their presuppositions and prejudices. "Recognition that science has discovered a wide range of truths is compatible with the conviction that a wide range of truths it has *not* discovered exists, and that its formulations of the truths it *has* discovered are one-sided, presenting only abstractions from the full truth."[21]

Scientists today are thus conscious of the accuracy of the famous parable told by Sir Arthur Eddington in 1929. It concerned a zoologist who decides to study deep-sea life by using a net of ropes on a two-inch mesh. After repeatedly lowering his net and each time studying what he caught, he concludes that there are no deep-sea fish less than two inches in length. Obviously the zoologist's method of fishing determined what he could catch. In the same way, science may still aim at knowing the real, but because it selects only publicly observable sense data, and because its abstract theories about these data are so limited by both culture and subjectivity, it is now no longer possible for scientists to claim that reality is only what they know.[22]

To what then are scientists committed in their pursuit of intelligibility? Quite simply to experimentation. It is experimental work that provides the strongest evidence today for scientific realism. For scientists cannot organize an experiment without believing that its object exists. While their beliefs *about* a particular object may undergo very significant change over time, they cannot even begin to organize any of their observations without asserting the object's existence. This has always been true, even when the object has not been observable. The electron is a good example. Kuhn would say that, when it was first discussed before 1900 in the context of classical physics, it had a meaning and significance radically different from its new status in quantum theory. But physicists today still use the same word to speak of what they presume is the same entity, even though they now remain more open to new ways of understanding its precise nature.[23]

Hence the realism scientists assert in practice is about entities, not about concepts, models or theories. The latter tend to be thought of much more frequently as "candidates for reality," with which scientists still aim to unlock the secret structures of nature, but about which they remain always skeptical, without any of those illusions of permanence so confidently claimed by the naive realism of the past. "There is no quicker way for a scientist to bring discredit upon himself and upon his profession," writes the eminent British zoologist Peter Medawar, "than roundly to declare . . . that science knows or soon will know the answers to all questions worth asking, and that questions which do not admit a scientific answer are in some way nonquestions or 'pseudoquestions' that only simpletons ask and only the gullible profess to be able to answer."[24]

This new "critical realism" is an acknowledgment by scientists that they know reality only imperfectly, and that their search for truth is always influenced by personal judgment. This search is also subject over time to continual public scrutiny, however, and this is what eventually provides the true test of its capacity to cope with new data and predict new phenomena. In other words, by criticizing competing theories we can steadily approximate objective truth. It is precisely this rational staying power of the scientific enterprise that finally yields genuine verisimilitude. Models and theories may indeed only approximate the real world, but with each new approximation science's grip on this world is tightened ever so slightly. For science is a way of thought, not merely a body of knowledge, and scientists now readily admit that the way they think has its own built-in limitation. Such contemporary modesty in truth claims has also had an unexpected result: many scientists in recent years have begun to listen with more respect to other truth claims about the real world, especially to those proposed by the insights of contemporary theology.

—— THE COMMITMENT OF THEOLOGY ——

When we turn now to the professional commitment of theologians, it is important to distinguish at the outset between religious faith experience and the intellectual reflection upon that experience which is the theologian's concern. "Faith seeking understanding" is the classic definition of theology. Hence the presupposition of the theological enterprise is that there is an identifiable sphere of human interaction with reality which results in a sense of the Absolute that transcends sense perception. In the case of Christians this is the central religious experience of God's self-disclosure through the revelatory events of the Bible. This initiative of God reconciled them, they believe, to God's own self, to others and to themselves, through the life, death, and resurrection of Jesus of Nazareth, who lived on the Jewish periphery of the Roman empire some two thousand years ago. In the person of Jesus they find the fullness of God and the decisive key to the meaning of human existence. This union with God in Jesus is mediated for them historically through the Christian Scriptures and through the teachings and sacramental rituals of the Christian faith community.

Christian theologians thus have a threefold data base on which to rest their intellectual analysis: the biblical narratives as testimony of the earliest witnesses to God's self-revelation, the tradition and worship of the Christian churches over the centuries, and the contemporary experience and life commitment of believing Christians. Theological analysis then seeks to explore, often with the aid of secular disciplines, the cognitive aspects of this total faith experience, which obviously includes other important aspects, such as those that are historical, social, liturgical, and institutional. The starting point is the fact that, from biblical times to the present, the Christian community has never doubted that it is truly in touch with a transcendent dimension of reality, that it encounters God living and operating here and now in the lives of its members. This type of experience is not limited to Christians, of course. William James concluded his seminal work on religious psychology at the turn of the century with an affirmation of its universal character; and Rudolf Otto's classic study of the "numinous" element in all religion shows it to be everywhere an awareness of mystery, majesty, and fascination.[25]

But what the theologian wants to know is the extent to which this experiential component, involving as it does existential decision and a total commitment of one's life, can indeed be captured in concepts and propositions. When will such cognitive formulations be more than purely subjective preference or personal taste? In what sense can they be said to communicate objective truth for the knower? For even though religious language normally functions in the contexts of worship and life-orientation, it nevertheless contains assertions about *what* one worships and to *what* one is oriented.[26] These assertions may not be verifiable experimentally, but religious people still believe that they have an objective reference, and that reasons can be advanced for holding them to be true. Thus the theological task of understanding and evaluating these cognitive claims of religion cannot be avoided.

Theological interpretation of biblical texts has had a checkered history. Premodern theology was certainly not hermeneutically naive in dealing with this first data base. Interpretative categories had long existed in the allegorical exegesis of Origen, Augustine, and Aquinas. In the religious turmoil of the sixteenth and seventeenth centuries, however, rigidity and authoritarianism was the order of the day for both Protestants and Catholics, and as a result biblical literalism generally prevailed. This was exemplified most blatantly in the public condemnation of Galileo in 1633. While knowledgeable people at the time were well aware of the deficiencies of geocentrism and attracted to the heliocentric theory of Copernicus, the Catholic Church had a special problem. For this geocentric cosmology had come to be identified with religious orthodoxy: it was part of that Aristotelian worldview within which all medieval theology had been constructed, and it was supported by a literal reading of biblical texts dealing with the heavens. Thus Galileo's repeated public proclamation that he had proved Copernican theory to be a fact (which even his supporters acknowledged he had not) appeared to be a threat to orthodoxy that had to be publicly eliminated.[27]

Such an authoritarian approach to biblical texts eventually had to face the stringency of the Enlightenment critique which took into account the autonomy of human reason. This proved to be a watershed that changed the whole direction of biblical hermeneutics, since until then theologians had assumed that religious faith always had to act as reason's guide. Tools of language and textual criticism were now taken much more seriously, and by the end of the nineteenth century, when the discovery of evolution seemed once again to contradict the Christian scriptures, biblical scholars were able to offer Church authorities more constructive ways to deal with the challenge than were available in the time of Galileo.

While biblical literalism still flourishes today among fundamentalist Christians, mainly as a source of certainty in a time of moral relativism and rapid cultural change, Roman Catholicism has abandoned it, as well as all mainline Protestant churches. For the scholarly analysis of scriptural texts has shown that the biblical writers believed themselves to be recording not infallible divine dictation, but rather events in their lives which they experienced as revelatory of God's presence, as in the history of Israel, for example, or in the person of Jesus. Hence most Christian theologians no longer think of their Scriptures as the ahistorical revelation of God, but as a divine revelation mediated by time and circumstance, whose meaning develops in the course of history. The biblical witness must inevitably be partial and limited, experienced and reported by fallible witnesses, as well as influenced by the thought forms of a particular historical period. Because there is no such thing as uninterpreted experience, there can therefore be no such thing in the Bible as an uninterpreted revelation of God.[28]

Just as Christian theology became progressively more open and tentative in regard to its understanding of Scripture, its first data base, so it also developed new attitudes toward its second base, the formal, doctrinal teachings of the living Christian tradition. Protestantism and Roman Catholicism followed very different paths, however, in reaching such new understandings. Liberal Protestant theologians of the nineteenth century, led by Friedrich Schleiermacher, initially sought ways to formulate traditional Christian doctrines in light of the then-current concerns of Scripture scholars for the human character of the biblical record. But their efforts gradually led them to deemphasize the revelatory character of the Bible altogether, and to derive their theological reflection on Christian faith primarily from an interpretation of religious experience. To this was added a strong reliance on philosophical reflection and ethical consciousness as important sources for our knowledge of God. But such increased emphasis on the human as an object of inquiry inevitably meant that there would be less and less place for Scripture and church tradition.

The neoorthodoxy of Karl Barth reacted strongly against this liberal Protestant neglect of historical revelation. Only God's self-disclosure, insisted Barth, not the human search for God, can be the starting point for theology. Christians must therefore recognize a radical discontinuity between God and God's revelation on the one hand, and human reason and culture on the other. God is totally transcendent to human persons, and this gap cannot be bridged from the human side, but only through God's coming in Jesus Christ. This insistence on the primacy of revelation, moreover, went hand in hand with a general acceptance by Barth of the results of critical biblical scholarship, which convinced him that the Bible speaks only of human creatureliness, sinfulness, and dependence on God, and says nothing at all about nature or cosmology or human cultural achievement. The human person, as the present receiver and interpreter of revelation, was consequently ignored and the capacity of reason correspondingly devalued. Human experience at particular points in history had relatively little importance; revelatory events of the past alone had true religious significance.[29]

Neoorthodoxy provoked its own reaction. The movement known as Christian existentialism put exclusive emphasis on contemporary experience and individual self-understanding: God can be encountered only in the immediacy of a personal relationship. The most influential of these theological existentialists, Rudolf Bultmann, insisted that to speak of God's activity as if it were somehow objective in historical events, as the Bible seems to do, is mythological. None of the events grounding traditional Christian teaching were really observable; they were all interior events of rebirth and transformation of the heart. The question to be asked by theology, therefore, is how this mythical imagery of Scripture can be translated into language about one's own existential situation and about new possibilities for one's life here and now. The Christian message, in other words, refers not to objective happenings in the past but exclusively to new understandings of ourselves and to a present transformation of our lives. These God accomplishes in us in the midst of the hope, despair, fear, and decision of our historical existence.[30]

Obviously the problem with Christian existentialism is not its concern for the personal lives and experiences of Christians, since these phenomena form the third data base on which contemporary theology rests its intellectual analysis. The problem is rather that existentialism as a theological approach totally privatizes Christianity, separating it from its historical community structures as well as from its belief that its traditional doctrines, however interpreted, are truth claims about objective realities. This is not to say that the religious practices of Christians cannot be understood as a way of life, or a set of attitudes and strategies for moral living, since this is obviously the way Christians speak about them. What constitutes the existentialist position, however, is a reliance on these experiences and practices that tends often to ignore the key historical role of doctrinal truth, the confession of which has always been central to Christian life.

Unlike Protestantism, Roman Catholicism dealt in a much more authoritative fashion with the implications of modern biblical criticism for traditional doctrinal teaching. Until the end of the nineteenth century, the study of the Bible had relatively low status in Catholic intellectual circles. But, as Catholic scholars gradually sought to acclimatize church teachings to the modern world, they began to use the same historical-critical methods as liberal Protestants in their search for a scientifically sound approach to Scripture. The reaction of Pius X to these intellectual efforts was repressive and harsh, less because of any particular doctrinal formulations (almost all of which are commonplace today) than because he perceived an implicit threat to church authority in the attempt to make scientific study the arbiter of religious truth. In 1907 he labeled all the efforts of these widely diverse scholars "Modernism" and condemned the movement en bloc as heresy.

Hence in the Roman Catholic Church there was never any specifically theological response to the so-called Modernist crisis comparable to the neoorthodox reaction to liberal Protestantism. The response was rather one of pure disciplinary authority, motivated by a need for submission, theological uniformity, and institutional stability. By 1910 the nascent Catholic intellectual elite was silenced, and all free theological inquiry and innovation effectively suppressed. A certain fundamentalist mentality now took over, ecclesiastical as well as biblical. It was not until 1943 that Catholic scholars were at last allowed to apply scientific methods to the study of Scripture, and not until the Second Vatican Council in the 1960s that official Catholic theology finally internalized the problems of modernity and responded to the "Modernist" challenge with genuinely theological argument.[31]

As we come to the end of the twentieth century, then, Protestantism has provided some badly needed correctives for Catholicism's rationalizing tendency, which usually overdeveloped the importance of neat propositional statements. Nevertheless, because theology's perennial thrust is for intelligibility, the issues of revelation and truth will not go away. The question theologians are now faced with, consequently, whether they be Protestant or Catholic, is how precisely to deal with these issues in the

future. Obviously the first step is to be aware of the limitations of one's
conceptual tools. Only fundamentalist Christians repudiate such limitations today. We have already noted some of these limitations as they have
affected our understanding of the biblical texts. Let us see now how these
conceptual tools are further restricted by the inevitable need of theology
to employ models and paradigms.

Theologians have come to recognize in recent years that their language
is much less scientific and much more metaphorical than previously realized, as well as much richer in those systematic and relatively permanent
metaphors called models. The awareness of Arthur Peacocke is typical:
"The model of God as personal, transcendent Creator, immanent in and
transforming his creation and especially man, i.e., of God as Creator, Re-
deemer, Sanctifier, is a root-metaphor which has a comprehensive role at
the summit of a hierarchy of theological models and metaphors expli-
cating religious experience."[32] Though less conceptually precise than
doctrines, religious models have always had a strong affective function,
evoking moral and spiritual response, commitment, and self-involvement,
especially in Christian liturgy. Thus God is referred to as Father, Mother,
Creator, Shepherd, Judge; Jesus as Christ, Son of God, King, Savior; the
Holy Spirit as Comforter and Advocate. Even abstract religious concepts
like "transcendent" and "immanent" contain a spatial metaphor.

Nevertheless, this Christian faith experience of God's self-disclosure
and personal relationship to us in Jesus clearly contains beliefs *about* God
and *about* the relationship. These beliefs *in* inevitably involve statements
that. While truly cognitive, these theological statements are not explicitly
descriptive, however, because the reality of God is simply beyond the capacity of language to express. As the parables of Jesus suggest, we are able
to speak of God only by analogy. This is because the religious encounter
is so open: there is no way to specify in advance or to control the experience. Because meaning is to be found exclusively in the event itself, it can
be captured only by symbol. Such cognition must always be partial and
inadequate, and yet it is precisely this gap between symbol and referent
that gives the theologian room for maneuver in making propositional
statements.[33] All words used in such statements must therefore inevitably
fall short of the concepts they signify.

If this limitation on religious language is so clear to theologians today,
what have they to offer in defense of the claim that such language actually
catches reality? Are religious models just useful fictions, whose only function is to express and evoke a certain psychological attitude or ethical

response? The answer would seem to lie in the crucial distinction between referring to God and describing God. A critical realism would say that a model comes into existence originally in order to help an individual or community to interpret an event or experience by imagining what cannot be observed. Subsequently linguistic communities and interpretative traditions perpetuate the model, thereby guaranteeing a continuity of reference and protecting the model against arbitrariness and distortion. Hence there is, as Ian Barbour notes, a genuine intersubjective testing among members of any given religious community. "The interpretation of initiating events, formative experiences, and subsequent individual and communal experiences goes through a long process of testing, filtering, and public validation in the history of the community. Some experiences recur and are accepted as normative, others are reinterpreted, ignored or discounted."[34] The more recurrent and widespread the experiences in question, the more secure the reference and hence the reality.

However, such intersubjective testing has its limitations. Janet Soskice makes the point well: "To be a realist about the referent is to be a fallibilist about knowledge of the referent. . . . So the theist may be mistaken in his beliefs *about* the source and cause of all. . . . for fixing a referent does not on this account guarantee that the referent meets a particular description."[35] Christian theology, in other words, tends too easily to forget that there is an "is not" in all metaphor. The confident personal witness and affirmation of God's self-revelation, therefore, does not mean that the reflective understanding and verbal expression of this knowledge can be anything more than approximate. These theological formulations, moreover, because they are to a large extent critical reflections on the life and thought of Christians at a particular time, will always be revisable, subject to a process of testing by the community. Nor is such revision a negative factor in the search for intelligibility. "Rational argument in theology," says Ian Barbour, "is not a single sequence of ideas, like a chain that is as weak as its weakest link. Instead, it is woven of many strands, like a cable many times stronger than its strongest strand."[36]

Not only is theological discourse limited by the use of models, however; it is also limited because, just like scientific discourse, it must take place within a certain paradigm, a certain broad set of metaphysical and methodological assumptions. Hans Küng has helped to show how Kuhn's analysis of historic changes in the world views of science can be applied also to theology.[37] Like "normal science," "normal theology" is generally conservative. Traditional questions and modes of thought are passed on by

particular theological communities; young theologians are initiated into
these community practices and do their theological work in the context
of community expectations. Before a paradigm change actually takes
place, there is a transitional period of uncertainty, during which normal
theology gets challenged, usually provoking strong reaction and resistance
to whatever might alter the status quo. The growing crisis finally peaks,
and eventually a sudden breakthrough takes place for a new interpretative
framework.

Küng lists five major paradigm changes in the history of Christian theology: from the apocalyptic paradigm of primitive Christianity to the
Hellenistic paradigm of the patristic period, and from there to the Augus-
tinian paradigm, the medieval Thomistic paradigm, the Reformation
Protestant and the Counter-Reformation Catholic paradigms, and finally
to the critical Enlightenment paradigm. This latter is presently being challenged by a contemporary ecumenical paradigm, according to Küng, the
full dimensions and implications of which are not yet known. Representatives of various traditional theologies, moreover, still cling to and
work within older paradigms: Orthodox within the Hellenistic paradigm,
fundamentalist Protestants within the Reformation paradigm, Roman
Catholics within the Counter-Reformation paradigm, and liberal Protestants within the Enlightenment paradigm. Because each of these paradigms arose in a specific time of crisis and uncertainty (such as the rise of
science during the Enlightenment), a long period of normal work and cumulative growth inevitably followed once the crisis had passed, in which
the scope of the paradigm was extended and all major changes resisted.

Küng takes pains to emphasize that in the course of each of these
paradigm shifts there is a root conceptual stability in the midst of comprehensive conceptual change, a continuity in the midst of discontinuity.
For the effort is always to reformulate the original tradition, not to re-
discover it: to communicate a fresh experience of the original biblical
message of God's self-revelation in Jesus. Within whatever paradigm
it takes place, therefore, Christian theology is always an effort to think
through what is believed to be the truth of the Christian faith. What is
distinctive about the present theological crisis is that so many cultural factors are also involved: secularization, religious pluralism, racism, sexism,
the turmoil of developing nations, the ambiguity of science and technology, environmental problems, and the threat of nuclear war. The experiences of women and of the Third World of being exploited, for

example, have been contributing for some time now to the correction of many endemic biases in the classical theological tradition.[38]

We have been discussing models and paradigm shifts in theology because we are trying better to understand the contemporary commitment of theologians to articulate the Christian faith experience. This commitment is worlds apart from the popular stereotype of theologians as closed-minded ideologues rigidly defending propositional statements which they expect all Christians to follow without question. For all these conceptualizations of God's revelation in Christ are now recognized as no less "candidates for reality" than the theories and models of science. All earlier theological models, based on historical and authoritarian understandings of beliefs, have by and large collapsed today, except in the minds of biblical or ecclesiastical fundamentalists. Naive realism has yielded to a sense of the complexity and tentative character of most theological issues, and all easy solutions risk looking like so many efforts to preserve the status quo. Theological understandings are coming rather to be seen as time-bound efforts to translate a historical message from the world of past experience to the world of the present. In short, theologians have as a group been experiencing for some time now a genuine modesty in regard to both what they know and how they know it. Their enterprise of understanding reality has therefore turned out to be as corrigible as that of science.[39]

―――― OBSTACLES TO CONVERSATION ――――

In these commitments of science and theology can be seen, I think, the two major contemporary efforts to grapple with and rationally to organize the human experience of reality. Although concerned with radically different subject matter (revelation in history has no parallel in science), the ultimate quest of each is for intelligibility rather than for the generation of observable data. Alfred North Whitehead, philosopher as well as mathematician, saw this relationship clearly: "The dogmas of religion are the attempts to formulate in precise terms the truths disclosed to the religious experience of mankind. In exactly the same way the dogmas of physical science are the attempts to formulate in precise terms the truths discovered by the sense perceptions of mankind."[40] A skeptical and qualified realism, moreover, has become the working assumption of by far the majority of scientists and theologians. The epistemology of science differs from that of theology, but, as we have seen, a common sociology of knowledge, arising from the dynamics of history and culture, can both critique and illumine the efforts of each.[41]

It would seem, then, that dialogue between these two intellectual enterprises should not only be possible but even welcomed. What proves to be intelligible in their observations is applied by science to prediction and control of nature, and by theology to questions of life's ultimate meaning, to the worship of God, and to personal responsibility. Hence theology tends naturally to use more "actor" language, science more "spectator" language. (As we saw, however, science has a much more human face than the popular stereotype allows.) The interaction of the two should consequently reveal a certain complementarity rather than conflict. For both are concerned with nature and the cosmos, the one as lawful structure, the other as related to God and to humankind. One would think that theology ought to be attentive to all discoveries of nature's structure, and that science ought to be open to hear with respect whatever theology has to say about relating these discoveries to the larger and more complex area of religious experience. We should expect, in other words, some fruitful exchange along the lines suggested by John Paul II.

Yet it is only with extreme reluctance that scientists and theologians can get themselves to speak with each other today, and it is important for us to understand why. Let us begin with theology. There is a certain legacy from the past here that is difficult to overcome, occasioned by the transition in the West from a medieval mentality to the modern critical mentality engendered by the Renaissance and solidified by the Enlightenment. The Christian churches generally resisted this transition, and finally adapted to it only after the new methodologies of philosophy and the natural sciences gained sufficient status and prestige. In the meantime, church authorities often overstepped the boundaries of theology to make pronouncements on questions that were answerable only in scientific terms and about which they totally lacked competence. Religious resistance to the heliocentric system of Copernicus thus lasted a long time, as did religious insistence that the evolution of living beings could not be true because it contradicted the account of creation in Genesis. Biological emergence of humans from animals was denied for over a century, and as late as 1950 the Catholic Church was still insisting officially that all humans originated from a numerically single pair. In the words of Karl Rahner:

> The Church has often shown too little understanding toward those branches of anthropology in which the material, biological reality of the human being

as such is validated. The Church's relation to genetics, to depth psychology, to the development of the social life and morals of humankind as conditioned by natural science was never especially benevolent, was not sufficiently differentiated. The Church was always quicker to say no than to say yes.[42]

Religious leaders on local, national and international levels are much more prudent and tactful today in what they say about science. This strategy enables them in effect to ignore scientific findings altogether, or to minimize their significance in relation to what they see as the overarching importance of human values. They justify such unconcern because Christian faith is addressed to the average person, and the work of scientists is usually inaccessible to this average consciousness. The fact that science has so often in the past played a surgical role in regard to deep-rooted religious beliefs is additionally a reason for distrust.[43] Science's cold light has thus always been seen as a threat. There is little recognition, for example, that Darwin's corrective to the biblical narrative of creation was indeed healthy for religion, releasing the early chapters of Genesis to function powerfully as the biblical authors clearly intended, namely as a story of the goodness of all creation as the work of a free and transcendent God, and of human dependence upon and alienation from God as the source of life.

Ironically, a new and healthy development in contemporary theology is having a further negative effect on this dialogue. This is the deprivatization effected by political and liberation movements acutely conscious of massive global suffering. These movements are eager to assuage such suffering with all the theological resources of the Christian tradition, and their sensitivity understandably has little interest in the religious implications of scientific discovery. Because theologians in these movements are reacting strongly against the existentialist disregard for the needs of human community, they naturally tend to regard all cosmological issues as distractions from Christian responsibility for the poor and oppressed. Indeed, one of their claims is that science as an enterprise serves mostly rich nations, with only a tiny percentage of its research aimed at problems typical of poor countries. This has naturally led them to emphasize the liberating message of the doctrine of redemption and to neglect any exploration of the doctrine of creation. Theologians sympathetic with both these movements are therefore seeking today to modify what they see as an overemphasis on society and history. They want to reintroduce into consideration the important third category of "world" or "cosmos," and to insist that human salvation cannot be divorced from that of the material universe, which Scripture says is also "groaning in pain."[44]

A final factor inhibiting the dialogue is awareness of the perennial danger of theology seeking to incorporate even the best science of the day, whose findings have truly become part of the intellectual culture of a particular period. This is, after all, what happened in the Middle Ages, when biblical theology was so merged with the cosmology of Ptolemy and Aristotle that it was impossible for the Church to respond flexibly when this cosmology was finally discredited. The great fear of those who argue this way is that attaching one's religious belief to contemporary science is a sure route to obsolescence: married to science today, a widow tomorrow, as Arthur Peacocke would say.

But there is a false supposition here, namely that the only objective theologians could possibly have in this dialogue would be to gain some new evidence to validate a particular traditional teaching. Such an aim would not be theological at all, however, and would really constitute a neglect of revelation and religious experience as the true supports of the teaching in favor of certain scientific data that would allegedly provide stronger support. If theologians were really to have this objective they would simply be looking for some new "God of the gaps" type of argument, like the classic example in which a creator God is invoked as a hypothesis to account for those puzzling aspects of the natural world that science for the present at least is unable to explain.[45] If, on the other hand, the true objective of theologians is to seek in science not new evidence for their teachings but rather new insight into them, then their search for the intelligibility of faith experience would in no way be compromised by dialogue. They would simply be recognizing that some features of our natural world have become so well established that it would be foolish for the theologian not to take them into account.

This reluctance of theologians to dialogue with scientists, which we have been discussing up to now, is matched today by an equal reluctance on the part of scientists. The reason is quite simply that in the eyes of scientists, religion constitutes a threat—not to themselves personally so much as to the integrity of their method, which seeks knowledge of universal causality. This will come as a surprise only to those whose image of science is still governed by the conventional stereotype: scientists as detached collectors of observable data, validating their theories by clear-cut criteria, and testing them against indisputable factual evidence. But this stereotype ignores the impact of their methodology on the personal lives of scientists, and attributes to them a confidence in their intellectual pursuit which, as we saw earlier, has been severely limited in recent years, and in some areas even eroded.

Consider, for example, this reaction of Albert Einstein, when faced with the full implications of the discovery that the universe was expanding at fantastic speeds: "It was as if the ground had been pulled out from under one, with no firm foundation to be seen anywhere, upon which one could have built." Or that of Wolfgang Pauli in the months before Heisenberg formulated a new theory of quantum mechanics: "At the moment physics is again terribly confused. In any case, it is too difficult for me, and I wish I had been a movie comedian or something of the sort and had never heard of physics."[46] In principle, however, this collapse of earlier mechanistic and positivist models served to free scientists to sense the ultimate mystery of reality, and as a result some actually became more open to religious insight. Werner Heisenberg, for example, could write: "Although I am convinced that scientific truth is unassailable in its own field, I never found it possible to dismiss the content of religious thinking.... Thus in the course of my life I have repeatedly been compelled to ponder on the relationship of these two regions of thought."[47]

But this greater openness to religion in the personal lives of scientists is only with the greatest difficulty translated into their professional lives where dialogue with theology must take place. Princeton sociologist Robert Wuthnow, after analyzing a number of recent studies of science vis-à-vis religion, concludes that the irreligiosity of most scientists is a "boundary posturing mechanism" to maintain the precarious reality of the work they do. That is to say,

> irreligiosity helps to maintain the plausibility of the scientific province by differentiating scientists (in their own minds) from the larger public who represent everyday reality and generally maintain stronger religious identifications. By helping to maintain the plausibility of the scientific role for the scientist, irreligiosity contributes to his or her role performance as a scientist, as indicated by higher productivity and greater attachment to the values of science.... [In short,] the more successfully scientists can extricate themselves from the realm of everyday reality, of which conventional religion is an important aspect, ... the more likely they are to make the transition successfully into the scientific role.[48]

In the mind of the average scientist, therefore, his or her work needs to be protected not from religion so much as from everyday life in which religion flourishes. The other phenomenon noted by Wuthnow is that "scientists seem more likely to *think of themselves* as religious persons than they are actually to engage in any of the conventional practices or beliefs associated with religion." This fact "suggests that scientists may be able to

maintain private, nonconventional religious orientations at the same time
that their public boundary-posturing activity calls on them to disidentify
with the conventional religious performances that are tainted by everyday reality." Wuthnow concludes that

> the proverbial conflict between religion and science may be more a function
> of the precariousness of science than of the precariousness of religion. Rather
> than religion being constantly on the run, so to speak, in the face of ever ad-
> vancing scientific knowledge, scientists have had to carve out a space in
> which to work by dissociating themselves from the powerful claims which re-
> ligion has had traditionally, and which it still appears to command over the
> everyday life of contemporary society.[49]

The religious beliefs and values of many scientists may thus appear to
them to be perfectly valid forms of personal faith, as long as this faith is
isolated from religious practice and closed to scientific scrutiny. They are
content to live in two equally legitimate but separated realms, between
which there can properly be neither conflict nor compromise. Werner
Heisenberg, whose words on religious commitment we quoted earlier,
could be quite explicit:

> The care to be taken in keeping the two languages, religious and scientific,
> apart from one another, should also include an *avoidance of any weakening of
> their content by blending them*. The correctness of tested scientific results cannot
> rationally be cast in doubt by religious thinking, and conversely, the ethical
> demands stemming from the heart of religious thinking ought not to be
> weakened by all too rational arguments from the field of science.[50]

This explains, of course, why most scientists feel so ill at ease in dialogue situations with theologians. They are suited neither by training nor
by disposition to grapple with the larger questions that tend to arise in
these discussions, such as those that touch on the history and philosophy
of science, as well as the relation of science to society, to ethics, or to the
history of religious thought. On the other hand, most theologians, as
we saw, are equally ill at ease, because as a group they find great difficulty
with the language of science. Their humanistic training hardly prepares
them to appreciate or to work with the rigorous insistence by scientists
on the importance of empirical, causal, and testable data. "God," says one
scientist, "is in the details of existence. And anyone who refuses to look
there is likely to be worshiping idols."[51]

Hence some significant effort is needed on both sides to overcome the
pull to isolation that arises naturally from the historical experiences of

each, as well as from their present methodologies and psychological concerns. The motivation to do this from the theological side has to come from the realization that, if God is in fact the all-encompassing reality Christian faith proclaims, then what science says about nature, whether physical, chemical, or biological, can never be irrelevant to a deeper experience of God. The language of science, moreover, is now the common possession of humanity as a whole, and not to use this language in understanding and communicating Christian teaching entails a serious risk of not being heard. Science, for its part, must recognize the religious quest as one of the major and permanent realities of human life, even in our present technological culture. Not to relate to this quest in any way at all is simply to impoverish science. Langdon Gilkey makes this point well:

> A scientific community that ignores the relation of its truth and its life to law, to morals, and to fundamental religious symbols. . . . only makes itself and its culture vulnerable to ideological capitulation. Ignorance of the religious in both its demonic and its creative forms can be even more fatal for a scientific culture than ignorance of new scientific and technological developments.[52]

It is important for all parties involved to recognize, moreover, that dialogue will tend to be strongly resisted by movements within Christianity that we mentioned earlier: fundamentalism (whether biblical or ecclesiastical), neoorthodoxy, and Christian existentialism. Though very different in many respects, each seeks to isolate theology by insisting that what is distinctive and constitutive of Christianity, namely revelation and commitment to a way of life, is totally absent from science. By supposition, therefore, we have two realms with no common interests or points of contact, and hence no possibility of communication. Between theological assertions and scientific assertions there can only be total separation. Impersonal nature is thus either of no religious importance or is important merely as the physical setting chosen by God for human redemption. Nor is it any accident that theologians in these movements tend to endorse positivism as the correct description of the scientific enterprise: such a view helps them emphasize the dichotomy all the more, since positivism asserts that sense data are the only reliable norm for knowledge, and that any religious statements which cannot be verified by such data must therefore be meaningless.

Nevertheless, there is a fundamental truth in these negative assessments of dialogue and it should be freely acknowledged: some language problem is inevitable in all discussions between theologians and scientists. A certain discrimination will be especially needed on the part of theologians in dealing with the extrascientific statements of scientists, and on the part of scientists in dealing with extratheological statements of theologians. The neuralgic issue is thus not the existence of such a language problem but its severity and the extent to which it can be resolved. In our earlier discussion of scientific and theological commitments we saw the many similarities as well as the key differences in these two approaches to knowledge: each intends to speak of reality (though for each the data and content of this reality are quite different), and each in recent years has become more tentative and modest in regard to what it actually knows. Science also appears to be less objective in its methodology than was previously thought, theology to be less subjective. Propositional statements in both languages are thus seen to be approximations of objective truth, as "candidates for reality," always open to modification and correction from new data, as well as from more accurate concepts, models, and theories. In spite of their mutual reluctance to dialogue, therefore, theologians and scientists are more ready today than in the past to show genuine respect for each other's truth claims.

But there will obviously be different ways for them to conceive the relationship between their respective languages, and some provisional agreement on this relationship ought perhaps to constitute an early goal of their interaction. How in practice might one language serve to illumine the other? Superficially one could say that science asks "how" questions about observable sense data, and religion asks "why" questions about personal goals and ultimate purpose. Such a distinction is too easily blurred however, since scientists obviously profess faith in the intelligibility of nature and have their own ultimate concerns in the pursuit of truth, and theologians are often curious to know how the world God created actually works.[53] This overlap of interest need pose no serious epistemological or methodological problem as long as theological language and concepts are not used to answer strictly scientific questions and vice versa.

Ian Barbour proposes the category of "levels" of knowledge as a way to relate the two languages.[54] This is a methodological concept that is common in science, where levels of analysis are relative both to the state of knowledge at the time and to the problem under investigation. Scientists use different abstract models and theories because they believe that there are different levels to be analyzed in the objective structure of the world. This structure in turn reveals levels of organic complexity in nature that chemistry and physics do not deal with, and in the case of humans there occur events of reflective intelligence whose complexity biology does not deal with. However, none of this implies that there exist separate strata or sharp boundaries in nature, and so these levels of activity, like levels of analysis and organization, are not seen to be mutually exclusive.

Hence the presence of distinctly higher-level phenomena in humans does not rule out in their case the laws of physics, chemistry, and molecular biology. When the language of theology makes assertions about human persons addressed by God, therefore, this likewise does not exclude any scientific statements regarding lower-level phenomena like atoms, neurons, and DNA molecules. There is, in other words, a continuous spectrum of levels in the total human unit, and these need to be addressed by language appropriate to the particular level in question. The reason all these languages, whether scientific or theological, ought to be able to communicate with each other is precisely their reference to this objective reality and unity of human beings, to which both science and theology bear witness.

Holmes Rolston deals with this language problem from another point of view, by emphasizing the fact that science and theology do not confront each other as closed but as open systems. The issue is thus not whether they are compatible as systems, but whether their different emphases do not simply reflect a common effort to render the universe and human beings as fully intelligible as possible. Science is mainly in search of physical causes, theology mainly in search of meanings and values. Tension exists between them at the points of their overlap because we all want our understandings of causes and meanings to cohere. "The warfare between science and theology is often a struggle to clarify to what extent causal explanations are compatible with or antagonistic to meaning explanations."[55]

Sometimes "precursors of meaning" may even appear in biological and sociological explanations, but a religious explanation is usually needed to provide a full account of meaning. Nor do such full accounts of meaning compete with causes. Rather, there is a "causal looseness" in matter itself, an unfinished openness and indeterminacy well documented by science. It is here that meanings are to be found, not in some "perforation of the natural by a supernatural order." Indeed, notes Rolston, warrants exist within the sciences for nonreductive causal explanations that allow for the influence and effectiveness of purpose. For the universe that science studies is not a mere sequence but a story, a struggle upward through matter, life, thought, history, and culture. Only a narrative can really capture what is going on. And it is precisely this need of humans for meaningful narrative that allows theology to complement the causality of science.

——— OPPORTUNITIES FOR THE FUTURE ———

Once their mutual reluctance is overcome and commitment made to achieve some mutual understandings, it is incumbent on both parties to be realistic about the dialogue. Hence we must now ask, finally, what objectives we can expect to achieve through this collaborative interaction between scientists and theologians. I believe that only one focus will make the conversation worthwhile for the two participants, at least initially, and that is the human person. There is, of course, a second focus of supreme importance today, namely the responsibility of human freedom for the use of science's progeny, technology. But this focus raises so many large and delicate questions of morality that it demands the participation and expertise of many thinkers from many fields in addition to those from the natural sciences and theology. Hence we shall touch briefly on this second focus only insofar as it is derivative of the first and a manifestation of the mysterious power of human freedom.

Only in recent years have scientists begun paying any attention at all to human beings. The sheer complexity of the human tended in the past to be totally overlooked. The sophisticated tools of relativity theory and quantum mechanics enabled physics to move with ease from the enormously simple and relatively empty structures of galaxies to the simple and equally empty structures of the subatomic world. Physicists never paused in this movement to notice the incredible intricacy of the human phenomenon midway between the immense and the infinitesimal. Biology and chemistry dealt with the molecular and genetic structures of living things, but, because reflective consciousness was restricted to the higher forms of life, there seemed to be good reason to regard it as a mere epiphenomenon of life. Human persons, each with more atoms in their makeup than stars in the universe, were thus relegated to just another animal species.

This situation is now slowly changing. A new science has emerged that challenges traditional science because of the order of being that it studies: that range of the very complex that exists between the range of the infinitely large and the infinitely small. Physicist Heinz Pagels recently explained this development:

> Science has explored the microcosmos and the macrocosmos; we have a good sense of the lay of the land. The great unexplored frontier is complexity. Com-

plex systems include the body and its organs, especially the brain, the economy, population and evolutionary systems. . . . Scientists, in a new interdisciplinary effort, have begun to meet the challenge of complex systems and, remarkably, are understanding how complexity can emerge from simplicity. . . . Some aspects of our moral behavior—behavior that either reflects or constitutes our moral values—seem extremely complex, but conceivably they arise from simple elements that can be understood. While science cannot judge, it can help us understand.[56]

Pagels believes that this new orientation of science is the first step toward a resolution of the apparently unresolvable conflict between the reductionist and the transcendental views of reality. For the first, life and even human culture is nothing but complex chemical reactions; for the second, human thinking so transcends the material world that the cultural matrix of art, religion, and science form an invisible universe of meaning. "The mind, it seems, is transcendent to nature. Yet according to the material sciences that transcendent realm must be materially supported and as such is subject to natural laws. Resolving this conflict is, and will remain, a primary intellectual challenge to our civilization for the next several centuries." Like many scientists, Pagels holds both views to be true, and does not want the conflict resolved by collapsing the differences in some simplistic way in favor of one or the other. But he does not want permanent dualism either, and he looks to the new concern of science for complexity as an eventual way out. "Where these new developments are headed no one can tell. But they portend a new synthesis of science that will overturn our traditional way of organizing reality."[57]

While science is coming to see the unusual character and significance of complex systems, theology, absorbed as it must be with the self-transcendence of human persons, is being forced by science to see these hearers of God's word in their true physical insignificance in the cosmos. We know today that the human species is one of about two and one-half million known species, a relatively recent arrival in the cosmos, living on a medium-sized planet orbiting an average star in the outer regions of an ordinary spiral galaxy, that has about a hundred billion other stars in it, and that exists in a universe with at least a billion other galaxies. Alpha Centauri, the nearest star to our sun in our Milky Way galaxy, is four light years away, which is the distance light travels in four years at the rate of 186,272 miles per second, or about 23 trillion miles. The traditional Christian message that humans are the ones for whom the material world primarily exists, when delivered in this context of overwhelming vastness, is not easily heard.

It is far more likely, as Karl Rahner has said, that Christians who think about these things will begin to feel themselves to be an accidental, marginal phenomenon, a chance product of a very localized evolutionary process that is itself known to abound in countless improbable accidents. They will then find even more dizzying the teaching that the eternal God who holds these billion galaxies in place actually became human on this tiny speck of planet. For most people the narrow horizon of everyday life will usually serve to neutralize this dizziness, but Rahner believes that Christians simply have to start getting used to this feeling of being lost in the cosmos. In other words, they must find a way to allow the scientific view of the world to coexist in their consciousness with the Christian view, without minimizing either their own cosmic insignificance or their importance and dignity as human persons. Indeed,

> their very *recognition* and *acceptance* of the fact of being lost in the cosmos actually raises them above it and enables them to realize it as an expression and a mediation of that ultimate experience of contingency which they, in virtue of their ancient faith, must perceive and accept before the infinite God as finite creatures. . . . In this way the feeling of cosmic dizziness can be understood as an element in the development of people's theological consciousness. . . . If people have to give up their feeling of being at home in the universe in exchange for the feeling of not being at home, which reflects the character of their religious experience, then this is at root a legitimate element of humankind's fate.[58]

Because of this physical insignificance of the human, and also because of the old scientific fiction of a totally objective observation, scientists usually do not notice the fact that the operation of their own minds is the most sophisticated and complex thing the material world has yet produced. In charting the size of the universe or the depths of the atom or the organic mechanisms of life, scientists are exercising powers of thought that are really the products of matter, in so far as it has at last come to know itself and to be capable of reflecting upon its world. Scientists who claim they can never find any signs of spirit among the objects they investigate fail to notice why this must be so. The reason, notes Langdon Gilkey, is that what they are investigating are all *objects*, lacking any inwardness and often existing in the past. The scientists themselves, as present knowing subjects doing the actual investigating, are simply left out. And so, if Carl Sagan is referring only to the exteriority of nature when he insists that the cosmos is all there is, he is clearly wrong: there is also Carl Sagan looking at the cosmos and trying to make sense of it.[59] Holmes Rolston makes this same point: the most significant thing in the known universe is immediately behind the eyes of the observer.

> In our three pounds of brain there may be more operational organization than in the whole of the Andromeda galaxy. The number of possible associations among the trillion neurons of a human brain, where each cell can "talk" to as many as a thousand other cells, may exceed the number of atoms in the universe. The number of possible genetic combinations in the offspring that a man and woman can conceive may exceed the number of atoms in the universe.[60]

Hence it is reasonable to expect that serious dialogue over time between scientists and theologians must eventually produce changes in how the human phenomenon is regarded. Already science has begun to recognize that, in the world of nature, more seems mysteriously to come from less: the universe is somehow right for the production of thought and freedom, which have come into being from what billions of years ago was originally matter strewn out into the universe by exploding stars. How is it that such a lifeless and mindless cosmic process should have accomplished this almost infinitely improbable feat? And how is it that physical reality is somehow adapted to our mode of knowing and so can be understood by us as observers? This baffling intelligibility inherent in the universe has struck more than one scientist with awe. "The most incomprehensible thing about the universe," Einstein once said, "is that it is comprehensible."[61] Is there not here at least a hint of some transcendence, an intimation of a wider reality than science has elected to investigate, a realization that science raises questions that its own methodology does not allow it to answer? Max Planck, the father of modern quantum theory, knew this well: "Science cannot solve the ultimate mystery of nature. And it is because in the last analysis we ourselves are part of the mystery we are trying to solve."[62]

If scientists should now be more willing than in the past to see their models of reality as partial, applicable only to certain restricted levels of reality, theologians should be no less willing to see their own models in the same way. For they can no longer pretend to understand the fullness of human history and cultural change apart from the dynamics of a physical nature and a cosmic process some fifteen billion years old. If in dialogue they are eager to say what Christian faith can contribute to the understanding of this process, they must also be ready to listen when scientists point to the theological impact of certain realities in the natural world. Because there is no reason to doubt that the human future will be any less the product of scientific discovery and research than the human past, there is also no reason to doubt that theology will continue to feel the effects of this influence. Traditionally theologians have been interested in persons primarily as social and historical beings, and this is why they are currently directing much of their energy to strategies for political and social reform. But this focus needs to be complemented now by that of the scientists, who are interested in persons primarily as *natural* beings. These scientists are just as much concerned with the human future as are the theologians, but their proposals must necessarily be in the context of the human relationships to matter and to its movement.

This mention of proposals for the future brings us now to the issue of human freedom in the dialogue. The immediate objective ought not be to discuss very complex ethical questions involving the uses of technology, but simply to acknowledge that science as well as theology must carry a burden of responsibility. This will not be as easy as one might expect, since not all scientists would agree that they have any role to play in this context. Some would say with Albert Einstein that "science can only ascertain what *is*, but not what *should be*, and outside of its domain value judgments of all kinds remain necessary. Religion, on the other hand, deals only with evaluation of human thought and action; it cannot justifiably speak of facts and relationships between facts."[63] While science as such obviously cannot resolve moral conflict, scientists themselves have to recognize that what they pursue in their research can reach dangerously beyond their immediate objectives. Theologians therefore have every right to insist that scientists recognize the full significance of free decision in their work. For their freedom inevitably involves them in something more than natural science, and that something is all too often freighted with social dilemmas and moral ambiguity.

This focus on the human person, which I believe to be the key to the dialogue's success, must eventually involve the two parties in some discussion of the relationship of matter to spirit insofar as this is to be seen in human beings. Such discussion must aim first of all at making the positions of each discussant intelligible to the other. Scientists will have the easier task here because, insofar as they think of the question at all, they will tend either toward dualism if they believe in God or toward materialism if they do not. The dualist, following Descartes and Newton, will think of mind and body as radically distinct, the extended material body functioning like any other machine, only inhabited by a "soul" as the principle of human subjectivity. In the current biological context these scientists would have an insurmountable difficulty explaining how a totally spiritual source of consciousness could have evolved from matter, just as Descartes and Newton in their day had no explanation of how the soul interacts with the body it inhabits (the "ghost in the machine" as Gilbert Ryle called it). Hence in the former case as in the latter, the creative intervention of God must fill the gap.

Most scientists, however, are materialists. They avoid the conceptual problems of mind/body dualism by equating mind with the brain. For these reductionists all interior consciousness, all mental states, are nothing but physical states of the central nervous system. While we do indeed have a conscious experience that we know directly, this experience exerts no causal power on the physical world; it is simply a concomitant of certain physical processes which are causally related to other physical processes. We are still machines, therefore, but now we have no "ghost." Geneticist Jacques Monod puts it succinctly: "Anything can be reduced to simple, obvious mechanical interactions. The cell is a machine. The animal is a machine. Man is a machine."[64] Such scientific materialism has its own problems, of course. Why should humans have such a thing as self-conscious experience in the first place? Why should such interior experience have developed at all in an evolutionary process if it had no biological function? How could it have been selected if it was irrelevant to survival?

Theologians, for their part, have in the past always held some version of spirit/matter dualism, in their case in order to articulate the transcendental character of human persons, their unlimited openness to hear and respond to God's self-disclosure. The traditional name for this higher spiritual dimension of the human came from the Greek concept of "soul," which by its very nature had to be distinct from the body to which it was joined. In this dualism, matter was usually undervalued as the physical matrix for the soul, which was alone seen as the depository of divine revelation as well as the instrument and direct object of salvation. By the turn of the century, when the discovery of evolution became impossible to deny, theologians usually reacted by saying that, while one might have to speak of the evolution of the human body, the spiritual and transcendent character of the human soul demanded a special creative intervention of God. In other words, there was another gap that had to be filled, this time at the moment of conception.

With our present knowledge of evolutionary theory and of genetics, however, theologians have become aware that they cannot draw any easy boundary between matter and spirit. Clearly there is no such dichotomy in the Bible: for biblical authors humans are psychosomatic unities. The body as a prison from which death liberates the soul is a Greek not a Hebrew idea. On the side of matter, what has helped theology is the full retrieval of Christian teaching on the resurrection and immortality of body and soul together. Matter can thus be taken more seriously when its future spiritual destiny is acknowledged. On the side of spirit, theologians eventually learned that evolutionary theory itself recognized a self-transcendence of the lower into the higher, of the less continually producing the unexpected and unpredictable more. This meant that body/soul dualism is no longer the only way to safeguard the irreducible spiritual principle in human persons. The theological focus has finally shifted, therefore, to the potential spirituality present in the actual dynamisms of matter, and to a new understanding of God's continuous creative presence and causality within the process of physical evolution. When in the ordinary course of this process homo sapiens appeared on the scene, an altogether different relationship developed between God and nature, for something radically new was now possible, a species that could consciously respond to a God who was personally present in knowledge and love to all members of the species.[65]

No one has done more to help theologians hammer out this middle position between dualism and materialism than Pierre Teilhard de Chardin. By profession a geologist and paleontologist, Teilhard faced earlier than most religious thinkers the full implications of evolution for understanding the relationship of matter and spirit. When he spoke to scientists he emphasized that the transition from life to thought was an example of what is common in nature: "In every domain, when anything exceeds a certain measurement, it suddenly changes its aspect, condition or nature. . . . Critical points have been reached, rungs in the ladder, involving a change of state—jumps of all sorts *in the course* of development." Exteriorly this movement of life involves the slow development of the nervous system and brain, but this increase in complexity corresponds experimentally to a slow interior growth of consciousness. Indeed, said Teilhard, "the story of life is no more than a movement of consciousness veiled by morphology." Like the temperature of boiling water, this psychic temperature in the cellular world was inevitably transformed at a single stroke, leaping across the threshold of reflection to thought, "a mutation from zero to everything." This interval, however, is "transexperimental, about which scientifically we can say nothing."[66]

To theologians, on the other hand, Teilhard spoke in a different vein:

> Need I repeat that I confine myself here to phenomena, i.e. to the experimental relations between consciousness and complexity, without prejudging the deeper causes which govern the whole issue? In virtue of the limitations imposed on our sensory knowledge by the play of the temporo-spacial series, it is only, it seems, *under the appearances* of a critical point that we can grasp experimentally the "hominizing" (spiritualizing) steps to reflection. But with that said, there is nothing to prevent the thinker who adopts a spiritual interpretation from positing (for reasons of a higher order and at a later stage of his dialectic), *under the phenomenal veil* of a revolutionary transformation, whatever "creative" operation or "special intervention" he likes.[67]

—— Conclusion ——

Let me summarize the main argument I have been making and draw two brief conclusions. The present dialogue between scientists and theologians is at best in its infancy: neither group, as a group, is well prepared to understand the sources, methods, or subject matter of the other. While there are ample historical reasons for this, as well as for the current reluctance to change it, the thought processes of each group have nevertheless undergone a remarkably similar development in recent decades. They have both become more modest regarding the certainty of what they know as well as more open to outside influences. Their epistemologies may differ because of the different types of human experience they investigate, but there is a common sociology of knowledge available to both, and this goes far toward explaining their common commitment to the intelligibility of reality as well as their growing respect for each other. Hence new opportunities do exist for dialogue today, especially if the participants limit their initial focus to what each can contribute to new insights into the human.

The first conclusion we can draw is that theologians are in a position to gain more from this dialogue, at least initially, than are scientists. This is undoubtedly why John Paul II directed his message primarily to them. For their neglect of physical nature, of all those forces present in the cosmos and in life, has been almost total. *That* God creates all that exists has usually been their only concern. *What* and precisely *how* God creates has been of little or no interest. Only within a dialogue process, therefore, is it possible for them to learn anything about the fantastic results of God's creative power, and the implications of these results for human persons and their relationship to God.

Such an experience cannot but affect the way theologians think about nature itself as a source of knowledge about God, creation, divine providence, and the mystery of evil. They must also begin to ask about the relation of such "natural theology" to the "theology of nature" long derived from biblical revelation, which emphasizes God's immanence in the world as well as transcendence to it. The source references in these pages are an indication of how extensive this questioning has already become. Outside the context of dialogue, moreover, new theological efforts must certainly be made to reformulate certain traditional Christian doctrines in the context of widely accepted scientific findings regarding the evolution of matter and the human person. Christology, original sin, redemption, the theology of death, and the material character of the afterlife are the most obvious areas raising new questions which theologians must somehow confront.[68]

Secondly, we must recognize that scientists will be interested in discussing their findings with theologians only in so far as theologians are willing to meet them on their own ground. For few scientists, even among those who are religiously committed and who readily acknowledge their models to be partial, are much interested in strictly theological questions. The most that can be expected, as we saw, is respect for the integrity of the theological enterprise as a search for its own particular intelligibility of human experience. This means that the focus of the dialogue proper must be on the scientific understanding of nature and the human person, and on what we can and cannot know about God from these findings. To quote Whitehead once more: "When we consider what religion is for mankind, and what science is, it is no exaggeration to say that the future course of history depends upon the decision of this generation as to the relations between them."[69]

Because their primary orientations are so different, as well as their tools of intelligibility, any concerns which are seen as common to both science and theology can never be pursued without friction or without constant need of adjustment at their points of overlap. For while we may no longer have two totally separate realms of discourse, we also have little likelihood of achieving a single integrated intellectual enterprise. A coherent vision of all things may indeed be the ultimate goal of the dialogue, but scientists as well as theologians will have to settle in the short run for a friendly collaborative sharing and scrutiny of their fallible insights into very different aspects of reality.

—— NOTES ——

1. The Pope's message to the conference is in the form of a letter to one of its organizers, George Coyne, and appears at the start of its proceedings: *Physics, Philosophy, and Theology: A Common Quest for Understanding*, ed. Robert J. Russell, William R. Stoeger, and George V. Coyne (Notre Dame, Ind.: Univ. of Notre Dame Press, 1988). It appears also in *Origins* 18/23 (Nov. 17, 1988): 375–78. See commentaries by Ernan McMullin, "A Common Quest for Understanding," *America* 160/5 (Feb. 11, 1989): 100–104, and by Michael J. Buckley, "Religion and Science; Paul Davies and John Paul II," *TS* 51 (1990): 310–24. See also *John Paul II on Science and Religion*, ed. Robert J. Russell, William R. Stoeger, and George V. Coyne (Notre Dame, Ind.: Univ. of Notre Dame Press, 1991).

2. Langdon Gilkey, "Nature, Reality and the Sacred: A Meditation in Science and Religion," *Zygon* 24 (1989): 285.

3. Jacob Bronowski, *The Ascent of Man* (Boston: Little Brown, 1974); Carl Sagan, *Cosmos* (New York: Random House, 1980), 4. An incisive critique of scientific reductionism is given by Arthur Peacocke, *God and the New Biology* (San Francisco: Harper & Row, 1986), 1–20.

4. Quoted by Heinz R. Pagels, *The Cosmic Code* (New York: Bantam Books, 1983), 187.

5. B. F. Skinner, *Beyond Freedom and Dignity* (New York: Free Press, 1965), 6, 447.

6. Steven Weinberg, *The First Three Minutes* (New York: Basic Books, 1977), 154.

7. Jacques Monod, *Chance and Necessity* (New York: Knopf, 1971), 180.

8. Quoted by Robert Jastrow, "Have Scientists Found God?" *New York Times Magazine*, June 25, 1978, 20. Jastrow was at the time the director of NASA's Goddard Institute for Space Studies.

9. Ibid., 24.

10. Ibid., 19.

11. From his paper at a conference on "The End of Science," as reported in the *New York Times*, "Week in Review," October 22, 1989, 18.

12. See the two overviews by Mary Hesse, "Cosmology as Myth," in *Cosmology and Theology*, ed. David Tracy and Nicholas Lash (New York: Seabury, 1983), 49–54, and "Retrospect," in *The Sciences and Theology in the Twentieth Cen-*

tury, ed. Arthur Peacocke (Notre Dame, Ind.: Univ. of Notre Dame Press, 1981), 281–91.

13. Thomas S. Kuhn, *The Structure of Scientific Revolutions*, 2nd ed. (Chicago: Univ. of Chicago Press, 1970). Kuhn's argument has been discussed at length in *Paradigms and Revolutions*, ed. Gary Gutting (Notre Dame, Ind.: Univ. of Notre Dame Press, 1980). David L. Hull, another historian of science, has recently proposed a very different biological model: the same kinds of forces responsible for shaping the rise and demise of species also act on the social and conceptual development of science. See his *Science as a Process* (Chicago: Univ. of Chicago Press, 1988).

14. John Polkinghorne, *One World* (Princeton: Princeton Univ. Press, 1986), 13.

15. Typical of the defensive reactions of scientists to Kuhn's thesis is that of Heinz R. Pagels, *The Dreams of Reason* (New York: Bantam, 1989), 260–64.

16. Kuhn's concept of paradigm influence within the scientific community has in recent years been given a much larger societal focus by a movement within the sociology of knowledge known as "the strong program." The myth of scientific neutrality, say these social historians, has made it possible today for government and industry to misuse both pure science and technology to achieve political and economic goals. The questions posed by scientists and the type of answers they seek thus originate, according to "the strong program," not within science but outside it.

As Ian Barbour perceptively notes, however, experimental data are the great corrective to this charge of cultural relativism. While such externalist sociological critiques may be a healthy antidote to internalist views of a purely rational science, they inevitably underestimate the constraints of data upon both outside influence and insider objectives. That is to say, one can justify neither scientific theory nor social ideology without some reproducible confirmatory data. See Barbour, *Religion in an Age of Science* (San Francisco: Harper & Row, 1990), 74–75. Other critiques of "the strong program" will be found in Arthur Peacocke, *Intimations of Reality* (Notre Dame, Ind.: Univ. of Notre Dame Press, 1984), 18–22; Martin Rudwick, "Senses of the Natural World and Senses of God: Another Look at the Historical Relation of Science and Religion," in *The Sciences and Theology*, ed. Peacocke, 241–61; Sal Restivo, "The Myth of the Kuhnian Revolution in the Sociology of Science," in *Sociological Theory 1983*, ed. Randall Collins (San Francisco: Jossey-Bass, 1983), 293–305.

17. Polkinghorne, *One World*, 12. See the more detailed discussion of these analogies by Michael Polanyi, *Personal Knowledge* (Chicago: Univ. of Chicago Press, 1958).

18. Quoted by Timothy Ferris, *Coming of Age in the Milky Way* (New York: Morrow, 1988), 288.

19. Quoted by Pagels, *Cosmic Code*, 13.

20. This purely instrumentalist view of scientific theories is defended by Mary Hesse and M. A. Arbib, *The Construction of Reality* (Cambridge: Cambridge

Univ. Press, 1981). See also the articles by Hesse (n. 12 above) and Ian Barbour, *Issues in Science and Religion* (New York: Harper Torchbook, 1971), 162–74.

21. David Ray Griffin, *The Reenchantment of Science* (Albany: State Univ. of New York Press, 1988), 9–10. See also Polkinghorne, *One World,* 17–25.

22. On this selectivity of science see Barbour, *Issues,* 264–66. The parable appears in Arthur Eddington, *The Nature of the Physical World* (Cambridge: Cambridge Univ. Press, 1928), 16.

23. Kuhn, *Structure,* 198–204. Unlike Kuhn, the philosopher Karl Popper insists on the importance of experimentation as a means of logically and deductively refuting scientific hypotheses. General laws and theories themselves, however, are not inductively derived from such observation, but rather have their origin in the imagination and intuition of the scientist. As such they can never be positively verified, but only shown by data to be false. There can thus be no absolute certainty in any scientific theory; the most we can expect is a gradual approximation to truth. Popper's understanding of science is to be found in his many books, including *The Logic of Scientific Discovery* (New York: Basic Books, 1959) and *Conjectures and Refutations* (London: Routledge & Kegan Paul, 1963). It should be noted that many philosophers of science would not agree with Popper that for a theory or principle to count as "scientific" it must conceivably be able to be proved wrong.

24. Peter Medawar, *Advice to a Young Scientist* (New York: Harper & Row, 1979), 31. Quoted by Polkinghorne, *One World,* 61. The "candidates for reality" phrase was coined by Rom Harré and used often in his writings, e.g., in *The Philosophies of Science* (New York: Oxford Univ. Press, 1972), 93 and *Theories and Things* (New York: Sheed & Ward, 1981), 22. See Peacocke, *Intimations,* 22–34.

25. William James, *The Varieties of Religious Experience* (New York: Collier, 1961); Rudolf Otto, *The Idea of the Holy* (New York: Oxford Univ. Press, 1958).

26. For an extensive discussion of the inevitable tension involved between the existential commitment of religious experience and the theologian's task of understanding and evaluating religious belief claims, see Barbour, *Issues,* 207–69.

27. In 1984 the Vatican formally acknowledged the error of this condemnation. See *Origins* 16 (1986): 122. Galileo's undoing was his insistence that he had proven heliocentrism beyond doubt and that church authorities must immediately reinterpret all biblical texts to the contrary. But the evidence he produced (the orbits of the moons of Jupiter and the waxing and waning of Venus, both seen with his telescope) was quite inconclusive at the time, and this gave his enemies on the papal commission their excuse for humiliating him: he was forced to abjure heliocentrism publicly and live under house arrest until his death.

Given Galileo's enormous contribution to science, recognized even in his lifetime, this episode in the history of theology and of the Church is both sad and fascinating, and its literature is very extensive. The best of the longer studies is Giorgio de Santillana, *The Crime of Galileo* (Chicago: Univ. of Chicago Press, 1955). An excellent short account is William R. Shed, "Galileo and the Church," in *God and Nature*, ed. David C. Lindberg and Donald L. Numbers (Berkeley: Univ. of California Press, 1986), 114–35. There is also the interesting theory regarding the true motivation behind Galileo's condemnation advanced by Pietro Redondi, *Galileo: Heretic* (Princeton: Princeton Univ. Press, 1987).

28. Barbour discusses this change in theological thinking in regard to scripture in *Issues*, 60–62, 96–105, 229–37.

29. On neoorthodoxy, see Barbour, *Issues*, 116–19, 229–32, 376–80.

30. Ibid., 119–21, 431–37.

31. For a brief overview of Modernism see the perceptive treatment by Roger Haight, "The Crisis of Modernism," *Compass* 8 (1990): 21–24. Two studies by Alec Vidler will provide fuller background and analysis: *A Variety of Catholic Modernists* (London: Cambridge Univ. Press, 1970) and *The Church in an Age of Revolution* (London: Penguin, 1971).

32. Peacocke, *Intimations*, 43.

33. See the keen analysis by Janet Soskice, *Metaphor and Religious Language* (Oxford: Oxford Univ. Press, 1985) summarized in her "Knowledge and Experience in Science and Religion: Can We Be Realists?" in *Physics, Philosophy, and Theology*, ed. Russell, Stoeger, and Coyne, 174–83. Polkinghorne, *One World*, 26–42, also deals trenchantly with this question.

34. Ian Barbour, *Religion*, 88. Barbour relies on the analysis of Soskice as well as his own extensive treatment in *Myths, Models and Paradigms* (New York: Harper & Row, 1974).

35. Soskice, *Metaphor*, 217. Quoted by Peacocke, *Intimations*, 45, who also relies on the work of Sally McFague, *Metaphorical Theology: Models of God in Religious Language* (Philadelphia: Fortress, 1982).

36. Barbour, *Religion*, 90. A recent statement by the Vatican's International Theological Commission has cautiously endorsed this need to reinterpret doctrinal statements in a contemporary context: "The definition of a dogma, therefore, is never just the end of a development, but always a new beginning as well . . . Such a contemporary interpretation of dogmas must take into account . . . the abiding validity of the truth and the actuality of the truth. . . . Consequently the work of theology, the historical study of the sources as well as dialogue with sciences dealing with humanity and its various cultures, with hermeneutics, linguistics and philosophy are of great importance for the contemporary interpretation of dogma. . . . Without doubt the permanent and valid content of the dogmas is to be distinguished from the way in which they are formulated. In any age the mystery of Christ surpasses the possibilities of formulation and thus eludes any final systematization" ("On the Interpretation of Dogmas," *Origins* 20 [1990]: 12).

37. Hans Küng, "Paradigm Change in Theology and Science," in *Theology For the Third Millennium* (New York: Doubleday, 1988), 123–69. See Barbour's discussion of Küng in *Religion*, 56–58.

38. See the papers of the many contributors to the symposium on *Paradigm Change in Theology*, ed. Hans Küng and David Tracy (New York: Crossroad, 1989), especially Anne E. Carr, "Feminist Theology in a New Paradigm," 397–407, and Leonardo Boff, "The Contribution of Liberation Theology to a New Paradigm," 408–23.

39. What I have described as the professional commitment of Christian theologians is how the vast majority go about practicing their craft today. The inverse of this approach has been developing for some time, however, in such nontheological areas as the history, sociology, and philosophy of religion. The former outlook assumes that religious language is the product of a distinctive historical experience of God and of one's relationship to God, whose primary and normative source for the Christian is the biblical narrative, expressed and communicated in more or less adequate ways by metaphors, symbols, and models. The latter outlook assumes that language is rather the producer of this experience, which in turn is its effect, not its cause. When applied to Christian doctrines, this alternative model says that their most important function is their use as rules of discourse and action. All authoritative Christian teaching is therefore to be regarded simply as rule theory.

George Lindbeck believes that this "cultural-linguistic" view of doctrine is better than what he calls the "experiential-expressivist" view, because it does not ghettoize theology by isolating it from close association with the best of nontheological thinking. He concedes, however, that "experiential-expressivism" may be better suited to the religious needs of modernity and is in fact the model habitually used by the generality of Christian theologians. He would also have to acknowledge, I think, that doctrines never appear in the tradition as no more than ways of speaking about certain Christian attitudes and practices. See his *The Nature of Doctrine: Religion and Theology in a Postliberal Age* (Philadelphia: Westminster, 1984).

40. Alfred North Whitehead, *Religion in the Making* (New York: New American Library, 1974), 57. Arthur Peacocke calls this unusual relationship "the two books," and gives one of its best summaries in *Creation and the World of Science* (Oxford: Clarendon, 1979), 1–38.

41. This contemporary critical realism thus asserts that we can know to some extent the truth about real objects, but clearly departs from traditional Western foundationalism by denying that our perception and inference can give us absolute certitude. This is because both scientists and theologians have come to recognize, each through their own distinctive experience of reality, that too many cultural, personal, and conceptual filters intervene between the knowing subject and the object known.

One could legitimately argue, of course, that the current crisis in both theological and scientific knowledge is more extensive and radical than I have indicated. Whether or not this is actually the case would not affect the main points I am making, namely that scientists and theologians generally aim at some intelligibility of the real, and that the truth claims of each are now far more modest and tentative than they were in the past. For an overview of developments that today raise questions about this search for intelligibility see, on the science side, James Gleick, *Chaos* (New York: Penguin, 1987), and Ilya Prigogine and Isabelle Stengers, *Order Out of Chaos* (New York: Bantam, 1984); on the theology side, David Tracy, *Plurality and Ambiguity* (San Francisco: Harper & Row, 1987), and Mark C. Taylor, *Deconstructing Theology* (New York: Crossroad, 1982).

42. Karl Rahner, "Science and Theology," in *Theological Investigations* 21 (New York: Crossroad, 1988), 25.

43. Polkinghorne, *One World,* 65, makes this point well.

44. See the critique by Tracy and Lash, *Cosmology and Theology,* 88–89. The biblical text referred to here is Rom. 8:22.

45. In a widely publicized allocution to the Pontifical Academy of Sciences in 1951, Pius XII appealed to the Big Bang model to confirm what he called the "classical proofs" for the existence of God and for a finite beginning of the universe in a divine act of creation. As was to be expected, scientists were generally upset by this misunderstanding and misuse of their theory for apologetic purposes. But many Catholic philosophers and theologians were equally disturbed, because they could find no direct connection between scientific statements about cosmic beginnings and biblical statements about the creative power of God. See *The Proofs for the Existence of God in the Light of Modern Natural Science: Address of Pope Pius XII to the Pontifical Academy of Sciences* (Washington: National Catholic Welfare Conference, 1952).

A more balanced epistemological evaluation is that of Ernan McMullin, "How Should Cosmology Relate to Theology?" in *Sciences and Theology,* ed. Peacocke, 39: "What one *could* readily say, however, is that if the universe began in time through the act of a Creator, from our vantage point it would look something like the Big Bang that cosmologists are now talking about. What one cannot say is, first, that the Christian doctrine of creation 'supports' the Big Bang model, or, second, that the Big Bang model 'supports' the Christian doctrine of creation." Finally, it is important to recognize that this doctrine is not a teaching about cosmological beginnings in time at all, but rather about the absolute dependence of everything on God at every moment; nor do biblical scholars believe that the Genesis story refers literally to such beginnings.

46. Quoted by Kuhn, *Structure,* 83–84.

47. Werner Heisenberg, "Scientific and Religious Truths," in *Quantum Questions,* ed. Ken Wilber (Boston: Shambhala, 1984), 39.

48. Robert Wuthnow, "Science and the Sacred," in *The Sacred in a Secular Age,* ed. Phillip E. Hammond (Berkeley: Univ. of California Press, 1985), 196–97.

49. Ibid., 198–99.

50. Heisenberg, "Scientific and Religious Truths," 43. Italics in original.

51. Pagels, *Dreams of Reason,* 312.

52. Langdon Gilkey, "The Creationist Issue: A Theologian's View," in *Cosmology and Theology,* ed. Tracy and Lash, 68.

53. Langdon Gilkey pressed this "why/how" distinction during his testimony against the creation scientists in their trial at Little Rock in 1981. The trial concerned an Arkansas law mandating the teaching of creation science in public schools if these schools taught evolution. Gilkey's strategy, which succeeded, was to defeat the arguments of biblical literalists, who through creation-science courses sought to propagate scientific conclusions derived from the Genesis story. See his account of the court proceedings in *Creationism on Trial* (San Francisco: Harper & Row, 1985). Gilkey himself holds a far more subtle understanding of the relationship (ibid., 161–208). For a discussion of the other court cases involved in this controversy, see my *Boundaries Dimly Perceived: Law, Religion, Education, and the Common Good* (Notre Dame, Ind.: Univ. of Notre Dame Press, 1990), 89–92.

54. Barbour, *Issues,* 335–37, 359–64.

55. Holmes Rolston III, *Science and Religion: A Critical Survey* (New York: Random House, 1987), 25. See also pages 22–26, 179–86, 219–24, 278–82, 311–17, 326–36. It is important to note that the concept of physical causality is not the same in the classical and contemporary worldviews. Before 1900 the natural world was regarded as mechanically determined and in principle totally predictable. Today indeterminacy is recognized at the microlevel and, because of the complexity of causal chains, unpredictability at the macrolevel. This causal uncertainty is compounded in the megaworld of intergalactic distances and cosmological processes unfolding over billions of years. While the scientific ideal still remains the discovery of causal dependency, there is now much more use of and reliance upon the tool of correlation between physical situations, which may or may not yield a causal connection. This tool will obviously be more central in some areas, such as biology and medicine, where physical causes are so much more difficult to determine. See Peacocke, *Creation and the World of Science,* 52–63.

56. Pagels, *Dreams of Reason,* 12, 329.

57. Ibid., 12–13.

58. Rahner, "Science and Theology," 50.

59. Gilkey, "Nature, Reality and the Sacred," 294.

60. Rolston, *Science and Religion,* 66.

61. Quoted by Ferris, *Coming of Age,* 385, from *Einstein: A Centenary Volume,* ed. A. P. French (Cambridge: Harvard Univ. Press, 1979), 53.

62. Quoted by John D. Barrow and Frank J. Tipler, *The Anthropic Cosmological Principle* (New York: Oxford Univ. Press, 1986), 123.

63. Albert Einstein, "Science and Religion," in *Quantum Questions,* ed. Wilber, 108.

64. Quoted by Barbour, *Religion,* 6. See also pages 196–97. We are focusing here, it should be noted, on the corporeal aspects of the human person which

we find combined with the extraordinary capacity for reflective consciousness. This approach to "matter" is able to provide an immediate common ground for scientists and theologians. Very few at this early stage in the dialogue will want to get involved in the more abstract philosophical question of some commonly agreed meaning for "matter." Theologians generally do not find this to be a pressing theological problem, and scientists as a group will have very different experimental experiences of "matter," depending on whether they are astrophysicists, particle physicists, physical chemists, or molecular biologists.

65. Rahner, "Science and Theology," 27–31, 41–46; Gabriel Daly, *Creation and Redemption* (Wilmington, Del.: Glazier, 1989), 49–55. Rahner and Daly note that one can still refer to this process, if one so wishes, as "the special creation of the human soul," because they both want to give a benign interpretation to the words of Pius XII in his 1950 encyclical *Humani generis*: "The Catholic faith obliges us to hold that souls are immediately created by God" (DS 3896). Rahner insists, however, that the ancient teaching tradition of the Christian Church on the origin of the human soul did not in fact hold this clearly. Hence the Pope could have meant only "to emphasize that the transcendentality of the human subject cannot be derived simply from its material presuppositions with their material foundations, since one must still make a distinction between body and soul (even if it is now more difficult than before to affirm their unity and diversity ontologically)" ("Science and Theology," 44). Daly merely remarks that "this teaching was never defined and there is no intrinsically compelling reason for holding that it is an indispensable model for treating human creation" (*Creation and Redemption*, 52).

66. Pierre Teilhard de Chardin, *The Phenomenon of Man* (New York: Harper Torchbook, 1965), 78, 168, 171, 172.

67. Ibid., 169, n. 1. We cannot do more here than to indicate the two main emphases of Teilhard. For a fuller understanding see the chapter on "The Birth of Thought" (ibid., 163–90) as well as "The Analysis of Life," in his *Activation of Energy* (New York: Harcourt Brace Jovanovich, 1971), 129–39.

68. The literature in this area of doctrinal reformulation is not as extensive as that in the first area. A few examples must suffice: Pierre Teilhard de Chardin, *Science and Christ* (New York: Harper & Row, 1968) and *Christianity and Evolution* (New York: Harcourt Brace Jovanovich, 1971); Karl Rahner, "Christology Within an Evolutionary View of the World," in *Theological Investigations* 5 (Baltimore: Helicon, 1966), 157–92; Gabriel Daly, *Creation and Redemption*, cited in note 65 above. On Teilhard's extensive efforts at reformulation, see my *Teilhard de Chardin and the Mystery of Christ* (New York: Harper & Row, 1966).

69. Alfred North Whitehead, *Science and the Modern World* (New York: Free Press, 1967), 181.

2. The Anthropic Principle in Cosmology and Theology

※

The so-called anthropic principle in its various formulations originated from the gradual recognition by scientists that the universe as we know it has to be almost exactly the way it is in order for intelligent life at some time to make its appearance. This assertion, actually the most general formulation of the anthropic principle, could be simply tautological ("intelligent life exists in the universe, so the universe is fit for intelligent life"). A clue to its being more than simply tautological is that the "way" the cosmos is, as well as its relationship to the "way" life is, presents science with some of its most astonishing findings and most baffling problems. A remark by Princeton physicist Freeman Dyson notes the puzzlement of not a few scientists: "As we look into the universe and identify the many accidents of physics and astronomy that have worked together to our benefit, it almost seems as if the universe must in some sense have known that we were coming."[1]

The issue with the anthropic principle, then, is not the fact that the cosmos is fit for intelligent life (which is obvious), but that it is *just* fit; not that it is right for producing us who observe it, but that it is right with such astonishing precision and seemingly against such great odds. For the laws of nature now appear to be constituted by a massive series of coincidences of enormous statistical improbability. A number of scientists have sought for some time to turn these coincidences into a methodological tool with which to gain a deeper understanding of the role of human observers in the cosmos. Not all scientists interested in an anthropic principle want to press it equally far as an explanatory tool, however, and some scientists worry that it is a distraction from the real work of science as science.

There is a history to the formulation of the anthropic principle, albeit a relatively short history. While its roots can be traced through many strands of traditional western philosophy, science, and theology (wherever the existence of intelligent human observers was thought to be a result of purposive tendencies in the universe, or wherever intelligent life was considered the goal of "creation"), it emerged in its modern "scientific" form in the late 1950s and early 1960s. Indeed, only in the 1970s did it achieve clear formulation in a variety of versions. Brandon Carter in 1974 distinguished a "weak" and a "strong" version of the principle, though the variations on each of these have since proven to be multiple and often confusing, for they are given different meanings by different authors.[2]

Generally, a "weak" form of the anthropic principle asserts simply that the universe must have certain properties if it is to contain intelligent observers like ourselves; and since we do exist in this universe, it does indeed have these properties. The principle in this form serves to call attention to what has led to the emergence of human beings (that is, to physical constants that are necessary conditions for the ultimate existence of intelligent entities) and to the vast contingencies that have been overcome in this development. Its anthropic force lies in its post-Copernican return to a focus on humanity as a point of interest in studies of the universe. It does not, however, offer an explanation of why this particular development has occurred; nor does it conclude that there are no other forms of intelligent life in our universe or in other possible universes.

The "strong" form of the anthropic principle asserts or implies that the existence of intelligent beings has in some way been built into the direction of the universe's development all along. We did not simply happen to come to be out of a multitude of possibilities, eventuating by chance. How *anthropos* has influenced the universe is theorized about in a number of ways. For example, the universe from the beginning may have had a design intrinsic to it; there may even have been a Designer who controlled the nature and process of the universe; or observers are necessary to give the universe existence, so that it must have within it the properties that allow, conduce to, or actually cause life finally to evolve. The strongest version of this principle (sometimes called the "final" anthropic principle) suggests that so important are intelligent beings to the universe that they will not cease to exist even if the universe as we know it ceases to exist in its present form.

The theological import of the many versions of the anthropic principle is potentially great. Though the problems and possibilities that the principle raises for theology are as serious as they are for science, it nonetheless challenges both theology and science to relate to one another less as rivals and more as coseekers of understanding of our world and our life. To appreciate this opportunity we could begin with the shared questions of theology and science regarding theories of "design." It is useful, however, first to examine more closely the discoveries by scientists that have fueled their interests in an anthropic principle of one sort or another. To do this is to enter into the puzzlement of astronomers and physicists as they in recent years gradually observed more and more of what has come to be called the fine-tuning of the universe. This fine-tuning is what has led many scientists to convictions and speculations regarding the role of humans in the cosmos.

———— THE FINE-TUNED UNIVERSE ————

Let us begin by noting the significance of a new branch of modern science barely over fifty years old: cosmology. This is the field of thought that deals with the origin and history of the universe as a whole, the science of matter in the very large. Long the province of philosophers and theologians, cosmology in the present century has incorporated for the first time the scientific methods of controlled observation and testing. What finally transformed the fashioning of cosmic models from a wholly speculative into an importantly empirical inquiry were two major advances in physics and one in astronomy. In physics Einstein's general theory of relativity established a comprehensive understanding of space and time whose impact was eventually felt in the study of subatomic particles and in the quantum theory of matter. The advance in astronomy was the development of powerful new optical telescopes, deployed by astronomers like Edwin Hubble in the 1920s to make the remarkable discovery that all galaxies are ballooning outward, those farthest away at fantastic speeds. Einstein thus provided cosmology's theoretical framework, while Hubble provided the beginnings of detailed observation of actual cosmic structure.

These discoveries about the universe eventually led mathematicians like Georges Lemaître and physicists like George Gamow to use the general theory of relativity to develop a cosmology that put the Hubble expansion in reverse. At earlier and earlier stages the cosmos was seen to contract, galaxies moving closer and closer together until, over billions of years of contraction, all matter was finally seen to be concentrated in a state infinitely small and infinitely dense, a single quantum of explosive energy now known as the Big Bang. In 1965 this model of cosmic origins received its strongest confirmation from an accidental discovery by two researchers at Bell Laboratories in New Jersey. Robert Wilson and Arno Penzias detected a pervasive incoming microwave radiation, the same from every direction, exactly the kind of faint "noise" that Gamow and others had predicted would be the present diluted heat residue from the energy of the primeval blast.[3]

Meanwhile, astronomers were using the velocity of the expanding galaxies to estimate the age of the universe as somewhere between ten and twenty billion years, a number which roughly corresponded with the ages of the oldest known stars, as well as being consistent with the very low temperature of the newly discovered background radiation. Finally, particle physicists began to apply quantum theory to this earliest moment in cosmic history, thereby forging for the first time a link between astronomy and nuclear physics. Henceforward, to understand the universe in the large, one also had to understand the very smallest entities in it.[4]

But when all of these scientists began systematically to investigate what the cosmos must have been like at its beginning (in order for it to end up as we know it today), they made some disconcerting discoveries. The most surprising was that, although the Big Bang ought statistically to have been a totally chaotic event, it was apparently the origin, against all probability, of an exquisitely fine-tuned set of cosmic laws. This surprise will be better understood by us if we realize, as Cambridge mathematician Stephen Hawking has pointed out, that the whole history of science has consisted in the gradual realization that events do not happen in an arbitrary manner, but that they reflect a certain underlying order.[5] Hence the question inevitably arose as to whether such order should apply not only to the laws of nature but also to whatever boundary conditions produced these laws at the start of the universe. The Big Bang, however, because it was an apparently random initial event without discernible cause, should in principle have been chaotic—for the simple reason that, in any random choice, there are vastly more disordered configurations that are possible than ordered ones.

We are not speaking here, it should be noted, about order in the sense of that complex organization we find in living organisms. This type of order could presumably arise spontaneously, or even with a certain degree of likelihood, as long as we presuppose the preexistence of some ensemble. In the case of life's initial appearance, this ensemble would have been the primeval cloud of fundamental particles, which must at least have had the potential to develop into complex replicating molecules. In the case of life's later evolution, this ensemble would have been the thousands of millions of organisms existing over millions of generations of time. It is this huge resource that enabled nature to experiment with any number of possible alternatives until a favorable mutation appeared and, isolated by natural selection within a certain environment, eventually became fixed in the genetic pool. The human eye is a good example of such ordered complexity: in spite of its delicate and intricate mechanism, there is nothing mysterious about its origin or design. Given the structure and function of the DNA molecule and the nature of the hereditary variations upon which natural selection operates, the adaptability of the eye for seeing is simply the natural effect of the long evolutionary process.

The Big Bang, however, was an absolute beginning; it would seem, then, to have to possess its own intrinsic symmetry or there would have been nothing to drive the subsequent orderly expansion. But from a scientific point of view, as physicist Paul Davies takes pains to emphasize, this offers a conundrum: "If the universe is simply an accident, the odds against it containing any appreciable order are ludicrously small. If the big bang was just a random event, then the probability seems *overwhelming* (a colossal understatement) that the emerging cosmic material would be in thermodynamic equilibrium at maximum entropy with zero order."[6] The reason is that mathematically the probability of random choice leading to an ordered state declines exponentially (doubling each time) relative to the degree of order demanded. An illustration would be the chances of a monkey, tinkering at random with a piano, finally playing a well-known tune. Obviously these chances are minuscule in an absolute sense, but they immediately become astronomically high when compared to the chances of a random initial explosion producing an order as delicate and precise as we intelligent beings find in our universe today.

The degree of accuracy we are talking about will become clear if we look more closely at the expansion process itself. Its incredibly delicate precision has long been a puzzle. "If," writes Hawking, "the rate of expansion one second after the big bang had been smaller by even one part in a hundred thousand million million, the universe would have recollapsed before it ever reached its present state."[7] On the other hand, an early increase in the expansion rate by one part in a million would have blown matter apart too rapidly for condensation into galaxies and stars to take place. To avoid these twin disasters, astrophysicists conclude that the rate of expansion in the first second had to have been fine-tuned to approximately one part in 10^{60}. This is an exponential number indicating a one followed by sixty zeros. Since 10^9 would be equivalent to a thousand million or billion, and 10^{12} to a million million or trillion, a number like 10^{60} in this context indicates an almost inconceivably low probability.[8]

Where do such numbers come from? Their source is present-day analysis of the current ratio between the energy from the Big Bang, which is still expanding the universe, and the force of gravity arising from the density of matter, which is gradually slowing down this expansion. Since the total amount of matter in the cosmos is not yet known, the overall effect of gravity's force is also not known, and so we cannot as of now predict whether or not this force will eventually reverse the expansion and finally collapse the universe billions of years hence into what cosmologists refer to as the Big Crunch. The determining factor is what is called "the critical density of matter," that amount of matter required to generate a gravitational pull that would halt expansion. Measurement by astronomers today of the density of visible matter in stars shows that we are now at just 10 percent of critical density, and therefore have about ten times too little matter in our universe to exert such gravitational pull. However, the present distribution and structure of galaxies are such that astronomers are constrained to postulate the existence of a very large amount of invisible matter. This so-called dark matter in and around galaxies could, astronomers say, increase the total mass density to as much as 30 percent of critical value, but this would still not be enough to halt expansion.[9]

This knowledge of how close we are today to critical density is extremely significant because we theorize that when expansion began at the Big Bang, the universe was still supercompressed and that the density of matter therefore must have been enormous.[10] The more densely compressed cosmic matter was, however, the stronger would have been the pull of gravity opposing expansion. And yet the density at the very beginning still had to be less than critical or the whole cosmos would have immediately collapsed and winked out of existence. How much less than critical? Princeton astrophysicist Robert Dicke once estimated that for us to be now within 10 percent of critical density means that the density of matter in a universe one second old had to have been so fine-tuned that it differed from critical density by less than one trillionth of one percent.[11] Paul Davies compares this degree of accuracy to aiming at, and actually hitting, a one-inch target on the other side of the universe some fifteen billion light years away.[12] "The cosmos," observes Ian Barbour, "seems to be balanced on a knife edge."[13]

This delicacy of balance holds true for the immensity of the universe: if its size were any smaller, then it would have run its course long before life had enough time to appear. For it is not possible for carbon-based life to get started at all except in second-generation stars and planets, which already possess the necessary carbon, oxygen, and other elements that come from the explosion of first-generation stars. Yet the stellar alchemy that cooks up these heavier chemical nuclei takes a long time to complete, ten billion years at the very least. The universe is thus so big precisely because it is so old: the more time that elapsed, the larger the cosmic expansion grew. At the age of five billion years, for example, there has to have been, according to relativity theory, an expansion to a distance of five billion light years across. Once life appeared from simple prebiotic molecules, about five billion more years were needed for it to evolve into the complex forms we know today. As expansion continued at this rate for this long a time, however, the originally very dense matter inevitably transformed itself into the present hundred billion stars in our Milky Way galaxy, with those billion more galaxies beyond it. The universe thus needs to be as big as it is in order to have evolved just one single carbon-based life form.[14]

Physicists make another point about immensity: the distance *between* stars has also had a decisive effect on the possibility of human existence in our particular world. In an ordinary galaxy such as our own Milky Way, for example, the average distribution is about one star every twenty trillion miles. This is the direct result of age: the more expansion time available, the more distance there will be between what is expanding. If the distance had been smaller by a factor of ten, however, there would have been high probability that some star, at some time during the almost five billion years that the earth had existed, would either have collided with our sun or at least have passed by it close enough for its own gravitational field to disrupt the present orbits of our sun's planets. In this context Freeman Dyson reminds us that in order to destroy life on earth, "it would not be necessary to pull the earth out of the solar system. It would be sufficient to pull the earth into a moderately eccentric elliptical orbit."[15] As the earth alternately approached and receded from the sun in this new orbit, it would become alternately too hot or too cold to support life. The overall emptiness of the cosmos, therefore, with these vast distances between stars, would seem to be a precondition for our existence, at least our existence on this planet in this galaxy.

Intelligent life on this earth thus ultimately depends upon what seems to be a network of interlocking and very tightly knit occurrences at the start of cosmic expansion. Highly unlikely though they were, all of them had to have taken place in exactly the way they did or life would never have come into being. The *a priori* chances of our particular human existence are thus vanishingly small, and this poses the enigma with which we began. Here is how Nobel laureate George Wald phrases it: "How did it happen that, with what seem to be so many other options, our universe came out just as it did? From our own self-centered point of view, that is the best way to make a universe: But what I want to know is, how did the universe find this out?" Putting such questions to nature, he acknowledges, is a difficult business. "Yet sometimes it is as though Nature was trying to tell us something, almost to shake us into listening."[16]

Cosmology as a branch of science does not concern itself primarily with questions of how the laws of the universe conduce to the emergence of intelligent life. Astronomers and particle physicists are now working closely together, but neither of them are particularly focused on the connections between the behavior of matter in its original form and the later appearance of life as part of matter. Life is the subject matter of biology, and intelligent life is the concern of psychologists. Yet there are cosmologists who press for cross-disciplinary theories, for a view of the whole, as it were. The point is not that life obeys the laws of physics or that life rules the laws of physics; it is that in some way the laws of physics conduce to the emergence of life. Enter the anthropic principle in weaker and stronger forms. The former offers a perspective for appreciating the fine-tunings of the universe; the latter takes these fine-tunings to "offer compelling evidence that something is 'going on' . . . [A] hidden principle seems to be at work, organizing the cosmos in a coherent way."[17]

─────── Cosmology and the "Weak" Version of the Principle ───────

The weak version of the anthropic principle, as we have already noted, articulates a point of logical consistency. That is, the fact that intelligent observers like ourselves exist entails a universe whose history makes our existence possible. The fact that life has come to be in our universe entails the kind of universe in which life is able to come to be. The point is not that the emergence of life caused the universe to be as it is or that the eventual appearance of intelligent beings functioned all along as a *telos* driving or pulling the universe to be the kind of universe it is. Rather, it is simply that we can look out upon our universe and expect to find the conditions we need in order to exist. Not surprisingly, this weak form of the anthropic principle is not particularly controversial among scientists, for it claims very little indeed.

Nonetheless, what is noteworthy about so seemingly trivial a principle is, first, that it expands our astonishment at the improbability of the ordered development of the universe to include our astonishment at the improbability of our own existence. The fundamental characteristics of the physical universe (as we have seen, for example, its size, age, and density), the independent constants of nature (such as the ratio of electron and proton masses, the pull between nucleons, etc.), are directly connected with the possibility of our own existence. Our location in space, for instance, can no longer be seen as typical. While our sun may have no particular status among stars or our earth among planets, we, as biological organisms, find ourselves living on a solid surface (when the vast majority of matter in the universe is in the form of gas clouds and hot plasma) that is just the right distance from a stable star (when most stars behave too erratically or cluster too closely to have steady planets). We could not, in other words, survive in the hostile environment typical of most of the known cosmos. Of all the planets in our solar system, ours is the only one with those great quantities of water essential for life, and with the sun both far enough away and near enough to give us exactly the temperature we need.[18] Our earth is thus a haven amid cosmic wastelands, apparently the only suitable environment around.

Our location in time is not less amazing. Life could arise only after a significant amount of carbon and other elements heavier than hydrogen had accumulated in the universe; this accumulation required a very long period of evolutionary change. Our "now" is thus necessarily a very restricted time interval; we must live in an epoch at least ten billion years after the Big Bang, because that is the minimum amount of time needed for intelligent life to develop—at least five billion years for the first generation stars to form and explode as supernovas, scattering their debris of heavy elements to form other stars and planets; and about two billion years more for the slow biological evolution toward thought. As the astronomer John Barrow and the mathematician Frank Tipler note in their massive study of the anthropic principle:

> ... the Anthropic Principle deepens our scientific understanding of the link between the inorganic and the organic worlds and reveals an intimate connection between the large and small-scale structure of the Universe. It enables us to elucidate the interconnections that exist between the laws and structures of

Nature to gain new insight into the chain of universal properties required to permit life. The realization that the possibility of biological evolution is strongly dependent upon the global structure of the Universe is truly surprising, and perhaps provokes us to consider that the existence of life may be no more, but no less, remarkable than the existence of the Universe itself.[19]

But if the anthropic principle helps us stand in awe of the improbabilities of our own coming to be, it does so because it offers us a vantage point for exploring the history and properties of the universe. It serves as a methodological principle, a principle of self-selection in our scientific studies. As such, it both privileges humanity in the universe and helps us to recognize the limits of what we come to understand. In a way, the introduction of intelligent observers into the center of cosmological studies constitutes the principle's truly radical departure from the tradition of modern scientific thinking. The significance of this departure will appear more clearly if we recall that modern science began as a revolt against the anthropocentrism of the pre-Copernican, Aristotelian approach to physical science. The new reasoning was based on a conviction that neither our earth nor our solar system had any privileged status in the universe, and that no other position anywhere else in the universe was privileged either. Treating all regions of the universe as exactly alike thus meant that the earth's position in space was in no way atypical. Employing this outlook as a methodological tool had the good effect initially of preventing cosmological findings from being dismissed as idiosyncrasies stemming from physical features peculiar to that tiny fraction of the universe inhabited by humans. And indeed, contemporary cosmological discoveries (of, for example, cosmic expansion and the sameness of cosmic background radiation in all directions) provide compelling evidence for large-scale spatial uniformity. While the weak version of the anthropic principle does not challenge the spatial uniformity of the cosmos, it does challenge a post-Copernican refusal to give any special status to human intelligence.

But to privilege human intelligent observers is not necessarily to yield to a self-serving arrogance that makes of humans the center of the universe. It is, as adherents of the weak anthropic principle argue, to try to make sense of the universe in a way that relates to humans and, at the same time, to take account of the limits of the perspective of the observers. "Human bodies are measuring instruments whose self-selection properties *must* be taken into account, just as astronomers *must* take into account the self-selection properties of optical telescopes."[20] While the anthropic principle aims to mediate between a pre- and a post-Copernican perspective, it introduces its own epistemic modesty of claim.

The weak version of the principle appears, then, innocuous because it is so weak. Who could object to scientific astonishment, or to efforts to hold together the various aspects of scientific exploration, or to a subtle restatement of the well-established principle of science, namely that it is essential to take into account the limitations of one's measuring apparatus when interpreting one's observations? In fact, some scientists and philosophers of science do object to the anthropic principle even in its weak form. Objections include the insistence that this principle is, after all, trivial and irrelevant to the task of science; and, more importantly, there are explanations for the seeming improbabilities and coincidences in the history of the universe.

The physicist Heinz Pagels has been among the sharpest critics of the anthropic principle, even in its weak form. He notes the problem thus:

> Physicists and cosmologists who appeal to anthropic reasoning seemed to me to be gratuitously abandoning the successful program of conventional physical science of understanding the quantitative properties of our universe on the basis of universal physical laws. Perhaps their exasperation and frustration in attempting to find a complete, quantitative account of the cosmic parameters that characterize our actual universe has gotten the better of them. . . . Unlike conventional physical principles, the anthropic principle is not subject to experimental falsification—the sure sign that it is not a scientific principle. No empirical resolution of its veracity is possible, and a debate about whether it is true or not could go on forever.[21]

Pagels is making a stronger charge than that the weak anthropic principle is unscientific. Like Stephen Jay Gould, William Drees, and others,[22] he scores the triviality of the principle and its inappropriateness as a selective point of view for science. More than this, however, he believes that it is invidious insofar as it prevents science from pursuing its proper search for fundamental explanations. Though in its weak form this principle may not aim to be explanatory, "the fact remains that the anthropic principle is an alternative approach to thinking about the mysteries of the universe, and in that respect detracts from real science. Physicists who dwell on it are, in effect, giving up on the attempt to find a truly fundamental explanation of the nature of things."[23]

As Pagels's position suggests, much of the unease of scientists with the weak anthropic principle is generated by its qualitative rather than quantitative approach to the fine-tuning of the universe. Cosmologists have reacted in two ways to the absence of hard quantitative explanation. One is to reaffirm a commitment to data; the other is far more speculative in character. Scientists who take the first way are convinced that a purely physical foundation must exist for all of the as yet unexplained coincidences in the universe, a foundation based on physical laws that are knowable in principle though they may not yet be known. The whole scientific enterprise, they say, is based on the belief that there are laws of nature that are universal, invariable, and verifiable, and that can eventually explain how everything in the universe is either necessary or happened to come out this way, including intelligent observers. Hence, they search for a more fundamental theory that would provide a completely physical explanation for the tightly knit character of the cosmos.

The most serious example of this kind of effort to date is the theory developed in 1981 by Alan Guth, then at the Stanford Linear Accelerator Center and now at MIT. Guth, and others after him, proposed that a 10^{-35} second after the Big Bang, the laws of physics could have produced a phase change by which the still ultra-compressed matter of the universe might have gone through an instantaneous and very rapid inflation, as when one pumps air into a balloon and it suddenly springs from its original crumpled state into a smooth and regular shape, thereafter expanding at a uniform rate. Why might such an inflation have occurred? Because there could well have been an excessive amount of energy available just before the symmetry of the four forces (gravity, electromagnetism, strong and weak nuclear forces) was broken at the 10^{-35} second point. If this is what actually happened, then we would no longer have to assume any fine-tuning in the initial density of matter at the Big Bang; it would simply have been a necessary consequence of the physics of the freezing that took place at 10^{-35} second.[24]

While one response to the apparent coincidences in the universe is to search for a more fundamental theory based on physical laws, the other is the attempt by a small group of cosmologists to provide some middle way between pure chance on the one hand and a purely physical explanation on the other (a middle way that combines both chance and the laws of physics). The result of their search is the many-worlds hypothesis. The most comprehensive many-worlds proposal is that of Hugh Everett of Princeton, based on his own interpretation of quantum theory. Whenever a measurement of a quantum system yields an experimental outcome for the observer, we must assume, says Everett, that all other possible outcomes are also realized, but not in the universe inhabited by the observer. Since acts of quantum measurement are taking place each second, any one universe must proliferate into countless separate universes, all equally real but with no access or interference between any of them. In such a context, the weak anthropic principle appears obvious and quite unremarkable: amid this vast array of coexisting universes there must in principle be at least one where all the conditions turn out to be just right for life.[25]

In contrast to the simultaneous worlds of Everett, John Archibald Wheeler, of the Center for Theoretical Physics at the University of Texas at Austin, proposes a cycle of successive worlds. For him it is cosmic oscillations that give reality to this conceptual device of world-ensemble. He envisages a universe forever expanding from a Big Bang, collapsing into a Big Crunch, and then expanding again from another Big Bang. Some of these "worlds" might last a million years, others a hundred billion. But most are "stillborn," in that the prevailing physical laws do not allow anything interesting to happen in them. Sooner or later, in one of these oscillations intelligent life must therefore make its appearance, like the winning combination of numbers in a lottery. It is thus not a cause for any surprise that in our world we should find nature to be so fine-tuned for the benefit of our existence.[26]

The different versions of the many-worlds hypothesis cannot be ruled out on the basis of conventional experiments in quantum mechanics, with which they are entirely consistent. Faced with the fact that minute changes in our world would apparently have precluded intelligent life, some cosmologists find little difficulty in opting for worlds adequately numerous and varied to ensure that this improbable situation would actually occur. But most cosmologists are unimpressed. These explanations are more philosophical than physical, they say, and are no substitute for a proper physical theory. As such, they suffer some of the same weaknesses as the anthropic principle. They also strain the imagination to the limit: it is actually more difficult to picture this multiplicity of worlds than it is to accept the coincidences which these worlds are introduced to explain.

It might be argued that even if a fundamental theory could be formulated that would explain how all of the physical constants in the universe can only have the values they have, we would still not have an explanation for the emergence of intelligent observers. The history of science is replete with examples of recalcitrant gaps in our understanding being eventually filled by some new theoretical synthesis. The synthesis that a comprehensive physical theory would provide, however, may simply push the problem back one stage. For even if all anthropic coincidences could be explained, it would still be remarkable that relationships dictated by scientific theory, which of themselves have nothing to say about life, should happen to be organized in just the fashion necessary for life's development.

The anthropic principle in its weak form does not, as we have seen, pretend to offer an *explanation* for the emergence of life and of intelligent observers. Yet the desire for an explanation of some sort appears strong in science as well as in philosophy and theology. Hence, there is a tendency to push the anthropic principle to include stronger claims. As Ernan McMullin points out, "The anthropic principle would tell us to *expect* these physical features, once we know that this is the universe that has man in it. But to expect them given the presence of man is not the same as to explain why they occur in the first place.... For the anthropic principle to function as explanation, the anthropic features of the universe must be explainable by their connection with human origins."[27] But to link the nature of the universe with a definite potentiality for the evolution of human beings (the universe is so finely tuned *in order that* there should be observers) is to change the formulation of the principle. It is to move from its weak version to its strong version. It is to introduce thereby the concept of teleology and the category of design.

—— COSMOLOGY AND THE "STRONG" —— VERSION OF THE PRINCIPLE

The weak version of the anthropic principle, then, notes the massive coincidences that have allowed the emergence of human beings in the universe, uses this emergence as a principle of selection in studying the universe, and all the while accepts the emergence as indeed simply coincidental. The strong version, dissatisfied with coincidence as the best theory of what has in fact come to be, hypothesizes an intrinsic order in the universe from the beginning. This order is purposive; it has a *telos*, a goal; and at least part of its *telos* is the production of intelligent beings. The connection between physical constants in the universe and the eventual appearance of human observers of the universe is not in every way contingent, not the result of sheer coincidence; rather, it is built into the structure and process of the universe from the start. Why would such a principle be of interest to scientists when it clearly represents a move from the physical to the metaphysical as a mode of explanation?

In part, the interest of cosmologists in the strong anthropic principle comes from the commonly experienced human drive to wholeness of explanation. If the many-worlds hypothesis cannot achieve this, something else must. Scientists are not immune to the force of Jon Leslie's analogy: I am sentenced to be shot, but when I stand before the firing squad the sharpshooters all miss me. Would it be reasonable to say, "Well, if they hadn't all missed, I obviously wouldn't be here to discuss the matter, so what is there to be curious about?"[28] In the case of the cosmos, we have the primeval explosion of the Big Bang that, instead of resulting in the chaos of a firing squad, was governed by physical laws of exquisite delicacy, the tiniest variation in which would have made the generation of life and mind impossible. Is it not important to look for some explanation?

Still, the majority of scientists no doubt walk away from such a question. Why do some of them pursue it even if this means moving outside the usual purview of science as it is contemporarily practiced? Several of them attribute their interest in the question, and in the strong anthropic principle as a clue to its answer, to personal "taste" or "style." "Whether you like the Anthropic Principle or not is a matter of taste," says Dyson. "I personally find it illuminating. It accords with the spirit of modern science that we have two complementary styles of explanation, the teleological style allowing a role for purpose in the universe at large, and the nonteleological style excluding purpose from phenomena within the strict jurisdiction of science."[29] Pagels, on the other hand, whose style is clearly nonteleological, is genuinely puzzled that "some scientists continue to honor the anthropic principle with their attention. At least part of the answer is beyond the reach of scientific analysis, and lies somewhere in the realm of personal taste and individual psychology." The other part of the answer he suspects goes like this:

> Perhaps the frustration and exasperation intrinsic to searching for a complete account of the cosmic parameters have gotten the better of some physicists and cosmologists. . . . Faced with questions that do not neatly fit into the framework of science, they are loath to resort to religious explanation; yet their curiosity will not let them leave matters unaddressed. Hence the anthropic principle. It is the closest that some atheists can get to God.[30]

But scientific interest in the strong anthropic principle clearly also goes beyond matters of taste. Since scientists approach and employ it *as scientists,* their sympathy to a strong version of the anthropic principle can often be correlated with the value they assign to the role of mind (or intelligence) in the cosmos. This in turn, at least for some scientists, seems to depend on the type and interpretation of data particular to their discipline. As Harold Morowitz speculates:

> What has happened is that biologists, who once postulated a privileged role for the human mind in nature's hierarchy, have been moving relentlessly toward the hardcore materialism that characterized nineteenth-century physics. At the same time, physicists, faced with compelling experimental evidence, have been moving away from strictly mechanical models of the universe to a view that sees the mind as playing an integral role in all physical events. It is as if the two disciplines were on fast-moving trains, going in opposite directions and not noticing what is happening across the tracks.[31]

One would not want to make too much of such speculation, though it is suggestive in important instances. For example, the molecular biologist Jacques Monod, Director of the Pasteur Institute in Paris and 1965 Nobel laureate in physiology, sees no role at all for mind. His well-known book, *Chance and Necessity,* seeks to show, he says, that there is no harmony whatsoever between humans and their world. Our species is a freak, whose number came up by pure chance in the cosmic Monte Carlo game. We are a quite accidental mutation in the otherwise fixed and invariable microscopic machine known as the genetic code. "Now does he at last realize that, like a gypsy, he lives on the boundary of an alien world. A world that is deaf to his music, just as indifferent to his hopes as it is to his suffering or his crimes."[32] While this represents only an aspect of Monod's thought, he nonetheless posits a kind of meaninglessness with the force of scientific dogma: "The cornerstone of the scientific method is the postulate that nature is objective. In other words, the *systematic* denial that 'true' knowledge can be got at by interpreting phenomena in terms of final causes—that is to say, of 'purpose.'"[33]

This narrow definition of valid scientific knowledge would, of course, exclude some of what others consider the most exciting aspects of modern cosmology. Yet it makes great sense from the point of view of molecular biology. For this field of science is based on reducing the complex behavior of living things to the simpler behavior of the protein and nucleic molecules out of which they are built. These all exist in well-defined states, and they react to their environment by changing from one state to another; the farther down we go in the size of these biological entities, the more mechanical we find their behavior to be. Modern physics, on the other hand, has shown that further reductions in size of entities reveal the exact opposite behavior. The component atoms of a divided molecule behave *less* mechanically than the whole molecule, while the nuclei and electrons of these atoms behave still less mechanically. Indeed, experiments have shown conclusively that it is hopeless to look for a description of any subatomic event independent of the observer making the experiment. Monod's postulate that nature is "objective" is thus not true for the subatomic realm.

Princeton's Freeman Dyson draws a striking comparison between this functioning of mind on the lowest level of reality and its more recognizable functioning at the psychological level of self-consciousness:

> I, as a physicist, cannot help suspecting that there is a logical connection between the two ways in which the mind appears in my universe. I cannot help thinking that our awareness of our own brains has something to do with the process which we call 'observation' in atomic physics. That is to say, I think our consciousness is not just a passive epiphenomenon carried along by the chemical events in our brains, but is an active agent forcing the molecular complexes to make choices between one quantum state and another. In other words, mind is already inherent in every electron, and the processes of human consciousness differ only in degree but not in kind from the processes of choice between quantum states which we call 'chance' when they are made by electrons.[34]

Hence mind appears to be irrelevant only at the in-between level of molecular biology. At the levels of self-consciousness and subatomic physics its role is crucial.

But the strong anthropic principle implies that mind functions on yet another level, on the level of the cosmos as a whole; and that its role is as crucial here as on the other levels. How it functions varies from one formulation of the strong anthropic principle to another. That is, the strong version that most cosmologists find interesting and plausible claims only that there is an order within the universe that is directed toward intelligence. Who or what is responsible for this order is not specified in the anthropic principle as such. Other versions of the principle, such as the further claim that intelligence orders the universe (as in a Divine Orderer giving the universe a design) or that intelligence makes the universe real (as in a form of idealism that holds that observers are not only the end product of the development of the universe but its necessary grantors of reality) are not necessary or even generally acknowledged as part of the meaning of the strong anthropic principle. This, however, points to the neuralgic issue in regard to the anthropic principle: the strong version neither asserts the existence of an ordering Mind, nor can it tell us why such a Mind might want to fine-tune everything so carefully just to ensure the evolution of observers; nor can it overwhelm the scientist's commitment to empirical research by imposing a form of idealism. Hence, whatever a scientist's interest in the strong anthropic principle, it appears to lead to little more than possibility or conjecture.

Unlike the weak form of the anthropic principle, the strong version is only marginally scientific at best. But does it at least have some validity as a philosophic principle? A few philosophers today believe that they can construct a valid argument regarding the design of the universe, but they seldom rely on the strong version of the anthropic principle. It is philosophically deficient because it relies to a great extent on a large gap in present scientific knowledge. If it is to be based only on the current scientific inability to explain the tightly knit character of the cosmos, then it suffers from all the weaknesses of a kind of philosophical "god of the gaps" remedy. And it must await in the history of science the development of more adequate theories that may or may not incorporate an anthropic principle.

The strong anthropic principle contains, then, an irreducible element of indeterminism and uncertitude, buttressed by assumption, conjecture, and extrapolation. It is vulnerable to exalted scientific claims as well as complacent philosophical and theological claims. As the philosopher Mary Midgley has argued, it risks turning science into a kind of promise of salvation well beyond its ability to deliver; it risks placing human hopes totally in the hands of science; it risks once again putting humans at the center of a scientific and philosophical enterprise that could just as well shape its goals from astonishment regarding the existence of species in the universe other than human.[35]

We may thus be forced to conclude that the anthropic principle in all of its forms may indeed point to, but can never of itself actually reach, an explanation of the fine-tuning of the universe and the existence of intelligent observers. It is possible, however, to confront the principle with another kind of knowledge altogether, thereby encountering a completely different kind of epistemological project, one with hitherto unexpected illuminative power. It is possible, in other words, to find a relationship between scientific data and the questions consequently posed, and the data of religious revelation regarding divine causality and the possibilities in creation.

────── THEOLOGY AND THE ANTHROPIC PRINCIPLE ──────

It is possible for a knowledge source other than science to validate a focus on the human and to press, along with science, for explanations like those aimed at in the anthropic principle. I refer to the relationship between the scientific data we have been considering and the data of Christian belief (though one might refer more broadly also to the data of belief in religious traditions other than Christian). Here we have a source of knowledge that readily acknowledges the theological implications of both a weak and a strong anthropic principle, whatever its value for science. What we must be clear about is that these theological implications have not one but two epistemological lines—lines that are in principle distinct, with radically different sources, subject matter, and modes of inquiry. Hence there is here no question of casting disparate data into a single mode, either deducing a divine creative and salvific action in Jesus Christ from the anthropic arguments of science or finding in Christian revelation information about the physical structure and specific history of the world.

There is an apt analogy here: these data are like two meridians on the sphere of the Christian mind. Because Christians believe God to be the source of each, the two can be examined critically at the equator for signs of both their present consonance and their possible future convergence at some pole of common vision.[36] On the Christian revelational meridian, for example, we have an affirmation of the central and unique importance of all human persons in God's eyes. This belief rests primarily on the historical witness to salvation present in the covenant with Israel and in the person of Jesus, as well as on the Christian community's and individual's experience of God's healing care and renewal of life. Even without knowledge of cosmic fine-tuning and its relation to intelligent observers, Christians can thus still believe in the astonishing significance of the human species in its own right as a major focus and goal of God's creative action. This action must necessarily permeate the whole history and expanse of physical matter, whatever these might in fact be, because it has as an ultimate cosmic eventuality the coming of Jesus Christ into the matter of human history. This coming takes place on a particular planet where the salvific influence of God is experienced in all things human, whether biological, intellectual, or cultural.

Hence, whatever science can tell us about the structure and behavior of matter in the universe is of immense importance for theology, insofar as it provides an insight into how God has actually been acting creatively in the realms of matter and energy. Christian revelation by itself says nothing about these specific realms, yet whatever science discovers about them, provisional though it may be, belongs to the totality of human knowing within which Christian faith must be lived. This is why the full anthropic principle in its two versions can have such illuminative power as a methodological tool for Christian scientists and theologians. On the meridian of science, this principle says not only that the emergence of intelligent life on earth has depended upon all the fine-tuning extending back to the Big Bang; it also suggests that the fact of intelligence in the universe actually requires that all of these delicately balanced laws of nature be exactly as they are. The principle as a scientific principle thus provides data otherwise lacking on the meridian of theology, where Christians believe they already know about God's design of the cosmos for human life, but have no idea how God actually has gone about this designing process. While neither meridian's data depend upon those of the other, the thoughtful Christian can obviously draw insight into reality from both.

The thoughtful scientist, on the other hand, might possibly as scientist do the same. For if there was in fact a Big Bang, as is generally accepted in science today, then this at least looks a lot like the act of a creator such as the one Christians (and others) have always believed in; or minimally, it is not incompatible with this belief. While the core Christian belief in creation is about the dependence of everything on God and not about how creation actually took (and takes) place, it is nevertheless possible for the scientist to find startling resemblances between the data of these two sources of knowing and to note their obvious link with the design implications of the strong anthropic principle. Astrophysicist Robert Jastrow is one such scientist. "At this moment," he writes, "it seems as though science will never be able to raise the curtain on the mystery of creation. For the scientist who has lived by his faith in the power of reason, the story ends like a bad dream. He has scaled the mountains of ignorance; he is about to conquer the highest peak; as he pulls himself over the final rock, he is greeted by a band of theologians who have been sitting there for centuries."[37]

Christians, for their part, ought to begin having second thoughts about the overly anthropocentric emphases that are usually to be found on their meridian. The data of science are clearly a corrective here. They suggest to Christians that, while God may always have intended us humans, we are obviously not the only thing on God's mind. The fine-tuning to be found at all levels of the cosmos points to a God intensely concerned with the potential riches of all matter, all energy, all forms of life. We may indeed be the privileged outcome of God's creative power, but that is because, in James Gustafson's insightful wording, we are *measurers* of all things, not because we are the *measure* of all things. [38] Among the millions and millions of living species, we alone appear to be capable of understanding the world we are in. Human intelligence is thus the most valuable (though clearly not the only valuable) product of our tightly knit cosmos. Our value as observers may be unique, but everything else has its own value, and this does not necessarily depend upon its relevance to us. One scientist has put it thus:

> Man is not the center of the universe as once we thought in our simplicity, but something much more wonderful—the arrow pointing the way to the final unification of the world in terms of life. Man alone constitutes the last-born, the freshest, the most complicated, the most subtle of all the successive layers of life. [39]

The single conclusion to be drawn from all we have said is that the anthropic principle constitutes a striking illustration of the role of myth in cosmology. Myth here refers to that perennial human drive to interpret the reality we know, thereby imaging from it those meaningful wholes within which we feel at home in our world. All enduring religious beliefs do this, as well as all cultural achievements in art, politics and social morality. The philosopher Leszek Kolakowski offers a trenchant analysis of this. [40] We all need myths for our lives, he maintains, no less than we need food, clothing, and a place to call home. Myth rescues whatever happens to us, as well as what we value, from meaningless contingency, discontinuity, and fragmentation. Myth roots us in the human community, enabling us to become part of an inherited, shared way of life. Through myths, especially religious myths, we tell stories of our existence, thereby escaping the tyranny of seemingly pointless and accidental events, as well as the terror of a world that appears indifferent to our needs and hopes.

Scientific knowing evidently operates on a very different level from myth. Its understanding of truth is reductive, aimed at knowing things in their physical reality and only insofar as they can be utilized in effective technological procedures. Science as such thus knows nothing of persons or of that prerogative of persons, freedom. Kolakowski notes that, while the mythical imagination seeks to cancel out the apparent indifference of the physical world, science again and again cancels out such canceling.

Most of the time, such canceling is not in any sense deliberate on the part of science, and can indeed have the very salutary effect of keeping religious myth in close touch with the physical world, ready to accept responsibility and to face courageously all the frustrations of that world.

But the effect in the opposite direction can be equally salutary, as I think the anthropic principle illustrates. For here many scientists find themselves willy-nilly focusing on human intelligence and consciousness as the key to making ultimate sense of a tightly knit cosmos. Such an attempt to find roots for nature in consciousness, however, is really to locate nature in a mythical order. Kolakowski makes the point well: "Reintegration, which is unattainable through a retreat from humanity, is possible only thanks to the conviction that I live in a universe which can be understood as similar to me in a certain respect, primarily as equipped with essential characteristics of my continuing existence." In this way "both the bond-creating role of myth in communal life and its integrational functions in organizing personal consciousness appear irreplaceable, and in particular irreplaceable in favor of beliefs regulated by the criteria of scientific knowledge."[41]

Three centuries of scientific investigation have in effect produced a totally new story of human existence, a radical change in human self-awareness: a universe born some fifteen billion years ago in the energy of a primordial fireball, which eventually produced myriad galaxies, within one of which, about five billion years ago, appeared a solar system where living cells mysteriously erupted on a single planet, followed by some three billion years of evolutionary change that finally produced a species that could think and act freely, and which fifty thousand years later could achieve the marvels of human culture and society. So far does this story go beyond the myths which once structured our understandings of the origins of human life that it constitutes in our time a major revelatory experience. It was thus inevitable that its sheer presence should produce a mythic energy within the scientific enterprise itself.

While science as such cannot answer questions of ultimate meaning, scientists as human persons are instinctively drawn by the human desire to interpret reality as a meaningful whole. In its weak version, the anthropic principle is an effort by some of these scientists to show how human activity and cosmic activity are mutually dependent, thereby reversing the Enlightenment tendency of the scientific community to reduce quality to quantity. In its strong version, so important for theology, the anthropic principle is a search for some design in the extraordinary story that science has been telling us, as well as for some indications that there may indeed be a Designer at work with some purpose and overall plan. In its entirety the principle sees the human species not as an accident of nature in the midst of a vast and senseless universe, but as an integral part of an ongoing and orderly cosmic process. This is myth-making at its best, a meditation on reality's ultimate meaning, an attempt by the scientific imagination to find in its own story signs of benevolence and hope.

—— NOTES ——

1. Freeman Dyson, "Energy in the Universe," *Scientific American* 225 (1971): 59.

2. It was in an address to the International Astronomical Union in 1974 that Brandon Carter, then a physicist at Cambridge and now at the Meudon Observatory in Paris, coined the term "anthropic principle" to explain scientifically the surprisingly ordered structure of the physical world. In doing so he was relying on the work in the late 1950s by Princeton's Robert Dicke, who in turn had utilized the research some thirty years earlier of Cambridge mathematician, Paul Dirac. Carter's principle was based, as were Dicke's conclusions, not on fundamental physics but on biology, and it offered for the first time a means of relating mind and observation directly to physical phenomena. The principle was subsequently examined in some detail by other physicists like Bernard Carr and Martin Rees and by philosophers of science like Ernan McMullin and John Leslie. A massive study of the principle was coauthored by astronomer John Barrow and mathematician Frank Tipler. Numerous popular discussions also began to appear in the writings of physicists Freeman Dyson, Paul Davies, and George Greenstein, biologists Arthur Peacocke and George Gale, and mathematicians Stephen Hawking and John Casti. For historical perspective on the principle, see John D. Barrow and Frank J. Tipler, *The Anthropic Cosmological Principle* (Oxford: Oxford Univ. Press, 1986), chaps. 2, 3; Brandon Carter, "Large Number Coincidences and the Anthropic Principle in Cosmology," in *Confrontation of Cosmological Theories with Observational Data*, ed. M. S. Longair (Dordrecht: Reidel, 1974), 291–98; B. J. Carr and M. J. Rees, "The Anthropic Principle and the Structure of the Physical World," *Nature* 278 (1979): 605–12; Ernan McMullin, "How Should Cosmology Relate to Theology?" in *The Sciences and Theology in the Twentieth Century*, ed. Arthur Peacocke (Notre Dame, Ind.: Univ. of Notre Dame Press, 1981), 40–46; John Leslie, "Anthropic Principle, World Ensemble, Design," *American Philosophical Quarterly* 19 (1982): 144–51; John L. Casti, *Paradigms Lost* (New York: Morrow, 1989), 479–91.

3. This faint microwave radiation was found to be exactly the same whichever direction the detector pointed, which meant that it was coming from

outside the earth's atmosphere. Also it was the same day or night and throughout the year, which indicated that is was coming from beyond the solar system, perhaps beyond the galaxy; otherwise, it would vary with the movement of the earth. We know now that this noise comes across most of the observable universe, and that the universe must therefore be the same in every direction. See Stephen W. Hawking, *A Brief History of Time* (New York: Bantam Books, 1988), 41.

4. For a more detailed history of this development see Heinz R. Pagels, *Perfect Symmetry* (New York: Simon & Schuster, 1985), 136–56. This relatively new field of science is surveyed in its entirety by Edward R. Harrison, *Cosmology: The Science of the Universe* (New York: Cambridge Univ. Press, 1981).

5. Hawking, *Brief History*, 122.

6. Paul Davies, *God and the New Physics* (New York: Simon & Schuster, 1983), 167–68.

7. Hawking, *Brief History*, 121–22.

8. See the analysis by Davies, *God and the New Physics*, 176–82. Note that the negative exponential numbers are abbreviated in the same way as the positive numbers: 10^{-3} would mean 0.001 or one thousandth, 10^{-6} would be one millionth, 10^{-12} one trillionth. In other words, a 10 with a negative number as exponent means that the decimal point should be moved this many places to the left.

9. Unseen matter is a disconcerting discovery. At best, astronomers now tell us, we can see only about 10 percent of what exists. At least 90 percent of mass in the universe, perhaps as much as 97 percent, gives off no visible light and no radiation at any wavelength. What this "dark matter" is made of is still a mystery, but its existence has been deduced from the gravitational dynamics of galaxies: the pull of their gravity on light from visible stars is much too strong to be explained by their luminous matter. See Lawrence M. Krause, *The Fifth Essence* (New York: Basic Books, 1989); and James Trefil, *The Dark Side of the Universe* (New York: Scribner's, 1988).

10. Astronomer Bernard Lovell gives the density of matter at 10^{-43} second after the big Bang as 5×10^{93} grams per cubic centimeter of space, and, after one second of expansion, as one gram per cubic centimeter. Today, after some fifteen billion years of expansion and with the almost bottomless emptiness of space between galaxies, he estimates the critical mean density to be 2×10^{-29} grams per cubic centimeter, or approximately one proton per cubic meter. *In the Center of Immensities* (New York: Harper & Row, 1978), 104–7.

11. See Alan Guth and Paul Steinhardt, "The Inflationary Universe," *Scientific American* 250 (1984): 120.

12. Davies, *God and the New Physics*, 179. A light year is the distance that light travels in a year at the rate of 186,272 miles per second, or just under six trillion miles.

13. Ian G. Barbour, *Religion in an Age of Science* (San Francisco: Harper & Row, 1990), 135. This knife edge may turn out to be exceedingly sharp. Cosmologists

refer to the phenomenon we have been discussing as the "flatness" of the universe: there is just barely enough space for the expansion to continue against the pull of gravity. But such flatness may in fact be necessary in order to stabilize the expansion. Recent calculations by Harvard physicist Sidney Coleman indicate that the universe could well be exactly flat, i.e., its present density may be exactly 1 or exactly equal to critical density, and that consequently it must always have been such. This should not be so surprising, cosmologists say, because it would be very peculiar for a universe so very close to critical density at its start, and at most of its evolutionary stages, to be in our epoch departing from this delicate equilibrium. If Coleman's calculations are correct, then eventually enough dark matter must be found to increase the critical mass from the present guess of 30 percent to exactly (or very nearly) 100 percent. See. M. Mitchell Waldrop, "The Quantum Wave Function of the Universe," *Science* 242 (1988): 1248–50.

14. This point is well made by John Polkinghorne, *One World* (Princeton: Princeton Univ. Press, 1986), 55–57; and by John D. Barrow and Joseph Silk, *The Left Hand of Creation* (New York: Basic Books, 1983), 204–5.

15. Freeman Dyson, *Disturbing the Universe* (New York: Harper & Row, 1979), 151.

16. Quoted in George Greenstein, *The Symbiotic Universe* (New York: Morrow, 1988), 188, 190.

17. Paul Davies, *The Accidental Universe* (New York: Cambridge Univ. Press, 1982), 110.

18. Ibid., 115.

19. Barrow and Tipler, *The Anthropic Cosmological Principle*, 4.

20. Ibid., 3.

21. Pagels, *Perfect Symmetry*, 359.

22. See, for example, Stephen Jay Gould, "Mind and Supermind," in *Physical Cosmology and Philosophy*, ed. John Leslie (New York: Macmillan Publishing Co., 1990), 181–88; Willem B. Drees, *Beyond the Big Bang: Quantum Cosmologies and God* (LaSalle, Ill.: Open Court, 1990).

23. Heinz Pagels, "A Cozy Cosmology," in *Physical Cosmology and Philosophy*, ed. Leslie, 180.

24. Guth's theory is explained at length by Hawking, *Brief History*, 127–32, and by Guth himself in Guth and Steinhardt, "The Inflationary Universe," 116–28.

25. See Hugh Everett, *Review of Modern Physics* 29 (1957): 454.

26. On the many-worlds hypothesis see Davies, *Accidental Universe*, 122–27, and *God and the New Physics*, 171–74; Leslie, "Anthropic Principle," 145–46. The many-worlds hypothesis has been incorporated also into the strong anthropic principle as part of the *requirement* for a teleologically ordered cosmos.

27. McMullin, "How Should Cosmology Relate to Theology?" 43–44.

28. Leslie, "Anthropic Principle," 150.

29. Freeman Dyson, *Infinite in All Directions* (New York: Harper & Row, 1989), 296.

30. Heinz R. Pagels, "A Cozy Cosmology," *The Sciences* 25 (1985): 38.

31. Harold J. Morowitz, "Rediscovering the Mind," in *The Mind's I*, ed. Douglas R. Hofstadter and Daniel C. Dennett (New York: Basic Books, 1981), 34.

32. Jacques Monod, *Chance and Necessity* (New York: Knopf, 1971), 172–73.

33. Ibid., 21.

34. Dyson, *Infinite in All Directions*, 249.

35. See the critique offered by Mary Midgley in her *Science as Salvation: A Modern Myth and Its Meaning* (London: Routledge, 1992).

36. The analogy is that of Pierre Teilhard de Chardin, *Toward the Future* (New York: Harcourt Brace Jovanovich, 1975), 165.

37. Robert Jastrow, *God and the Astronomers* (New York: Norton, 1978), 116.

38. James M. Gustafson, *Ethics from a Theocentric Perspective*, vol. 1 (Chicago: Univ. of Chicago Press, 1981), 82.

39. Pierre Teilhard de Chardin, *The Phenomenon of Man* (New York: Harper & Row, 1959), 224.

40. Leszek Kolakowski, *The Presence of Myth* (Chicago: Univ. of Chicago Press, 1989).

41. Ibid., 118.

3. Theology and the
Heisenberg Uncertainty Principle

All scientific investigation seeks to conform thought to successful instrumental discoveries in the natural world. Unlike advances in cosmology, however, by which we have come to an in-depth understanding of the very large, the success of quantum mechanics has revealed a subatomic world whose nature is so baffling and enigmatic that physicists have simply had to suspend their disbelief. While they find the mathematical precision of the theory to be lucid and in nearly perfect conformity with experiment, they are forced to acknowledge its utter absurdity in relation to the world of everyday experience. "I don't understand it," says Nobel laureate Richard Feynman, "nobody does."[1] Feynman is referring to the fact that those clear-cut physical processes of classic Newtonian physics, with specific causes inexorably determining specific effects at specific moments in time, now appear at their subatomic level to dissolve into constituent roots that, while able in large part to be rationally structured, are nevertheless elusive and probabilistic, characterized by fitfulness and shadowy unreliability.

With some striking exceptions, as we shall see, physicists have generally been content to exploit the extraordinary predictive and explanatory power of quantum theory, not troubling themselves very much with what it seems to be saying about the nature of physical reality. Theologians, on the other hand, have tended by and large to ignore the theory altogether, and to confine their understanding of creation to the more secure world of Newtonian laws, content in the belief that this is the world that God has made and continues to guide with delicate providential care. Relatively few have been willing to familiarize themselves with the anomalies of quantum reality, or to grapple with their revolutionary implications for understanding divine grace and human freedom, God's creative action in the world, and indeed the doctrine of God itself. The major reason is undoubtedly the abstract mathematical character of quantum physics, which appears to them (as well as to most humanists) to be unrelated to immediate human experience or even to common sense.

Yet what theologians have failed to recognize is that this challenge to strict Newtonian determinism has meant the beginning of a whole new vision of the physical. Reality's atomic core has been found to be intelligible, but at the same time random, blurry, and apparently radically open. This is why, in the words of John Polkinghorne, "Quantum theory is arguably the great cultural achievement of our century. It is too important to be the preserve and pleasure of professionals alone."[2] The following pages thus seek to facilitate the moving of quantum theory into the preserve of theology. First, however, we must make a serious effort to understand it. So we shall begin with an overview of the theory itself, postponing until the second section those questions about its meaning, raised initially by its puzzled founders in the 1920s and subsequently by those seeking either to soften or to highlight its startling conclusions. We shall then, in the third section, be better able adequately to deal with the theory's theological significance, and perhaps to understand the extraordinary remark of British astronomer Sir Arthur Eddington that religion became possible for the reasonable scientist about the year 1927.[3]

──── The Loss of Certainty ────

The discovery of what has come to be called the "microworld" culminated in the overthrow of Newton's principle of strict determinism in nature, an achievement whose symbol has become Werner Heisenberg's uncertainty principle. The revolutionary character of this discovery will become evident as we begin to track its very spasmodic development beginning at the turn of the century. This development was controlled neither by pressure from the scientific community nor by the ingenuity of speculative minds playfully devising an alternative to classical physics, but exclusively by the natural world imposing itself on the human mind. The slow and tedious process of interpreting experimental results eventually led to the stark realization that at the subatomic level of reality there is an intrinsic limitation on the human capacity to know the material world.

The story began quietly enough in Berlin in 1900, where Max Planck had already spent years wrestling with the theory behind experiments on a phenomenon called 'black-body radiation'.[4] The existence of radiation itself had been recognized ever since Michael Faraday and James Clerk Maxwell demonstrated that electricity and magnetism were two aspects of a single force, electromagnetism. There was, they found, an electromagnetic spectrum, radiation waves ranging from very high frequency gamma rays through visible light waves to very low frequency radio waves. However, the so-called black bodies posed a special radiation problem for physicists: in so far as actual bodies approximated these more closely, they became nonreflecting and colorless, and yet they suddenly glowed brighter as they got hotter, their glow changing colors as their temperatures increased or decreased. There thus appeared to be a continuous thermal agitation over the whole range of the electromagnetic spectrum.

Physicists knew that the reason must be an energy exchange: as the temperature of the black object was increased, energy was being slowly added in the form of heat and taken off in the form of light radiation, emitted in different colors and intensity depending on the wavelength or frequency of the particular light (red light first, with its lower frequency and longer wavelength, then yellow and green light, finally blue and ultraviolet light, with their very high frequencies and very short wavelengths). When Planck followed classical physics, however, and assumed that this energy seeped in and out of the heated body continuously, his theory of how the emitted light should be distributed bore no relationship to what was actually being observed. For there was no smooth transition from color to color, from one energy frequency to another on the radiation spectrum. Planck was therefore forced to conclude that theory and observation could only be brought into agreement if one supposed that the light energy being measured was not radiating continuously but was being given off in something like packets.

This hypothesis, to which Planck said he was "driven by an act of desperation," is now recognized as one of the great leaps of human intuition, an incredible feat of the imagination. Planck confided to his son at the time that he might have made a discovery comparable in importance to those of Newton, and no physicist today would say that he was exaggerating. For the first time light radiation was recognized as existing in tiny bundles, its propagation perforated by 'jumps'. Planck called these granules of electromagnetic energy 'quanta', after the Latin for "how much." The glow of colored light from the heated black body thus only *appeared* to increase steadily with temperature change, in the same way that a row of tightly spaced microscopic dots will appear to the eye as a straight line.

These discrete movements of light radiation were simply too small and too numerous for the human eye to separate out.

Planck also realized that these quanta did not all carry the same amount of energy. The energy seemed to depend on the frequency or 'pitch' of the light wave in question: the higher the frequency of a wave and the shorter its length, the larger the amount of energy delivered in a single quantum of radiation. Red light would thus have much less energy than blue or ultraviolet light, because its frequency was lower and its wavelength longer. Planck was able to measure this wave energy by using a very precise number which connected the energy of a wave to its frequency through a proportionality. He called this number, which later became known as 'Planck's constant', the 'quantum of action', and he designated it by the letter h. The amount of energy of each light quantum of a particular color, he said, is equal to the frequency of its wave crests multiplied by h. Even though minuscule by standards of everyday life, h was shown in subsequent experiments not to be zero. Hence the energy of any particular quantum, however small, could also never be zero, which meant that the electromagnetic energy of light radiation had to be regarded not as continuous in structure but as bitty and discrete.

The general acceptance of this last statement actually owed more to Einstein than to Planck, who limited himself to describing the processes by which the energy of light radiation was emitted and absorbed. Einstein made the much more radical assertion that electromagnetic energy itself is quantized, and he actually showed this in 1905 by applying Planck's quantum hypothesis to explain the so-called 'photoelectric effect.' At the time, physicists believed that when electrons were ejected from metals under the influence of a light beam, the reason was the continuous intensity or brightness of the light. Einstein, however, following Planck, saw that such ejection occurred only when the light had the proper color or frequency, regardless of its brightness. He then hypothesized that all light waves had to be made up of large numbers of discrete light quanta, which he called 'photons', whose energy bombardment was what dislodged the electrons. Eventually he was able to prove that the energy of these dislodged electrons was in strict proportion to the frequency (and therefore the energy) of the light used to dislodge them. This discovery won Einstein the Nobel Prize in 1921. Two years later the experiments of the American physicist Arthur Compton finally proved beyond doubt that light waves are indeed constituted by the illusive photons whose existence Einstein had predicted.

Early in the century everyone believed that the atom was the most elementary structure and was without component parts. But in England in 1911 Ernest Rutherford, an experimental physicist already well known for discoveries in radioactivity, found that particles with a positive electrical charge bounded back when they hit an atom. Since like electrical charges repel each other, Rutherford knew that the source could not be the electron, which carried a negative electrical charge. Eventually he was able to demonstrate that some other positively charged entity had to be concentrated in a point-like entity at the center of the atom, which turned out to be the nucleus. In other words the atom was not a simple but a compound system. After this discovery, however, scientists still needed some description of what was going on inside the atom. What were electrons *doing* in the neighborhood of the nucleus? An answer was provided in 1913 by the theory of a young Danish physicist, Niels Bohr, which eventually won him the Nobel Prize. After observing Rutherford's work in Manchester, Bohr took the daring step of applying the quantum findings of Planck and Einstein to electrons moving around the atomic nucleus.

Bohr postulated that this movement of electrons around a nucleus had to take place not just at any distance but at very specified distances and in essentially stationary energy states. These he provisionally (and incorrectly, as it turned out) compared to the orbits of planets in a solar system. The state with lowest energy, he said, is that closest to the nucleus, while states with higher energy are further away. Since Bohr was working with the hydrogen atom which had only one electron, he could measure very precisely both the energy states of this single electron as well as the quanta of colored light emitted when this hydrogen atom was disturbed.

Bohr found that when there was an influx of energy the electron 'jumped' from a lower to a higher state, sometimes leaping over intermediate states, depending on the amount of energy delivered. When, on the other hand, the atom lost energy, the electron 'jumped' from a higher to a lower state. In both cases the energy difference between states would appear in the form of light radiation, namely light quanta that corresponded to the frequency (color) of the light multiplied by h. This emitted energy was also always equal to the energy of the electron's jump. None of this, of course, could be pictured in space and time. "I cannot describe these transitions," Bohr admitted. "They are not motions in any classical sense. They are something new that I don't understand."[5]

Physicists now had from Einstein a theory of light radiation that spoke of discrete particles in terms of frequency (a property of waves), and from

Bohr a theory of atomic structure which measured energy loss and increase in terms of electron jumps from one stationary energy state to another. There was never any doubt, moreover, that light was a wave, since the experiments of Thomas Young in the early nineteenth century had proved this beyond doubt and were recognized as still valid. Nevertheless, when light waves interacted with matter they also clearly manifested the discrete character of particles, giving energy to matter as well as taking energy from matter in quantized packets. Little progress was made in understanding this mysterious wave-particle duality until 1923, when Louis de Broglie, a young Parisian physicist, "lifted a corner of the great veil" (as Einstein put it),[6] and pointed to a way out of the dilemma: perhaps this wave-particle duality was not restricted to light but was in fact a universal phenomenon.

If light radiation, de Broglie reasoned, which was clearly an electromagnetic wave, could sometimes behave like a particle, might not the electron, which was clearly a particle, sometimes behave like a wave? He then proved that it actually did so behave by deducing what the electron's wavelength must be. This insight was later confirmed by reproducing for electrons the experiment that Thomas Young had performed on visible light.[7] There was, in other words, such a thing as a matter wave, whose energy and frequency were related through Planck's constant in exactly the same way as in radiation waves. It thus became clear for the first time that not only did all radiation behave like waves and particles, but matter behaved this way too.

De Broglie had finally connected the quantum nature of radiation energy with the paradox of wave-particle duality. All that was needed now was a concise mathematical formula that would express and govern how something like a matter wave could move and propagate itself. This was supplied in 1926 by the Viennese physicist Erwin Schrödinger, who was stimulated by de Broglie's discovery to work out his own famous 'wave equation'. Again focusing on the simple hydrogen atom, Schrödinger specified mathematically the wave shape that the single hydrogen electron would have to obey outside the nucleus. He showed that it was not a spherical entity (as was previously supposed) nor did it move around the hydrogen nucleus in a circular orbit. Instead it was literally "smeared out" in a certain quantized orbit about the nucleus, like a resonating violin string of a given length, whose harmonics are restricted as well as stabilized by the nature of its vibrations. Schrödinger himself seemed to think that electrons as well as other subatomic particles must be similar to clouds or fogbanks, with intrinsically fuzzy boundaries. He finally argued that they were not really particles at all, but pure and simple matter waves, and that the particle idea had been wrong to begin with.

Six months after Schrödinger published his 'wave mechanics', his German counterpart, Max Born, announced in Göttingen his own interpretation of the de Broglie–Schrödinger equations. Whereas Schrödinger was convinced that he was describing things that were real in an objective sense (*something* was waving), Born was just as convinced that the waves in question were 'probability waves', mathematical abstractions that gave one information, allowing one to say of an electron circling a nucleus that it had a certain probability of being found "here" and a certain probability of being found "there." He believed, moreover, that too much evidence showed electrons to be true particles, with sharply defined locations, very unlike those amorphous Schrödinger clouds.

What Schrödinger had actually accomplished, Born said, was to demonstrate mathematically that we can know these locations only approximately. The spreading of the wave thus did not mean that the electron itself was spreading; what was spreading was the likelihood of finding it more or less distant from the nucleus. This probability was a function (the square) of the wave's amplitude, which will be largest at its crest and trough, and smaller anywhere in between. Schrödinger's equation therefore states that these probability amplitudes, when squared, will tell us where the electron is likely to be found. Born thus conceived the wave–particle duality in exactly the opposite way from Schrödinger: it is the particle that is real, with its wave representing the probability of its location.

At this point we should note that in mid-1925, just before Schrödinger produced his wave mechanics, a young German physicist named Werner Heisenberg discovered a way to explain Planck's idea of the quantum by organizing experimental data into mathematical tables through a method he called 'matrix mechanics'. Like Schrödinger's equation, this was a theory to explain the behavior of the microscopic world. But whereas Schrödinger located the source of subatomic change in what atoms were made of, namely their states as matter waves, Heisenberg focused on what they were seen by observation actually to be doing, namely their energy transitions as seen in lines on the light spectrum. In one physicist's theatrical metaphor, "Schrödinger moved the scenery with the actors standing still, whilst Heisenberg left the scenery untouched and let the actors move around."[8] Because Heisenberg's tables enabled one to calculate the probabilities of particle motion under certain initial conditions, his theory was understandably quite congenial to someone like Born. But within a year Schrödinger was able to show that matrix mechanics was mathematically equivalent to his wave mechanics and was in fact simply a different representation of the same theory. One could thus move from one representation of the theory to another by the rules of translation, as one might move from one language to another to find different words to describe the same object.

The person who finally completed this transformation, incorporating wave mechanics and matrix mechanics into the general principles of quantum field theory known as 'quantum mechanics', was the brilliant Cambridge physicist Paul Dirac. He accomplished this in 1928 with his 'superposition principle', which demonstrated mathematically that one state of a particle (it is "here") can actually be combined with another state (it is "there"). This combination (or superposition) of states underlines in a striking manner the two most unexpected and most difficult features of the quantum world, namely its statistical character and its unpicturability. John Polkinghorne explains that

> the superposition of a state with an electron "here" and a state with an electron "there" does not produce a state with the electron at some point between "here" or "there" but a state in which the electron can be found either "here" or "there", with probabilities which depend . . . on the balance between the two states. If the state is mostly "here" with just an admixture of "there," then the electron will much more frequently be found "here" rather than "there." On any particular occasion of measurement, however, we are unable to predict which possibility will be realized.[9]

Dirac also finally solved the apparent paradox of wave-particle duality with which physicists had been living for twenty-five years (although he acknowledged the impossibility of translating his mathematical solution into the language of everyday life).[10] For it is the superposition of different states that gives the particle the spatial extension associated with a quantum field or wave, and it is the excitations of the field or wave that enable it to be interpreted as countable packets of energy or particles. Such superposition is, moreover, the essence of waves, which, through the phenomenon of interference,[11] can be added together to reinforce each other at crests or to cancel each other out at troughs. Probability waves are thus mathematical calculations of tendencies to happen, the strength of any particular outcome depending on the degree of its probability. This is why Heisenberg could say of such a wave that it was "a quantitative version of the old concept of 'potentia' in Aristotelian philosophy. It introduced something standing in the middle between the idea of an event and the actual event, a strange kind of physical reality just in the middle between possibility and actuality."[12]

Up to now we have been looking at how an understanding of the quantum world developed over the first quarter of this century. By 1928 all its structure and mechanics were well understood, at least mathematically: if left undisturbed, all matter at this subatomic level evolves with regularity and continuity, generating its potentialities in accordance with the Schrödinger wave equation which represents all its possibilities. If we ask for no specific information about these possibilities, nature gives us no specific answer. However, if by some large-scale measuring instrument we look from the outside to see what is going on in this realm, then our intervention creates a disturbance. An electron that is in a superposition of possibilities of being "here" or "there" is forced to "choose," to actualize one possibility, all other possibilities ceasing to exist.

Because this disturbance of the electron is a measurement of some sort, its result must be registered on some macroscopic device operating in the world of everyday life, such as a pointer coming to rest at some mark indicating "here" or "there." Such registration is in fact a most important moment in quantum theory and has a special name. It is called "the collapse of the wave packet," because the electron in superposition is considered to be a packet of waves of different wavelengths or velocities, which observation collapses to a single measurable particle. The smoothly propagating Schrödinger wave is thus violated by contact with large-scale matter, its packet suddenly forced to jump from multiple potentiality to actuality. While presumably this goes on all the time, in all parts of the universe, such collapse can only be observed if the large-scale matter happens to be some measuring device. Since these waves are packets of probability, moreover, there is no way to know beforehand the precise result of the measurement.[13]

Now it might be supposed that such collapse, actualizing as it does one of the potentialities, would yield certain knowledge. But this turns out not to be the case. Before the measurement there is no way of knowing, other than by some probability distribution, which of the myriad possibilities is going to be actualized, but afterward the content of detailed measurement turns out to be just as uncertain. In 1927 Heisenberg incorporated all these experiences into his celebrated 'uncertainty principle', arguably the most adequate single statement of quantum theory. The reader will better appreciate its significance if we first describe what happens when one repeats with photons or electrons Thomas Young's famous two-slit experiment of the last century. (The first quantum physicists all had to use photons; the extremely short wavelength of electrons ruled out their use until about 1960.) For however weird and mysterious quantum theory may appear, its acid test is whether it does or does not agree with experiment. In that experimental context one physicist wryly comments, "Everything is against quantum theory except the facts."[14]

As we saw,[15] when Young's experiment is done by filtering sunlight through two narrow slits of a screen, the wall behind is illuminated by an interference pattern caused by the light's diffraction at the slits, proving that light is a wave, since only waves are subject to interference. The pattern of light on the wall thus appears as one of alternating bands of light and dark areas. Now if instead of ordinary sunlight, large numbers of photons are shot through two closely spaced parallel slits in a metal foil toward a photographic plate, the same interference pattern will be found. The dots made on the plate by the impinging photons will form alternating bands of light and dark areas, and so will display (not surprisingly) the wave character of the photons. (This is because the photons will accumulate, in accordance with quantum theory, in those regions where the probability amplitudes are greatest, and totally avoid those regions where they are zero.) On the other hand, if we direct these photons in a steady stream through a single slit, they will then display (again not surprisingly) a single spot on the photographic plate without any interference pattern. (This is because two slits are needed for interference; the pattern depends on the reinforcement or cancellation of two trains of waves.)

Note that, although in both cases the photographic plate is recording the impact of individual photons, this obviously does not tell us, in the first case, through which of the two slits any single photon passed. If, however, we try to make the experiment more precise by shooting one photon at a time through these two slits, we still find the interference pattern; it just takes longer to build up. So the question is this: as each individual photon arrives at the photographic plate, which slit did it pass through? Surely it must have passed through only *one* of the slits? Yet the interference pattern before us on the screen requires *two* overlapping wave trains, one from each slit. If we suppose that the photon went through slit #1, then slit #2 should have been irrelevant and could just as well have been closed. But if we then close slit #2 and shoot this photon again, there is no interference pattern. The same happens if we close slit #1 and shoot the photon: no interference. Yet what possible difference can it make whether the slit through which the photon did *not* pass is open or not?

What, then, is causing the buildup of interference when only one photon at a time is shot through? In the early 1920s, Bohr gave a tentative resolution of this paradox, but it was weird: the indivisible photon is going through *both* slits and so must be interfering with itself. This bizarre conclusion was eventually confirmed by Dirac's superposition principle: the motion of each photon as it hits the screen is a combination of state one ('passed through slit #1') and state two ('passed through slit #2'). The two states overlap and combine, like two movie films projected simultaneously onto the same screen. Hence if we stop the experiment here, the most we can do is to follow Born's formula: square the probability amplitude of the photon's wave to calculate the likelihood of its having gone through one or the other slit. At this point in the experiment we have absolutely no way of knowing for sure.

Of course we can continue the experiment. We can install some device at each of the slits that will click if a photon goes through. Sometimes the click will be at slit #1 and sometimes at slit #2, so now we shall be able to know what we could not know before. However, this new knowledge will come at a price. For by intervening to spy on the photon in this way we alter the experiment and immediately do away with the interference pattern. Why? Because the measuring click forces a collapse of the wave packet and signals to us that the photon is no longer in that superposition of location states that was causing the interference pattern on the photographic plate. The probability is now zero that the photon can be anywhere other than where we have found it to be.

But by reducing its range of possible location states to the width of this very narrow slit, our measuring device also brings about a very large range of superimposed velocity states. In other words, we lose all knowledge of where the photon is going once it has passed through the slit at which we have located it. There is now equal probability of its hitting the photographic plate absolutely anywhere. Our certainty regarding its position has in effect left us totally uncertain about its subsequent path to the photographic plate. Only with a second measurement at some subsequent point will it be possible to reduce this superposition of velocity states to a single state that will tell us about the path and speed of the photon. "I remember," wrote Heisenberg late in his life, discussions with Bohr which went through many hours till very late at night and ended almost in despair; and when at the end of the discussion I went alone for a walk in the neighboring park I repeated to myself again and again the question: Can nature possibly be as absurd as it seemed to us in these atomic experiments?[16]

Heisenberg was nevertheless able to use experiments like these finally to formulate his uncertainty principle. Before enunciating it, however, let us pause a moment. It is important to be clear about the magnitude of the atom, the behavior of whose particles the principle seeks to clarify. The diameter of an atom is about one hundred millionth of an inch. Yet this tiny microscopic entity consists mostly of vast regions of empty space, in which the even smaller electrons move around a nucleus one ten thousandth the size of the whole atom. This nucleus contains smaller particles still, protons and neutrons, with spatial dimensions of almost a millionth of a millionth (a trillionth) of an inch. An atom is thus huge compared to its nucleus. To see this nucleus we would have to blow up the atom to the size of the Houston Astrodome. The nucleus would then be about the size of a grain of salt, and electrons, which have about two thousand times less mass than a nuclear particle, would be comparable to specks of dust whirling around in the vast space of the dome.

The initial task undertaken by quantum physicists, as we just saw in experiments like that of the two slits, was to chart the behavior of these subatomic particles, which meant finding out where the particle was at any given moment, as well as where it was going and how fast it was going there. For only when these variables were known could any predictions be made or laws formulated regarding future behavior. The first experiments were able to locate the position of a particle relatively easily by shining on it a light which had a very high frequency and a very short wavelength, and then measuring the distance between the short wave crests of the light to locate the particle.

But physicists now encountered a problem they had not found in charting the behavior of energy quanta in the macroworld. For the light particles (or photons) they were using, with their very short wavelength and high frequency, also had a very high energy. These photons could therefore locate a particle's position with great accuracy, but their energy was found to disturb the particle's momentum (its mass multiplied by its velocity), so that the direction and speed became much less clear. If, however, they used light with a lower frequency (hence with longer wavelength and less energy) to "see" the particular particle, its direction and speed could be known much more accurately but its position would then be much less clear. (The same held true when radiation other than light was used to "see" subatomic particles: the smaller the wavelength of this radiation, the higher was its energy and the greater the disturbance introduced into the subatomic realm.)

These experiments, similar to that of the two slits, were the basis in 1927 for Heisenberg's formulation of his uncertainty principle, which may be stated thus: the more accurately one knows by repeated experiment the position of any subatomic particle, the less accurately one knows its momentum, and vice versa. The quantum state of a subatomic particle (its position and momentum) can thus never be known or predicted with certainty. There is, in other words, a minimum amount of uncertainty, an irreducible fuzziness, which we can never escape in our observations of the subatomic world, a certain limit on the accuracy with which position and momentum can be simultaneously known.

Heisenberg said that this minimum uncertainty could be quantified: the amount of our uncertainty regarding a particle's position multiplied by the amount of uncertainty regarding its momentum is a constant, namely Planck's quantum of action or h. This number is extremely small, but, as we saw, it is not zero and was contained in Planck's proportionality between wave energy and frequency. It constitutes, said Heisenberg, an absolute limitation on our knowledge of the subatomic world. That is to say, we may be more or less uncertain about any given phenomenon taking place in that world, but we must always remain at least *this* uncertain about the totality of what is taking place. Planck's 'constant' thus achieved in subatomic theory a significance comparable to that of the absolute speed of light in relativity theory.[17]

The upshot of the uncertainty principle was the gradual recognition that science can get only so close to the underpinnings of nature. At the level of Planck's constant the centuries-old quest to know must stop. We are simply unable to make a measuring mesh of reality that is fine enough to tell us everything that is going on in spaces less than one hundred millionth of an inch. There is, in other words, an intrinsic limit to the precision of scientific investigation at this level. Something will always be hidden from the observer by the fitfulness of the quantum jump symbolized by Planck's quantum of action. Quantum chance is thus radically different from chance in everyday life, where two events whose causes can be completely known suddenly and unaccountably connect with each other (a speeding car and a child crossing a street to a neighbor's house). In the microworld there is no way to know everything about what causes a particular event. We can give no complete retrospective explanation of what we have seen an individual particle do. Causality as such is not eliminated, because physical situations still depend on each other. But they do so probabilistically: all we have from the past is a range of potentialities for the future. The corollary of such uncertainty is therefore unpredictability: in so far as there is an observational limit to our measurement, the particle's future behavior becomes to that extent also indeterminate and probabilistic.

Classical physics, on the other hand, worked on the premise that all effects are products of their antecedent causes, and that to discover the cause of a thing is to explain it. Newton's equations could thus measure quite accurately the present position and momentum of moving objects (earth, sun, moon), and calculate exactly their future as well as their past behavior (eclipses, seasons), something still true of very large bodies. But, as double-slit experiments and those like them demonstrate, when we get down to the physical foundations of these bodies, we may know everything knowable about antecedent conditions, and still not be able to predict what individual particles will actually do. (We shall say more in Section 3 about agreement and correlation between these two apparently different descriptions of the physical world.)[18] This is why Bohr could write:

> We have been forced step by step to forego a causal description of the behavior of individual atoms in space and time, and to reckon with a free choice on the part of nature between various possibilities to which only probability considerations can be applied.[19]

Bohr himself tended to think in terms of a 'complementarity principle'. That is to say, position and momentum are complementary notions. Dirac may have enabled us to understand wave-particle duality without paradox *before* we intrude into the quantum state, but once we decide to intervene to get specific information, we must choose a measuring situation appropriate to either wave or particle, under conditions that are mutually exclusive. Which specific behavior the particle reveals thus depends on which behavior we inquire about. Hence the experiment, as well as our description of its results, constitutes our choice between a wave model or a particle model. We cannot have both simultaneously. Bohr insists, however, that this experimental restriction should not be seen as a defeat, because quantum theory shows these descriptive limits to be inherent in nature itself. Subatomic processes simply do not admit the exact descriptions of classical physics; they do not define themselves with that precise conjugation of position and momentum that has long been axiomatic in the macroworld of everyday experience.

—— THE MEANING FOR SCIENCE ——

The discovery of the curiously elusive objects of the quantum world has modified in very substantial ways the scientific understanding of reality. Since the late 1920s science has recognized that an inescapable randomness and discontinuity appears whenever one attempts to extract by measurement any information from the regularity of Schrödinger's smoothly propagating wave. The collapse of this wave packet is always traumatic, because there is no way to determine its outcome on any particular occasion. While the probability for some particular behavior can be specified exactly (with predictions that have been accurately measured up to one part in ten billion), no precise earlier behavior can be assigned as cause for the event that actually takes place. Intervening into the protean realm of quanta thus always involves the element of surprise. Each event is unique. Exactly the same two experiments will very likely not give the same results, because the connections between the experiments themselves are never necessary but only probabilistic.

All this has not, however, resulted in any problem for quantum theory. Its mathematical precision and range of predictive power have provided marvellously clear explanations for many ordinary-scale physical phenomena, including the very existence as well as the stability of solid bodies, the melting, freezing, and boiling of liquids, the behavior of transistors and television screens, as well as much that takes place in biology and genetics. There is nevertheless a big problem. "The greatest paradox about quantum theory," notes one physicist, "is that after more than fifty years of successful exploitation of its techniques its interpretation still remains a matter of dispute. We all agree on how to do the sums, and our answers fit experiment like a glove, but we cannot all agree on what is going on."[20] This inability to explain either predictions or results means that no single picture of reality has emerged from all the mathematical precision. Are natural processes at their roots intrinsically indeterministic? Or is the whole problem one of epistemology, a limitation of our knowledge forced upon us by the nature of the experiments involved? Is it possible, perhaps, that quantum theory as we know it, in spite of its usefulness in so many fields, is still incomplete, and that strict causation prevails after all?

Einstein, for one, held with stubborn tenacity to this last conviction. He found the specter of indeterminacy in nature to be abhorrent, and its demonstration in quantum theory appalled him. He kept insisting to the end of his life that there could be no such thing as hybrid photons or electrons going through two slits. There had to be causes as yet unknown for what we observe in this experiment; more careful observation must eventually determine through which slit the photon or electron went. "I find the idea quite intolerable," he wrote in a letter to Born in 1924, "that an electron exposed to radiation should choose *of its own free will*, not only its moment to jump off, but also its direction. In that case, I would rather be a cobbler, or even an employee in a gaming-house, than a physicist." And in another letter: "I am quite convinced that someone will eventually come up with a theory whose objects, connected by laws, are not probabilities but considered facts."[21]

What so deeply disturbed Einstein was obviously chance. All during the late 1920s and early 1930s he engaged in (and lost) debate after debate with Bohr on the validity of the uncertainty principle. He finally gave up, but he never gave in. He used to refer to God as "the Old One," a Deity who he said was "the God of Spinoza," an 'infinite substance', the higher cosmic order of an impersonal nature for which he had the deepest respect but which had no concern for the destinies and actions of human persons. "I am at all events convinced that *He* does not play dice."[22] His intransigence in this matter eventually tended to isolate him from the physics community. Heisenberg tells of spending an entire afternoon with him at Princeton in the fall of 1954, when he was nearing the end of his life. To his surprise, "Einstein's whole interest was focused on the interpretation of quantum theory. . . . The remark 'But you cannot believe, surely, that God plays at dice' was several times repeated, almost as a reproach." Heisenberg later reflected on the encounter: "He knew what enormous changes in science he had brought about in his own lifetime, and he also knew how hard it is—in science as in life—to accommodate oneself to changes of that size."[23]

Nor was Einstein the only one. Schrödinger consistently stood by his side. "You must surely understand, Bohr," Heisenberg quotes him as saying, "that the whole idea of quantum jumps necessarily leads to nonsense. . . . If we are still going to have to put up with these damn quantum jumps, I am sorry that I ever had anything to do with quantum theory."[24] He was referring, of course, to the fact that, while he himself believed in the reality of his wave equation as something independent and determined, Bohr and the others were interpreting it probabilistically to mean that external observation could abruptly alter it by collapsing the wave packet. Such a sudden jump, with its randomness and uncertainty, violated what Schrödinger considered his equation's elegance. To vent his irritation, he wrote a sardonic essay in 1935 which included the now famous "Schrödinger cat" paradox, the point of which was to show that this interpretation of theirs would lead to obvious nonsense, namely that the macroworld would have to be subject to the same uncertainty and subjectivity.

Suppose, he said, a cat is shut up in a steel chamber with a flask of lethal gas, some radioactive material with a fifty-fifty chance that one of its atoms will decay within an hour, and a device to smash the flask if it detects an atom's decay. At hour's end is the cat dead or alive? If orthodox quantum theory is applied, Schrödinger said, and the cat is treated along with the radioactive material as a total quantum system with its own wave packet of probabilities, then the answer has to be that we do not know until someone looks in the box. For the cat is a superposition of states, with a probability of $1/2$ that decay of an atom has occurred and the cat is dead, and $1/2$ that it has not and the cat is alive. But this is manifestly absurd. Must the cat be suspended between "dead" and "alive," depending on whether or not the wave packet is collapsed by opening the box? If the lid is not lifted and the cat goes unobserved, must it remain indefinitely in schizophrenic unreality? Common sense says that the cat's fate must be certain and independent of observation. Why then does such common sense not hold for subatomic particles as well? If quantum theory cannot describe macroscopic objects like cats, how can it be valid for microscopic atoms?[25]

These reactions of Einstein and Schrödinger represent quite well the first interpretation of the uncertainty principle: our uncertainty simply represents our ignorance. Embraced by a small minority of physicists, including originally Planck and de Broglie, this approach insists that a subatomic particle does *not* behave in two completely different ways, one when nobody is looking and one when it is being observed. Its behavior is completely determined, and any observations to the contrary simply reflect the incompleteness of quantum theory and our temporary lack of knowledge of the causal laws involved. For how could such dynamic flux produce our macroworld where objects are actual and fixed? The probabilities we calculate thus cannot exist in nature itself: they are epistemological in origin, not ontological, and in no way dependent on some subjective observation. Quantum measurement is therefore really the same as Newtonian measurement: whatever cloudiness it may have is either the result of experimental clumsiness or else exists exclusively in the mind of the person making the measurement.

Before we go on to those interpretations of the uncertainty principle that take the act of measurement more seriously,[26] it would be well to recognize the radical pragmatism of the vast majority of working physicists. They put high value on quantum theory because it is an unusually effective machine-like tool for predicting and explaining natural phenomena, such as the stability of the atom and the structure of the periodic table of the elements. But questions about the ultimate reality of these phenomena generally have little interest for them. They confine themselves to the theory's mathematical precision and simply ignore the weirdness of what they investigate. Apparently the average quantum mechanic is about as philosophically minded as the average garage mechanic.[27]

Nevertheless, the way working physicists deal with the quantum objects they study, as well as the way they speak about them, indicate that they regard them very realistically. They accord Schrödinger's wave equation a status beyond a mere calculating device, treating the weaving patterns of its packet as a quantum state that is objective in nature, independent of anyone's perception. In spite of the peculiarities of its collapse (which we are able to observe and measure instrumentally), this wraith-like entity is presumed to be the form that reality takes in the subatomic world.[28] This combined pragmaticism and realism of the average physicist have received very different emphases in the major interpretations of quantum theory that seek to explain uncertainty.

The first is the celebrated 'Copenhagen interpretation', the received orthodoxy followed to this day by most physicists. With Bohr as chief architect, its emphasis falls upon the fact that the statistical probabilities of microscopic particle activity are inseparable from the macroscopic measuring instruments we choose to know them with (and by extension from the conscious observer doing the measuring). This necessarily puts a fundamental limitation on our knowledge. Whether uncertainty really exists on the lower level we cannot say. It is thus impossible to know whether there is a one-to-one correspondence between quantum theory and quantum reality. For that reality only exists for us in a process carried out with macro measuring instruments. Only after the wave packet has collapsed and transformed itself into a single state in our macro-world, can we say anything at all about the original superposition in the microworld.

What then is responsible for this knowledge limitation? At first both Bohr and Heisenberg believed that it had to be the observation process itself. But this idea turned out to be incapable of explaining the unpredictability of particle behavior when no experimental intrusion is involved. It was then that Bohr and others saw a larger significance for the complementarity principle described earlier. The real source of limitation is conceptual: by choosing different experimental situations we decide which of our conceptual schemes (position or momentum, time or energy) the particle must manifest.[29] No meaningful value can be given to one partner of these pairs while we are measuring the other. We 'fix' at the macroscopic level of consciousness something from the micro-world, thereby showing ourselves to be the initiators of what we observe. The conscious observer is thus responsible for the wave packet's collapse. Bohr especially emphasized the positivistic aspect of this knowledge: we can assert nothing about this quantum world until a measurement is taken; it is scientifically meaningless to assign physical existence to the elementary phenomena themselves. Our epistemology must therefore be agnostic. What may or may not be going on before the measurement is knowable only within a certain probability.[30]

While most physicists subscribe to Bohr's insistence on the central importance of the measuring process, very few, including Heisenberg, would follow him and others in their consciousness-only approach. For if our limited knowledge gets fixed only when a conscious observer is involved in the experiment, then we must suppose something very odd: a computer printout that is left unread does not collapse the wave packet or record any definitive information about a particle until someone comes along to read it. This was one of the points Schrödinger was making with the sarcasm of his famous cat paradox.[31] Bohr also had to face the charge of introducing a radical dualism into nature: unknowable quantum entities totally distinct and separate from our macroworld until connected in a single measuring event by some macro measuring device. Physicists as a group, on the contrary, tend to think of the natural world as a unity, and to recognize that measuring instruments are made out of quantum constituents just like everything else.

Eventually Heisenberg broke with Bohr on a much deeper issue. He never abandoned the central Copenhagen tenet that our knowledge of particle indeterminacy comes at the moment of the wave packet's collapse. What he insisted on in his later writings was that this indeterminacy exists *before* the collapse and is indeed an objective part of the very structure of subatomic reality. He refused, in other words, to be agnostic about such reality. Subatomic particles, he believed, were simply not like entities in everyday life, all of which have precise positions and velocities easily accessible to measurement. They are rather superpositions of different dynamic states, entities with a range of potentialities, "tendencies to exist" in a variety of possible ways. We discover uncertainty in the electron's behavior with instruments and consciousness because that is the behavior that is intrinsic to the particle's reality, independent of observation. Ontology thus controls epistemology, not the other way around.

"The observation," said Heisenberg, "selects of all possible events the actual one that has taken place.... Therefore, the transition from the 'possible' to the 'actual' takes place during the act of observation."[32] As we saw earlier, he believed that such objective indeterminism in microprocesses was a restoration of Aristotle's concept of *potentia*, a plasticity in nature, a capacity for the novel and the unpredictable.[33] The observer's influence in the measurement process thus does not consist in disturbing a previously precise though unknown value (position/momentum, time/energy), but of forcing one of many potentialities to be actualized. The observer's action in this way becomes part of the atomic entity's real and objective history. Einstein was not wrong, then, because he insisted that particles must be real, but because he believed that they had to be real *things*, objectively there, like realities in the macroworld. His realism was 'classical' or 'Newtonian'—observation could have no impact on the reality of things. He, of all people, ought to have been able to recognize that matter, dematerialized at its roots into energy packets, could be just as physical as the matter of everyday life.

There have been two attempts in recent years to escape the quantum measurement paradox that is central to the interpretations of Bohr and Heisenberg, one within conventional quantum theory and one outside it. Working within conventional quantum theory, a small group of cosmologists, led by Princeton's Hugh Everett III in the late 1950s, looked for a way to apply quantum theory to Einstein's general theory of relativity by assuming that the entire universe can be treated as a gigantic evolving Schrödinger wave, responsible for the wave packets of all lesser entities derived from it. The result was the 'many-worlds hypothesis', a daring proposal completely consistent with quantum theory, which sought to reconcile the continuity of the Schrödinger wave with the discontinuity and multiplicity of empirical experience.

The bizarre and completely untestable claim was that *all* possibilities in any given superposition are actualized whenever a measurement is made. That is to say, to accommodate the demands of the cosmic wave, the individual particle and the measuring device together are split into as many copies as there are possible outcomes for the particular measurement. These realities then exist on parallel planes of existence, incapable of communicating in any way, each with a different copy of the conscious observer. There would thus be one world with a dead Schrödinger cat and another world with a live one. Since there is no collapse of the wave packet into one single reality, there is obviously no measurement problem and no role for the observer. Such a wanton ontological extravagance, however, with entities multiplying at this incredible rate, has turned out to have appeal for very few cosmologists. "It is enough," comments one critic dryly, "to make poor William of Occam turn in his grave."[34]

The second attempt to escape the quantum measurement paradox along with its indeterminism is that of the late University of London physicist David Bohm. Elaborated as a result of conversations with Einstein in the 1950s, and put in final form in his influential 1980 book *Wholeness and the Implicate Order*, Bohm's theory seeks to replace conventional quantum mechanics by turning physics around, as it were, starting with the whole instead of with parts. "We proposed that a new notion of order is involved here, which we called the *implicate order*," he writes. "In terms of the implicate order one may say that everything is enfolded in everything. This contrasts with the *explicate order* now dominant in physics in which things are *unfolded* in the sense that each thing lies in its own particular region of space (and time) and outside the regions belonging to other things."[35] One of Bohm's analogies is that of a TV signal with information enfolded in an electromagnetic wave, which the TV receiver unfolds in a visual image. So also, he says, beneath the world of surface phenomena, there is an undivided seamless whole, and it is this 'underworld' that is the domain of quantum objects.[36]

This philosophic vision of wholeness, along with other Bohm insights, has gained him something of a cult following among a small group of physicists and philosophers of science who believe that his views as scientist and philosopher are underestimated. His refusal to cooperate in principle with Senator McCarthy's Un-American Activities Committee in the early 1950s, which forced him out of his professorship at Princeton and prompted his move to England, undoubtedly enhances today an already impressive career in theoretical physics. His scientific originality, however, stems from his early dissatisfaction with conventional interpretations of quantum theory and his attempts to vindicate Einstein's conviction that all events in the microworld are determined by specific causes, even though these may not be known or even knowable. Bohm's theory is thus one of 'hidden variables'. It assumes the validity of quantum mechanics but reinterprets it as a deterministic theory in terms of hidden causes that may be forever experimentally inaccessible to us. It is precisely because of this ignorance, he says, that our knowledge of the microworld has to be statistical, like the actuarial knowledge of a life insurance company, whose individual clients may die of causes it cannot know. The uncertainty principle is thus quite valid: indeterminacy is indeed real, but it is not final.

To ground his theory, Bohm first overcame the mathematical difficulties associated with the concept of a 'pilot' wave, proposed originally by de Broglie in the 1920s. He then conceived each quantum object as both a particle in the explicate order and as a 'pilot' wave in the implicate order. This wave's function is to carry information about the environment, thereby guiding the particle half by telling it what to do. If the pilot wave senses the presence of a measuring device, for example, it immediately notifies the particle, which then accommodates its behavior to the kind of attribute the device is designed to measure. Such a wave would thus have no difficulty in going through both slits in the two-slit experiment. Bohm has been able to show, moreover, that this deterministic and classically realistic approach can actually work mathematically, with experimental results identical to those of conventional quantum theory.

Nevertheless, most of Bohm's colleagues remain dubious and have tended to relegate his work to the periphery of quantum physics. The chief reason is that in order to accomplish his mathematical *tour de force*, Bohm has to invoke an experimentally unverifiable 'pilot' wave, a 'variable' cause that is in principle forever 'hidden'. Such undetectability is simply too high a price to pay for the rigid Einsteinian determinism Bohm achieves by postulating his pilot wave. Indeed, this is supposed to be a *real* wave, not a probability wave, with an identity separate from the quantum object as particle, whereas the whole history of quantum mechanics affirms wave-particle inseparability. (It might be different, say Bohm's critics, if the results of one of his experiments were able to produce evidence that would distinguish the consequences of his theory from those of standard quantum theory.) Some physicists also claim that Bohm's approach must be restricted to the area of nonrelativistic quantum theory; that is, it is not as capable as conventional quantum theory of giving an account of the behavior of very small particles whose velocities approach the speed of light.

Finally, Bohm's ingenious mathematical equations appear to be much too contrived and arbitrary to be convincing, they say—too lacking in the elegance and simplicity that characterize equations of the standard theory, qualities that have come to be accepted as hallmarks of scientific truth.[37]

These already ambiguous relationships between Bohm and his critics have been thrown into even sharper relief by a quite different problem, one that has recently become the subject of much heated discussion: nonlocality. 'Locality', or 'local causality', as it is also called, means that the causal influence of one entity upon another cannot propagate faster than the speed of light; 'nonlocality', on the other hand, means that it can, and so calls into question the absolute in Einstein's special theory of relativity. Common sense would obviously opt for local causality: what happens at the same moment in two places some distance apart cannot be connected if there are no physical forces operating in between, the fastest of which is light. This touchy question of nonlocality or nonlocal causality arose originally as a result of one of Einstein's celebrated thought experiments, which he kept devising during his debates with Bohr to show that quantum theory, however consistent, had to be incomplete. In 1935 his collaborators on the most famous of these experiments were Boris Podolsky and Nathan Rosen, and so the experiment has gone ever since by the name of the EPR paradox.

According to strict quantum theory, said EPR, each member of an original particle pair, even if separated, always carries an imprint of the other. (If the spin of one particle is "down," for example, that of the other is "up," and vice versa.) Hence certain experimental situations could theoretically be devised in which the arbitrary choice of how one particle is to be observed in a particular region of space would seemingly have an instantaneous (nonlocal, faster-than-light) effect upon the second particle, which splits off and is now very distant from the first. For while the uncertainty principle says that one cannot simultaneously specify exactly both position and velocity of the first particle, it appears that one could predict exactly, and without measurement, the position and velocity of the second particle as an immediate consequence of whatever measurement is made on the first.

But how would the second particle find out what position and velocity the first is going to manifest to the observer? Is this not supposed to be a matter of statistical probability alone? EPR's conclusion was that the communication between the particles would have to be instantaneous, with a speed faster than light. But, said EPR, such "spooky action at a distance" (or nonlocality) is both counterintuitive and physically impossible. Hence the probability descriptions of quantum theory must be incomplete: the second particle must somehow already have its own definite position and velocity before the first particle is measured, which means that there have to be specific, if unknown, causes at work ('hidden variables'), acting on both particles to determine their individual outcomes.[38]

In the debate itself Bohr's positivism, with its strong emphasis on classical measuring instruments, managed to achieve a pyrrhic victory by answering EPR on Bohr's own terms. Einstein was assuming, Bohr said, that the second particle is isolated and that its position and velocity have objective reality before they are measured. But quantum theory's standard interpretation requires a more holistic approach; the atom is a total system in whose vibrant possibilities the separate identity of elementary particles is lost. Hence the position and velocity of both particles have no meaning until they are directly measured. Before measurement, the two particles, even if an enormous distance apart, are still encompassed by a single wave packet. When a measurement is taken they form, together with the observer and the measuring apparatus, a single individual experimental situation whose results obey the Heisenberg uncertainty principle. Choosing to measure one member of a particle pair in a certain way, therefore, also inevitably and immediately influences what we can know about the other.

Once the debate was over, however, physicists were faced with the real issue, and it startled them: the EPR experiment really did seem to show that, if quantum theory were complete, then it was violating local causality, perhaps the most staunchly held principle in physics. Could information possibly be getting around this fast in the quantum world?[39] Or was the theory really incomplete, with unknown specific causes, as Einstein said? For thirty years EPR's conclusions were debated, until in 1964 a then-unknown Northern Irish theoretical physicist working at the CERN nuclear research center near Geneva, John Bell, finally broke the impasse by giving Einstein's thought experiment an existence outside the mind. His six-page paper, published in the first volume of an obscure journal, has come to be known as 'Bell's theorem'. It consisted of a mathematical formula ('Bell's inequality') which could be independently checked by experiment and so was able to put "spooky action at a distance" to an empirical test.

'Bell's inequality' started with the two assumptions central to EPR's claim of unknown causes or 'hidden variables': classical realism (particles are objectively there at all times, whether observed or not) and local causality (no causal influence can be communicated between separated particles faster than the speed of light). Bell then showed that any such hidden variable theory, with a strong commitment to both particle objectivity and local causality, could not reproduce all the statistical predictions of quantum mechanics. To conform experimentally to the statistical probabilities of standard quantum theory, one or another of these assumptions had to be abandoned. In other words, experimental agreement with the uncertainty principle has to mean either that particles are not objective in the classical sense or that there is instantaneous nonlocal communication between them. This discovery of Bell is now regarded by many as one of the most important in the history of science.[40]

Mainline quantum theorists, who never took all that seriously the classical objectivity of subatomic particles, had little difficulty making the choice imposed on them by Bell's theorem. If they were positivists like Bohr, they tended to be agnostic about all reality in the microworld until it was observed. For nature at this level appears to them as no more than an inference from pointers on some measuring device or from the reasoning of the conscious measurers. If they were critical realists like Heisenberg, they did not regard particles as real *things* but as real 'tendencies to exist', totally unlike realities in the macroworld. Hence these physicists could easily opt for local causality. They usually reasoned, as Bohr did in the EPR debate, that separated particles from an original particle pair must always be considered a unity within a single wave packet. Only after an observation can they be regarded and discussed as having separate identities, thereby unveiling previously unknown aspects of the separated particle's motion.

Unlike Bohr, however, these physicists now have to deal with recent experiments that not only confirm Bell's theorem but actually have on record instances of what looks very much like nonlocal causality between photons.[41] While they obviously have to accept these experimental results, they tend to interpret them differently, namely as pointing to a new understanding of *local* causality: particles that are once together remain together no matter how far apart their subsequent separation; nature must be envisioned in organic terms, as systems in symbiotic relationship. The present position of mainline quantum theorists is thus that there has to be more cohesion between the fundamental constituents of nature than they could ever have previously suspected.[42]

Physicists like Bohm, and Bell himself, on the other hand, because strongly committed to Einstein's classical realism, also had no difficulty

choosing between Bell's options. As we saw, every quantum particle for
Bohm is immediately connected with every other by its nonobservable
pilot wave, which is the dynamic medium of nonlocality in the implicate
order. In very subtle ways the universe is in instantaneous communication
in all its parts. This underlying holistic order is what determines the explicate order through the 'hidden variables' of the pilot waves. Fluctuations
in these waves are what cause the statistical probabilities perceived in experiment and codified in Heisenberg's uncertainty principle. The classical
concept of local causality thus becomes irrelevant; particles discontiguous
and without causal influence in the explicate order are none the less correlated, by their pilot waves, becoming contiguous in the implicate order
and unfolded from its unbroken wholeness.[43]

Bell's theorem and its numerous confirmations have thus had significant impact on how physicists now think about the meaning of uncertainty in quantum mechanics. For the first time there are experiments by
which the various philosophic interpretations we have been discussing can
to some extent at least be empirically tested. One consequence is that a
theory like Bohm's, combining classical realism and radical nonlocal
holism, even though indistinguishable experimentally from conventional
quantum theory, is now grudgingly recognized as a scientifically legitimate challenge to the interpretations of Bohr and Heisenberg. A second
consequence is that some physicists have begun to think of classical objectivity and local causality as complementary concepts, different rep-
resentations of the same underlying wholeness of quantum reality, neither
of which can fully explain the type of world we live in. In this sense, observing scientists really create their interpretations of the fuzzy quantum
world by opting beforehand for one or other of these concepts. These
interpretations will then always be able to confirm from the available experimental evidence the invalidity of the other concept.[44]

Even more important is the third consequence: whether conceived as
ontological or epistemological or both, uncertainty appears to be at the
heart of every interpretation of microworld reality. Quantum theory may
be mathematically harmonious and precise, but it remains profoundly
mysterious and disturbing when examined in the context of everyday
life. We still have no answer, for example, to the enigma of quantum
measurement. Why does such measurement collapse the wave packet,
producing a single outcome from multiple potentialities? How does the
act of observation transform quantum entities into ordinary objects?
Precisely where does the fitful quantum world interlock with reliable laboratory instruments to produce definite answers whenever interrogated?

Nor have physicists yet even begun to explore what is implied about nature by recent data on the nonlocal interrelationships between particles. Can there actually be such a togetherness in the microworld that spatial separation of particles cannot divide them?[45] Is subatomic reality really such an unbroken whole that it cannot be described atomistically?

Finally, we must recognize that there is nothing absolutely inevitable about conventional quantum theory, even though most quantum physicists today still find it rationally coherent and compelling.[46] This inability of any single model to give an exhaustive account of subatomic phenomena has resulted in a restoration of that modesty that science had largely lost in the nineteenth century. An image of Heinz Pagels captures well this resignation to the uncertainty that must be lived with in our encounter with the world of the very small. "We can imagine that quantum reality is like a sealed box," he writes, "out of which we receive messages. We can ask questions about the contents of the box but never actually see what is inside it. We have found a theory—the quantum theory—of the messages and it is consistent. But there is no way to visualize the contents of the box."[47] As we shall see in the following section, theology asks very different questions about this box and its contents.

───── THE MEANING FOR THEOLOGY ─────

Before assessing the meaning of quantum theory for theology, it would be well to recall what scientists and Christian theologians have in common. Both assume that they can make some sense out of the data of their respective disciplines, that observations of the physical world and Christian experiences of God and God's creation are more or less intelligible. Both are also aware of the partial character of all human knowledge: scientists recognize that their observations and theories can never encompass the existing universe in its totality, and theologians are aware that their language and concepts can never exhaust the reality of God. Hence both construct models and paradigms in order to interpret as best they can the data available to them at any particular time. Since one of theology's tasks is to interact with contemporary culture, theologians must also periodically reassess the impact of scientific discoveries on their current understanding of the Christian tradition.[48] This is why various findings of science inevitably find their way into the subject matter of theology.

But this interrelationship will always be complex. While theologians must somehow incorporate current scientific explanations into their wider conceptual schemes, they must also, as Frederick Ferré cautions, make efforts to distance themselves from the theories of science that are dominant at any given time. For the scientific enterprise, as its history makes abundantly clear, is highly corrigible both in principle and in practice. Scientific claims that are related to the data of Christian faith can thus never be seen as foundational. In any testing of the consonance of such claims with theology's interpretation of these data, the latter will always constitute the normative counterweight.[49] Nevertheless, this corrigibility of science cannot be an excuse for theology shirking the hard task of grappling here and now with the implications of these claims. For theology is also corrigible. If current scientific models and paradigms eventually change, then their theological meanings will also have to change. In the meantime, theologians seeking to focus their reflection and critique will have to settle for, and make a concerted effort to understand, whatever data and theories are generally accepted at present by the scientific community as a whole.

When we ask about the meaning of quantum theory for theology, then, we have to start with the fact that all physicists today find this strange world to be both intelligible and capable of yielding definite observational answers whenever it is interrogated. While the true nature of quantum reality is still a highly contentious issue, as we saw in Section 2, most physicists nevertheless interpret its uncertainty as a principle of genuine indeterminacy and not merely as a principle of ignorance. (I leave aside the third option, the many-worlds hypothesis, as simply too bizarre for theological consideration, though it is not, as we noted earlier, inconsistent with quantum theory.) The reason is undoubtedly that the majority tend to be critical realists, convinced that what we know through experiment is a close approximation to what is actually there.[50]

This close link between epistemology and ontology is not difficult to understand, given the early history of quantum theory discussed in Section 1. Hence even though deterministic versions like David Bohm's are as empirically adequate as the conventional version, they exercise little appeal for physicists because they deny the ontologically open character of quantum entities manifested in the unpredictability of quantum process. It is therefore important that theologians reflect seriously on the scientific data we have been discussing before committing themselves too quickly to a relatively uncomplicated understanding of divine action in nature based on some hidden determinism in the microworld.

The latter would indeed be an easy escape from the dilemmas of quantum uncertainty. For instead of Einstein's unknown causes operating through mechanistic laws, God would become the ultimate Hidden Variable working at the roots of reality, orchestrating particle activity to obey the statistical probability of experiment. Such a God would be the polar opposite of the absent God of deism, in total control at all times of each and every quantum event, even though to the scientist such an event would appear to be without any completely knowable cause and governed by chance. Nor would a conviction of such control have to mean that God would be intervening in the particle world as an outside physical force, since particles in a superposition of states are without definite position or movement, and so no intervening force would be required to change them. God would simply be determining whatever actual value is to be realized from this range of particle potentialities. Whenever a wave packet collapsed, this would be God selecting some value to be actualized. Divine activity in the microworld would in this way be reduced to crass predestination.[51]

As we shall see presently, there is good reason that this understanding of God as the true Hidden Variable has such appeal, but there is also a root theological problem that has to be recognized: unless one holds predestination at the human level (a rare theological position today), God's providential involvement with human freedom will have to be understood as totally different from God's action in the processes of the natural world. On one level there would be openness and flexibility, on the other a rigid determinism. Such a position would be consistent, of course, with a spirit-matter dualism, but as I have explained elsewhere,[52] theologians in recent years have become aware that they can no longer draw any easy boundary between matter and spirit, and that a body-soul dualism is no longer the only way to safeguard the irreducible spiritual principle in persons. If, on the other hand, we conceive humans to be psychosomatic unities, with spirit no longer appearing as an intruder into matter, then we are forced to conclude that God's providential activity ought to be a seamless web, operating in the same way both 'top-down' through the mechanisms of human freedom and 'bottom-up' through the mechanisms of nature. We shall get a better sense of why this might well be so if we take a moment to evaluate three important facts about the micro and macro worlds.

First, since nature is a unity there obviously has to be some relationship between these two worlds, and quantum physicists have long connected them by what has come to be called the 'correspondence principle'. Its key rests with the magnitude of h, Planck's quantum of action, whose finiteness is basic to quantum theory. However, this number only has significance inside the atom, in sizes and distances less than one hundred millionth of an inch. As these become larger, h becomes so small as to be considered zero, thereby making the probabilities of statistical laws look more and more like certitudes and quantum theory more and more like classical physics. There will thus be an emergent upward movement of quantum reality. A camera with a zoom lens powerful enough to focus from the microscopic up to the macroscopic would actually find an unbroken unity. For all objects from the macroworld, including human beings, are composed of billions, perhaps trillions, of particles, all of them in a superposition of states. But the mass of these everyday objects is so enormous compared with h that any uncertainty of position and momentum becomes vanishingly small, and it will be impossible to distinguish probabilities at one end from certainties at the other. What exists in the macroworld is consequently the statistical averaging of particle motion. While Schrödinger's wave equation thus holds true as well for everyday life, Robert Oppenheimer reminds us that

> this equation, when applied to the familiar context of massive bodies and great distances, where the quantum of action is in fact negligibly small, will describe for us waves so reasonably concentrated in space, so little dispersed about their average wave length, that the Newtonian orbit reappears in its unaltered classical path.[53]

The second important fact is that in recent years the clockwork Newtonian regularity of planetary motion has come to be regarded not as the paradigm of what goes on in the macroworld but rather as the exception. There is now general agreement that only a small fraction of natural occurrences can be described in this way, and that physical processes are dominated overall by irregular behavior. Predictability, in other words, is no longer the norm: almost all complex dynamic systems are recognized as unstable. This does not mean that their movements are just downward toward disorder, however, because statistical science also reveals an urge toward unexpected structure in what is to all appearances random. Fluctuations of quite ordinary systems like the atmosphere, for example, or like pendula, magnets, and even insect populations, usually tend to emerge into orderly wholes. Their properties are thus found to manifest the same complex interplay of flexibility and lawful process that characterizes entities at the quantum level. This 'orderly disorder' has today become the object of a special field of applied mathematics known as 'chaos theory'. Indeed, many see this new understanding of structured chaos at the macro-level as a third revolution in science, in Thomas Kuhn's sense of that term,[54] next to those of Newtonian and quantum mechanics that preceded it.

Chaos theory is still in its infancy, yet it has already placed complex systems beyond the grip of any mechanistic determinism. The reason is that such systems can reach wildly unpredictable results from very simple initial conditions. While these conditions are in principle mathematically sufficient to project the entire future behavior of the system, they turn out in fact to be unknowable. This gives rise to what James Gleick only half-jokingly refers to as "the Butterfly Effect—the notion that a butterfly stirring the air in Peking can transform storm centers next month in New York."[55] For the storm is what is called a 'nonlinear system', one open to an almost infinitely multiplying variety of possible behaviors, the tiniest information error about it escalating exponentially with time.

No amount of computerized data can eliminate such complexity, moreover, and vast amounts of it are needed simply to keep pace with the system (unlike calculations about the solar system, for example, which can easily keep well ahead of its movements). All power of prediction is therefore lost. Does such a degree of randomness go beyond mere subjective ignorance? Does chaos theory show it to be intrinsic to these macro systems? "If apparently open behavior is associated with apparently deterministic equations," asks Polkinghorne, "which is to be taken to have the greater ontological seriousness—the behavior or the equations? Which is the approximation and which is the reality?"[56]

These two facts regarding the relationship and functioning of micro- and macroworlds, combined with what we have already seen to be the case with quantum reality, point to an overall looseness and dynamic in-stability in physical nature that have found ample confirmation in the instabilities of biological evolution. Events behave as though without specific cause, yet a certain order always manages to be generated from the initial chaos, producing the ever-changing yet ever-stable world of every-day life. Novelty now becomes both plausible and feasible, because the passage of time discloses which of innumerable possibilities gets actual-ized. "Only when a system behaves in a sufficiently random way," write two well-known analysts of the phenomenon, "may the difference be-tween past and future, and therefore irreversibility, enter into its description. . . . The arrow of time is a manifestation that the future is not given."[57]

The philosopher Karl Popper has said the same: "The greatest riddle of cosmology may well be ... that the universe is in a sense creative."[58]

This potential in nature for partial self-determination emerges into full flower, however, when we consider the third important fact: the experience of human freedom. This experience has had very divergent interpretations from psychology. Approaching the human person from the outside, using spectator language, strict behaviorists understand this phenomenon deterministically, believing that freedom is just an illusion or that it is simply a negative absence of interference. Others, the cognitive psychologists, are more concerned to approach the human person from the inside, using actor language, and to defend self-determination by appealing to everyday thinking and acting. In this perspective one's choices are acts of the whole person and much more than the mere absence of interference. We are indeed circumscribed by such normal human constraints as the past events of our lives, our physical condition, social surroundings and personality traits. But we nevertheless learn from our immediate experience of deliberation and action that we retain at our psychic roots the positive power to determine future goals and to initiate responsible moral choice.[59] Christians would obviously follow this second approach, which means that there would be a certain degree of indeterminacy in human freedom that is not unlike that of the quantum world as most physicists understand it, although as far as we know the quantum character of brain particles does not provide the physical basis for human psychological states.[60]

The significance of these three important facts for God's providential guidance of the world should now be clear. I want to suggest that the best way to understand how God might be acting in the indeterminacy of the subatomic realm is by analogy with the traditional theology of how divine initiative relates to the indeterminacy of human freedom. The Christian tradition has long recognized God's continuous presence and activity in the depths of the human personality, meshing somehow with the dynamics of human thought and initiative in order to help persons choose what is best for their present and future spiritual growth. The name given by the tradition to this presence is 'grace', and the tradition has always taught that humans may freely reject it. Augustine's formulation of the teaching in the early fifth century is still striking: "God is more inward to me than my most inward self."[61] Unfortunately, even religious persons do not often advert to this teaching, no doubt because humans generally tend to equate freedom with autonomy and self-sufficiency. Nevertheless, recognition of

God's gracious presence and action in every human life has always been an essential Christian belief.

Christian tradition perceived this presence and activity of God very differently, however, when it came to the world of matter. For many centuries physical reality appeared to be totally regulated, sustained in existence by God's creative power and quite unrelated to the human. Newton's rigid mechanistic paradigm of nature's deterministic motion italicized this theological model and gave it scientific legitimacy. Its settled order thus made it unnecessary to think of God's action as in any way analogous to God's presence to the dynamics of human choice. Hence when it came to the contingent cosmos, Christian theology was tinged with its own distinctive brand of deism, softened only by belief in the possibility, on certain rare occasions, of divine intervention by miraculous *tours de force*. Modern science changed all this by offering a totally new understanding of the physical world, as well as the human connection to it through biological evolution. Theology was thus challenged to reopen the question of how God related to these newly found dynamisms in nature.

Until recently few theologians took this challenge seriously. Most ignored the discoveries of quantum theory in the 1920s, for example, and continued to defend on religious and philosophical grounds the limitations imposed upon divine and human freedom by nature's apparent determinism. At the same time scientists like Eddington were seeing light from the opposite direction. Eddington could make the type of remark about religious belief that I referred to in the introduction because he recognized "that 1927 has seen the final overthrow of strict causality by Heisenberg, Bohr, Born and others."[62] There was now to be found in nature itself an alternative to deism, some room for maneuvre in the laxity of the quantum world for a God active in history and individual lives. Eddington's fellow astronomer Sir James Jeans had a similar reaction: "Mind no longer appears as an accidental intruder in the realm of matter."[63] Or again: "The old physics showed us a universe that looked more like a prison. . . . The new physics shows us a universe which looks as though it might conceivably form a suitable dwelling place for free man, . . . a home in which it may at least be possible to mould events to our desires."[64]

How, then, might theology go about extending the Christian understanding of God's interface with the human to God's interface with quantum reality? A warning of Thomas Aquinas at this point should prevent us from regarding the answer to this question as a mere exercise in a natural theology divorced from revelation. "Sometimes," he says, "errors about creation can lead one away from the truth of faith and induce a false knowledge of God."[65] The answer must thus be viewed as part of a Christian theology of nature; not as something extrinsic to faith experience, but as an effort to understand more fully God's self-revelation in Jesus. We want to know the extent to which we can speak as Christians of God's continuous interaction with the looseness we find in the microworld. We consequently seek a religious response to the strangeness of quantum reality, something Lonergan once referred to in another context as *intellectus quaerens fidem*, understanding in search of faith.[66]

This search can never be completely successful, however, because our analogy's primary focus, God's relationship to free persons, will always be slightly blurred. We have in the tradition no really satisfying model for this interaction, so we should not be surprised if we find difficulty in extending it to the quantum world. For Christians have always found themselves in a double bind: too much emphasis on God's omnipotence tends to impinge upon freedom, but too much autonomy for persons sets them adrift, allowing little room for God to help them give direction and meaning to their lives. Hence the perennial problem of balancing freedom with order, novelty in the world with stability, the flexibility of process with the reliability of law. Christians actually experience all these dynamisms operating in human life, but have never had any tight rationale to explain their interaction in the dialectic of grace and freedom.

Nor is this situation inconsistent with God's own mystery, "a patient and subtle Creator, content to achieve his purpose through the unfolding of process and accepting thereby a measure of the vulnerability and precariousness which always characterize the gift of freedom by love."[67] In any case, two things would seem to be true: that the human world is on a continuum with the microworld, mediated by larger biological matter, and that what is common to the activity of both free persons and quantum particles is that each is an example of what has been termed 'weak causality',[68] in which what is determined by the past is a range of potentialities for the future. Since some determinism is always present, we have an assurance of continuity; but since more than one alternative is open, we can also expect the unexpected.

While individual events may be undetermined, however, the involvement of large numbers in both realms nonetheless results in certain statistical regularities. Thus microscopic realities combining randomly with other microscopic realities mysteriously result in enough regularity in physical phenomena on the macroscopic level to justify our speaking of 'laws' on this level. We therefore see the correspondence principle at work once more: quantum physics somehow turns smoothly into Newtonian physics. None of this means, of course, that free decisions are derivative from this atomic indeterminacy. It is precisely because they are phenomena of quality rather than quantity, arising from human agency and experience as integrative events, that the potentialities of human choice are so different from purely physical phenomena, and so much less susceptible to scientific analysis and control.

The complexity as well as the consistency of God's causality in the world can thus be seen at work in the psychosomatic unity of human beings. On the most fundamental level there is the experience of radical contingency, of an existence that need not be, and so has to be received from God. God's creative power must thus continuously communicate existence to persons, from their deepest quantum roots up to their most sophisticated intellectual and volitional powers.[69] Moreover, since behavior follows from existence, this means that God must also be communicating existence to the behavior of persons, whether it be that of their quantum particles, biological systems,[70] or free decisions. Does this mean that God is somehow a cause of this behavior? Of course, but obviously not a cause like other causes, differing from them only in power. For when it comes to human behavior, God is what Aquinas refers to as the 'primary' cause, a cause at the level of existence. Any particular behavior is thus totally that of the creature, or 'secondary' cause, doing whatever it is inclined to do naturally in whatever way it naturally does it, and totally that of God communicating existence to the creature and to its behavior.[71]

Hence there would in principle be no gaps in any scientific account of such behavior, which would be complete on its own level. For God's presence and causality would be veiled within the total process, and would not suddenly appear in some gap which for a time science might have some trouble explaining. This is not to say that there is no gap at all in the process: continuing evolution is itself incomplete. But this is simply another way of saying that the process as we know it, both material and personal, is still open and flexible enough for secondary causes to function naturally in its ongoing development. Their behavior on their own level would thus also be the hidden action of God on another level, maintaining in existence these naturally behaving secondary causes. In this sense whatever any natural entity is doing is itself what God's continuous creative action must also be doing.

But Christians know that the range of God's causality has to be wider than simply sustaining in being this natural functioning of people and

things. Otherwise the depth of human suffering, especially innocent suffering, the sheer scale of its pain and tragic waste, would be a scandal too
great even for those of committed religious faith.[72] Christians thus look
to the Bible, which shows us a God who constantly plans for the good of
individuals and society and whose intentions get realized in history, from
Israel's rescue in Egypt to the coming of the Kingdom in the redemptive
life, death, and resurrection of Jesus, and in the animating presence of his
Spirit to the early church. The God of the Bible is thus no impotent spectator of the cosmic drama. Divine omnipotence clearly makes a difference
in events, but it unfailingly manifests itself not as coercive power but as
sovereign love. Both sciences and psychology make us aware today how
this steadfast love of God, the *hesed* of the Hebrew scriptures, might be
able to influence events: there is some room for maneuvre in the hidden
looseness of the unfolding quantum process and in the unpredictable
openness of persons to persuasion.

Here then, it would seem, are the 'causal joints' of divine action, to use
Austin Farrer's phrase, points at which the future comes into being, where
greater good can be brought out of evil, where God's intentions can be
actualized without denying to creation the freedom given it to be itself in
a flexible process that is structurally open. By analogy with human intentionality, where the mind's action is veiled yet guides the body to move
naturally, this divine intentionality gently interacts with the human, not
by way of an energy push from outside but by way of new information
suggesting the right direction to follow.[73] In this way God is at once both
transcendent to human action and intimately involved with it. St. Paul tells
us that these loving intentions of God extend to all matter as well, which
"groans" for redemption no less than do men and women, a groaning that
presumably must have begun some fifteen billion years ago when the
Spirit first hovered over the formlessness of the quantum void.[74] Perhaps nowhere today is this encounter of matter with the Spirit of Jesus
more visible than in the sacramental life of the church, especially in the
Eucharist.

Does this mean that God is after all controlling the cosmic process? To
a certain extent yes, it does, but not in the sense that God rigidly determines quantum events, any more than this is the case in God's involvement with free human decisions. There may be no inherent limitation
in God's power to achieve plans and intentions, but there clearly appears
to be a voluntary self-limitation. God's loving presence and guidance, in
other words, is not that of a puppeteer. Paul speaks of a divine *kenosis*, an
"emptying" into matter in the person of Jesus, and of Jesus' subsequent ac-

ceptance of the precariousness of the fully human.[75] God plainly took risks in Jesus: things could and did go wrong for him. The revelation of his passion shows us a divine love whose distinctive power lies in its acceptance of all the bitterness of human fallibility and malice, and in its embrace of vulnerability, suffering and death. "Christ," says Paul, "is the power and wisdom of God. For God's foolishness is wiser than human wisdom, and God's weakness is stronger than human strength."[76] The power of God's Word is thus that of forgiveness, patience, and persuasion.

Is it not then reasonable to suppose that these redemptive events in Jesus' life in the realm of human freedom are simply the further manifestation of that loving self-limitation of God in the realm of matter? From this perspective the vulnerability of the divine Word in history would be a reflection of a certain precariousness in the creative process itself, and the indeterminacy of quantum reality would illustrate this divine patience at matter's roots. Because God relates to every creature according to its nature, these roots would be allowed to explore their own potential, because matter's nature, like freedom's nature, is to do precisely this. Our world must consequently contain within itself the possibility of physical events which are both good and bad for individual persons. "It is inevitably," says Polkinghorne, "a world with ragged edges, where order and disorder interlace each other and where the exploration of possibility by chance will lead not only to the evolution of systems of increasing complexity, but also to the evolution of systems imperfectly formed and malfunctioning." God seems to be mysteriously content "to achieve his purposes through the unfolding of process. It is possible that Love can only work in such a way, out of respect for the beloved."[77]

The God of Jesus is thus neither a maker of clocks nor a thrower of dice, but the one ceaselessly at work bringing overall direction and order to the undetermined realms of matter and spirit, "an Improviser of unsurpassed ingenuity," to use Arthur Peacocke's phrase.[78] This mysterious process may at times stun and baffle us, but as Christians we nevertheless assert that it constitutes not an obstacle to but a vehicle for God's love, that it does not contradict God's providential care but somehow illumines it. Wave packets propagate and collapse, sparrows fall to the ground, humans freely decide for good or for ill, yet hairs of the head nevertheless get numbered, elusive quantum particles eventually statistically stabilize, and "where sin increased, grace abounded all the more."[79]

On the level of things, the world may not be tightly ordered, but it is ordered nonetheless. Over time, randomness gets smoothed out into statistical law, God acting as a principle of concretion, continuously bringing the definitive out of the novel and the ambiguous.[80] On the human level too, persons live in an economy of divine superabundance. The depths of human suffering remain impenetrable, but the scandal of their mystery is not meant to be dissolved so much as overwhelmed. Underneath both levels God thus remains, *vis-à-vis* creation, the ultimate Hidden Variable. If indeed there are any dice, theology would say they are loaded.

—— CONCLUSION ——

The burden of this chapter has been that the Heisenberg uncertainty principle has become the symbol of indeterminacy in natural process, and that thus far mainline Christian theology has not adequately dealt with its religious meaning. My chief contention is that, if the quantum world exists the way the vast majority of physicists says it exists, then God's presence at this blurry level of reality must be conceived by analogy with the classic understanding of God's presence at the level of persons, namely as a sign of the freedom given to creation to be itself. God's action meshes dynamically with the potentialities inherent in the behavior we see at both levels, without disturbing the natural probability patterns at either level.

Statistics are consequently not a mask for ignorance but rather a description of how things really are. What we have are probability distributions in which one alternative is actualized under God's guidance, with no physical force needed on God's part. The subatomic particle and the free human being both behave in accordance with the respective natures given to them by God, the one randomly, the other reflectively. God thus intersects with nature from the top down through human agency and from the bottom up through quantum uncertainty. We humans stand, says Freeman Dyson, "midway between the unpredictability of matter and the unpredictability of God. . . . We have learned that matter is weird stuff. It is weird enough so that it does not limit God's freedom to make it do what he pleases."[81]

We might draw two conclusions from what has been said. First, the discovery of quantum reality should help greatly in the ongoing task of formulating models for God's action in the world. This task is always urgent, because such models, though much less precise than doctrines, usually carry much greater conceptual power. Theologians have traditionally been more attracted to models stressing God as the transcendent source of order in nature than to those stressing God as immanent source of novelty. Hence there was a preference in the past for God as king and ruler, as the potter working with clay, even for a time as the divine clock-maker, with nature as the law-abiding machine. These models were always softened, of course, by the interpersonal model of God as immanent to free decision, as well as by the general rejection of human predestination. But there was seldom any prominence given to the model of God's continuous creation, which mostly lay dormant along with the medieval concept of primary causality. Only in recent years have they both re-emerged to stimulate new models able to deal with those dynamisms in nature where God is not the only agent.

Imaginative attempts have been under way for some time to work on this major theological problem, all of them stressing God's immanence in a continuously creative process. American theologian Sallie McFague has emphasized feminine models: the world as God's body (developing "within" God but distinct from the whole of God's being) and that of God as Mother, Lover, and Friend.[82] Perhaps the most striking model is that of British biochemist and theologian Arthur Peacocke, who speaks of God as a Composer. He uses this musical analogy because he sees the creative potentialities of the universe as inherent, as given by God, to be impro-vised and orchestrated (and so successively disclosed) in the way a master composer would expand a very simple tune into an elaborate fugue or symphony. What we find in the world is thus "the interplay between an expectation based on past experience ('law') and an openness to the new ('chance' in the sense that the listener cannot predict or control it)."[83] Eventually to evolve human persons in this way, however, brought into existence new and hazardous possibilities, exposing the Composer to re-jection, so that in the human species God now suffers with and through creation.

The second conclusion is that the irreducible uncertainty in the micro-world, to which science has long become resigned, should encourage theology to live more easily with the mystery of God's active presence in the lives of free persons. For human reality is clearly rooted in quantum re-ality, and hence theology's classic inability to speak with any precision to the divine-human relationship at the level of freedom can more easily be extended to our corresponding inability to clarify God's action at the quantum level. This is actually in keeping with theology's ancient apo-phatic tradition: God is hidden and wholly other; our religious language is radically inadequate to address the divine mystery; the theological task is not so much better to understand this mystery as better to locate it.

Nor does this mean that the genuine discoveries of quantum behavior ought not to raise legitimate theological questions that transcend the purely scientific. The point is that quantum mechanics seems to contain its own apophatic element, and theologians who arrive on this particular scientific scene late and a little out of breath, as Lonergan would say, should not underestimate the weirdness of the data they find, nor assume that they can deal with it any easier than they can with the data of religious experience. "Seek simplicity," says Whitehead, "and distrust it."[84] The desire to control reality by intellectual oversimplification is as endemic to theology as it is to science. Finding too much order in the world can be as bad as finding too much novelty. Hence the perennial need to recognize that there are limits to what can be known and that these limits must be respected and lived with. The hopeful element here, however, as Holmes Rolston points out, is that such limitation "can caution us not to worry overmuch if our theologies are multidimensional, approximate, conflicting and unsettled. Even our failures, instabilities and insecurities can be a form of providence."[85]

——— NOTES ———

1. Richard Feynman, *QED: The Strange Theory of Light and Matter* (Princeton: Princeton Univ. Press, 1985), 9.

2. John Polkinghorne, *The Quantum World* (Princeton: Princeton Univ. Press, 1985), ix. This is by far the most illuminating brief treatment of this complex subject for the nonprofessional. The author summarizes its salient points in "The Quantum World," in *Physics, Philosophy, and Theology: A Common Quest for Understanding*, ed. Robert J. Russell, William R. Stoeger, and George V. Coyne (Notre Dame, Ind.: Univ. of Notre Dame Press, 1988), 333–42.

3. Arthur Eddington, *The Nature of the Physical World* (Cambridge: Cambridge Univ. Press, 1928), 350. Quoted by Erwin N. Hiebert, "Modern Physics and Christian Faith," in *God and Nature*, ed. David C. Lindberg and Ronald L. Numbers (Berkeley: Univ. of California Press, 1986), 432. See text for note 62 below.

4. For the following historical account I rely on Polkinghorne, *Quantum World*, 5–31; Werner Heisenberg, *Physics and Philosophy* (New York: Harper Torchbook, 1962), 30–43; Heinz Pagels, *The Cosmic Code* (New York: Bantam Books, 1983), 11–65; J. Robert Oppenheimer, *Atom and Void* (Princeton: Princeton Univ. Press, 1989), 3–63, 113–32; Stephen W. Hawking, *A Brief History of Time* (New York: Bantam Books, 1988), 53–61; Gary Zukav, *The Dancing Wu Li Masters* (New York: Bantam Books, 1980), 48–103.

5. Quoted by Polkinghorne, *Quantum World*, 123.

6. R. W. Clark, *Einstein* (Cleveland: World, 1971), 335. Quoted by Richard Schlegel, *Superposition and Interaction* (Chicago: Univ. of Chicago Press, 1980), 34.

7. In 1803 Thomas Young established beyond question the wave behavior of light by his famous two-slit experiment. He filtered sunlight through two razor-like slits of a screen so that the light shined against a wall. Since the width of the slits was less than the wavelength of the sunlight, the light "diffracted" or spread itself out as it passed through the slits toward the wall. The projection on the wall should thus simply have shown the sum of this diffracted light from the two slits. But instead the wall was illuminated by alternating bands of light and darkness, a phenomenon known as "interference," something that only waves create. That is to say, the waves of diffracted light from the two slits overlapped in some places and enforced each other (the dark bands), but cancelled each other out in other places (the light bands). This is exactly what happens when ocean waves move toward a harbor protected by a jetty with two openings for ships to pass through. When the large waves go through the narrow openings they bend around the openings (or diffract), spending themselves out in a curve on the other side and exhibiting an interference pattern: at some points they toss up and down strongly, because at those points the crests of waves from each opening are merging and re-inforcing each other; at other points the water is quiescent, because at those points the crest of a wave from one opening is merging with the trough of a wave from the other, cancelling out the wave effect altogether. Young's experiment was eventually performed with photons and electrons, using a photographic plate for a wall and obtaining the same results. See text for note 15 below.

8. Polkinghorne, *Quantum World*, 29. In addition to the formulations of quantum theory by Schrödinger and Heisenberg, there is a third approach known as "path-integral" or "sum over histories," initially proposed by Paul Dirac and fully developed by Richard Feynman around 1950. Feynman's method consists of calculating all the possible past trajectories of a particle (its paths or histories), and arriving, via the probability amplitude of each path, at the most likely path by which the particle reached its observed state. Feynman's approach is thus able to bypass the Schrödinger equation and to reach the probability amplitudes directly, though most physicists regard it as a much more complicated and unwieldy procedure. See A. Zee, *Fearful Symmetry* (New York: Macmillan, 1986), 138–46. Feynman himself gives a book-length demonstration of his method in *QED*.

9. Polkinghorne, *Quantum World*, 23–24.

10. See Richard Schlegel, "The Return of Man in Quantum Physics," in *The Sciences and Theology in the Twentieth Century*, ed. Arthur Peacocke (Notre Dame, Ind.: Univ. of Notre Dame Press, 1981), 144.

11. See note 7 above.

12. Heisenberg, *Physics*, 41.

13. The account that follows of experiments, as well as of the principles of uncertainty and complementarity, is taken from Heisenberg, *Physics*, 50–52; Polkinghorne, *Quantum World*, 31–59; Schlegel, *Superposition*, 3–79; Pagels,

Cosmic Code, 75–124; Roger Penrose, *The Emperor's New Mind* (New York: Oxford Univ. Press, 1989), 228–56.

14. Schlegel, *Superposition,* 55.

15. See note 7 above.

16. Heisenberg, *Physics,* 42.

17. We should note here that the uncertainty principle applies only to what are called conjugate realities, variable pairs like position/momentum, time/ energy. Thus the more accurately we know the energy state of a particle, the less accurately we can know the amount of time that it is likely to remain in that state, and vice versa. But there would be no problem, at least in principle, in getting an accurate simultaneous measurement of a particle's position and energy or of its momentum and energy. See John L. Casti, *Paradigms Lost* (New York: Morrow, 1989), 435–38.

18. As we shall see also, in recent years physicists have discovered that the mechanically determined stability of these very large bodies is untypical behavior in the macroworld. See text for notes 53 and 55.

19. Niels Bohr, *Atomic Theory and the Description of Nature* (New York: Macmillan, 1934), 4.

20. John Polkinghorne, *One World* (Princeton: Princeton Univ. Press, 1986), 41.

21. Max Born, ed., *The Born–Einstein Letters* (New York: Walker, 1971), 82, 158. Quoted by Timothy Ferris, *Coming of Age in the Milky Way* (New York: Morrow, 1988), 290. Italics in original.

22. Born, *Born–Einstein Letters,* 90–91. Quoted by Abraham Pais, *"Subtle is the Lord . . ."* (New York: Oxford Univ. Press, 1982), 443.

23. Werner Heisenberg, *Encounters with Einstein* (Princeton: Princeton Univ. Press, 1983), 121–22. Einstein knew he had become an obstinate heretic to his colleagues. In 1949 he wrote to Born: "I am generally regarded as a sort of petrified object, rendered blind and deaf by the years. I find this role not too distasteful, as it corresponds very well with my temperament." Quoted by Pais, *Subtle,* 462.

24. Quoted by Walter Moore, *Schrödinger* (New York: Cambridge Univ. Press, 1989), 227–28.

25. Schrödinger's narrative of his cat paradox is given in ibid., 306–9. Few of his adversaries actually held the uncompromising idealist position that the cat's situation depended on the awareness of some human consciousness. Most would have said that the cat's macroworld consciousness would be the point at which information regarding life or death became irreversible, thereby collapsing the probabilities of the wave packet (unlike the electron in the two-slit experiment which has no such awareness). Even without such consciousness, information about the atom's decay would be irreversibly registered in the macroworld by the device that smashes the flask. This clever thought experiment has been much analyzed over the years. See the discussion by Penrose, *New Mind,* 290–93, and by Pagels, *Cosmic Code,* 125–31.

26. For the various interpretations of quantum theory described here I am indebted to Schlegel, *Superposition*, 162–96; Polkinghorne, *Quantum World*, 60–69; Casti, *Paradigms*, 429-75; Ian Barbour, *Religion in an Age of Science* (San Francisco: Harper & Row, 1990), 94–108; Paul Davies, *God and the New Physics* (New York: Simon & Schuster, 1983), 100–118; Paul Davies and J. R. Brown, eds., *The Ghost in the Atom* (New York: Cambridge Univ. Press, 1986), 11–39.

27. Polkinghorne, *Quantum World*, 33.

28. Ibid., 80–82. The revolutionary character of changes in scientific theory, as well as what the sociology of knowledge says about the impact of community expectations on scientific discovery, have made not a few philosophers of science highly skeptical about the relation of scientific statements to ontological patterns in the physical world. The vast majority of scientists, however, while little concerned with metaphysical claims about the nature of reality, remains convinced that their consistent experimental success involves objects that are actually there. They do not claim that their knowledge is exhaustive, but they nevertheless believe it to be reliable. On this question see the collection of essays edited by Jarrett Leplin, *Scientific Realism* (Berkeley: Univ. of California Press, 1985).

29. See note 17 and text for note 19 above. Bohr's life and the Copenhagen interpretation are studied in depth in Abraham Pais, "Niels Bohr's Times," in *Physics, Philosophy and Polity* (New York: Oxford Univ. Press, 1991).

30. It is not all that clear how agnostic Bohr actually was. While his theory is certainly positivistic, he himself once went further in a private conversation with a friend: "There is no quantum world. There is only an abstract quantum physical description. It is wrong to think that the task of physics is to find out how nature *is*. Physics concerns what we can say about nature" (Quoted by Polkinghorne, *Quantum World*, 79). A positivistic outlook is, moreover, curious in its own right, really a downgrading of the quantum world into simply a way of speaking. Polkinghorne refers to a comment by Richard Feynman: it is like asking us to believe that the historian who makes a statement about Napoleon simply means that there are books in libraries which make assertions similar to his own. For the positivist, quantum theory deals only in sources; whether there are past events or not becomes irrelevant. See ibid., 78.

31. See text for note 25 above.

32. Heisenberg, *Physics*, 54.

33. See note 12 above. Aristotle understood "matter" to be pure potentiality for natural being, something not yet organized into a specific "form," which is what gives structure to matter and enables it to be known. Heisenberg sees the interaction of observation as having the role of Aristotle's "form," enabling us to know one of the several possible outcomes contained in the wave packet. The parallel is not exact, however, since this interaction between measuring apparatus and microworld would be seen by almost all physicists to be just as physical as the outcome that is actualized. There does not seem, in other words, to be a

distinctive role for "form" in the Aristotelian sense. See Schlegel, *Superposition*, 21–22; 171–72.

34. Polkinghorne, *Quantum World,* 68. Nevertheless, a number of physicists do take this hypothesis quite seriously. See B. S. DeWitt and Niel Graham, eds., *The Many-Worlds Interpretation of Quantum Mechanics* (Princeton: Princeton Univ. Press, 1973).

35. David Bohm, *Wholeness and the Implicate Order* (Boston: Routledge & Kegan Paul, 1982), 177. The word "implicate" comes from the verb "to implicate," meaning "to fold inwards" or "to fold together." Bohm gives a much briefer explanation of this mainly philosophical outlook in "The Implicate Order: A New Approach to the Nature of Reality," in *Beyond Mechanism*, ed. David L. Schindler (New York: Univ. Press of America, 1986), 13–37; and in "Hidden Variables and the Implicate Order," *Zygon* 20 (1985): 111–24.

36. Bohm's favorite analogy is that of the universe as a giant hologram, which is a special kind of photograph in which the optics of light encode in each segment three-dimensional information about the whole lit-up object. The tiniest piece cut out of the hologram, if illuminated with laser light, will be able to unfold the total image photographed. See Bohm, *Wholeness,* 145–47.

37. See Polkinghorne, *Quantum World,* 11–12. See also the June 1985 issue of *Zygon,* which is wholly devoted to Bohm and his theory. Interestingly enough, the reaction of Einstein was that Bohm's interpretation was too glib and simple, "too cheap," as he put it in a letter to Born, in spite of Bohm's defense of determinism. Einstein was apparently looking for a much more profound rediscovery of quantum phenomena, not simply a new interpretation that added a few variables and left quantum mechanics as a whole undisturbed. See Jeremy Bernstein, *Quantum Profiles* (Princeton: Princeton Univ. Press, 1991), 66.

38. This brief summary does scant justice both to the sophistication of the EPR experiment and to the dilemmas resulting for quantum theory's interpretation. Much fuller treatments are given in Pagels, *Cosmic Code,* 137–52; Schlegel, *Superposition,* 142–60; Polkinghorne, *Quantum World,* 70–77; Casti, *Paradigms,* 167–76; Penrose, *New Mind,* 279–87.

39. There is a resonance here with an idea proposed early in the century by Ernst Mach regarding relationships among the very large. 'Mach's principle' was a claim that the physical behavior of objects on earth is influenced by properties of the universe as a whole; that the inertia of the planet, for example, has its origins in the far depths of the universe. Mach's principle has never been verified experimentally and may indeed be unverifiable. Nevertheless, Einstein acknowledged that Mach's ideas influenced him greatly in formulating his theory of general relativity. See Paul Davies, *Superforce* (New York: Simon & Schuster, 1984), 209–16.

40. Bell's actual experiment is complex and need not be addressed here, since for the purposes of our discussion it is his conclusion that is important. More on Bell's theorem and its confirmation, as well as on Bell himself, will be found in

Bernstein, *Profiles*, 50–89; James T. Cushing and Ernan McMullin, eds., *Philosophical Consequences of Quantum Theory: Reflections on Bell's Theorem* (Notre Dame: Univ. of Notre Dame Press, 1989); F. David Peat, *Einstein's Moon: Bell's Theorem and the Curious Quest for Quantum Reality* (Chicago: Contemporary Books, 1990).

41. In 1982 and 1983 a number of experiments on Bell's theorem, performed by Alain Aspect and his collaborators at the Institute of Optics in Paris, found evidence of real nonlocal quantum effects between photons up to distances of twenty-six to thirty meters. However, these effects need not necessarily be interpreted as transmitting the type of message required by faster-than-light communication. Some physicists interpret them as examples of instantaneous correlation rather than instantaneous causality. In Pagels's words: "one can instantaneously change the cross-correlation of two random sequences of events on other sides of the galaxy. But the cross-correlation of two sets of widely separated events is not a local object and the information it may contain cannot be used to violate the principle of local causality. . . . Because each pattern is truly random we cannot use Bell's experiments to uncover real nonlocality—only a kind of after-the-fact nonlocality. And the latter only if we accept the objective existence of photons irrespective of whether we actually observe their state" (Pagels, *Cosmic Code*, 152–59). See other references in note 38 above.

42. See Polkinghorne, *Quantum World,* 73–74: "The natural way to interpret the EPR experiment is not that it shows up the incompleteness of quantum theory but that it *manifests the falsity of naive locality.* For quantum systems it seems that once they have met there is never true parting. They enjoy a lasting degree of real togetherness." Italics added.

43. The analogy here is of two TV screens showing images of a moving object taken from different angles. The two images are correlated, but one image does not causally influence the other, nor is there any way to send messages between the two sets, so the prohibition of communication faster-than-light is not violated. See Bohm, *Wholeness*, 186–89.

44. See, for example, Pagels, *Cosmic Code*, 164. Bell, for one, although on Einstein's side regarding classical realism and causality, recognized that the latter's insistence on picturable objectivity contradicted the experimental evidence. "So for me, it is a pity that Einstein's idea doesn't work. The reasonable thing just doesn't work" (Bernstein, *Profiles*, 84).

45. At the end of his philosophical study of the work of Bell and others, Michael Redhead cites Karl Popper's remark that our theories are "nets designed by us to catch the world," and then adds: "We had better face up to the fact that quantum mechanics has landed some pretty queer fish" *(Incompleteness, Nonlocality and Realism* [New York: Oxford Univ. Press, 1989], 169).

46. Oxford mathematical physicist Roger Penrose, for example, believes, as did Einstein, that there will one day be a more profound understanding of

nature: "It is my personal view that even quantum theory is a stop-gap, inadequate in certain essentials for providing a complete picture of the world in which we live" (*New Mind*, 226).

47. Pagels, *Cosmic Code*, 163.

48. See my treatment of this interrelationship in "Theology and Science: A New Commitment to Dialogue," *Theological Studies* 52 (1991): 289–329. Also reprinted as chapter 1 of this book.

49. Frederick Ferré, "Science, Religion and Experience," in Eugene Thomas Long, ed., *Experience, Reason and God* (Washington: Catholic Univ. of America Press, 1980), 106–8.

50. See Heisenberg, *Physics*, 167–86: "Language and Reality in Modern Physics." John Polkinghorne underlines this point in "The Nature of Physical Reality." *Zygon* 26 (1991): 228–330.

51. William G. Pollard, a British theologian and nuclear physicist, comes close to defending exactly this position, though his argumentation has much more subtlety than can be conveyed in a single paragraph. See his *Chance and Providence* (New York: Scribner's, 1958), excellent analyses of which will be found in D. J. Bartholomew, *God of Chance* (London: SCM Press, 1984), 125–33, and in Ian Barbour, *Issues in Science and Religion* (New York: Harper Torchbook, 1971), 428–30. Pollard's book defends divine predestination at all levels of creation, including the human.

52. See note 48 above.

53. Oppenheimer, *Atom*, 48.

54. Thomas S. Kuhn, *The Structure of Scientific Revolutions,* 2nd ed., (Chicago: Univ. of Chicago Press, 1970). An overview of Kuhn's thought will be found in the article cited in note 48 above.

55. James Gleick, *Chaos* (New York: Penguin, 1987), 8. For other treatments of this "new science," see Paul Davies, *The Cosmic Blueprint* (New York: Simon & Schuster, 1989); John L. Casti, *Searching for Certainty* (New York: Morrow, 1990); Ilya Prigogine and Isabelle Stengers, *Order Out of Chaos* (New York: Bantam, 1984).

56. Polkinghorne, "Physical Reality," 229.

57. Prigogine and Stengers, *Order*, 16. They note that in a strict Newtonian worldview the universe was static and time was impotent: the future was completely determined by the present and in some sense already contained in the present. The laws of thermodynamics reintroduced change, but the second law insisted that all such change is part of an inexorable decay and degeneration. Einstein, for one, identified the intelligible with the immutable. "For us convinced physicists," he wrote just months before he died, "the distinction between past, present and future is an illusion, although a persistent one" (Quoted by Prigogine and Stengers, *Order*, 294). On this large question of time see Davies, *Blueprint*, 2–19; Pagels, *Cosmic Code*, 106–9; Hawking, *Brief History*, 143–53; Peter

Coveney and Roger Highfield, *The Arrow of Time* (New York: Fawcett Columbine, 1991).

58. Karl Popper and John Eccles, *The Self and Its Brain* (Berlin: Springer International, 1977), 61. Quoted by Davies, *Blueprint*, 5.

59. See B. F. Skinner, *Beyond Freedom and Dignity* (New York: Knopf, 1971), as representative of the first approach, and Abraham H. Maslow, *Toward a Psychology of Being* (New York: Van Nostrand, 1968), as representative of the second.

60. Physicists like Eddington and Compton believed that quantum indeterminacy was ontological and so provided a physical basis for human self-determination. But neurophysiologists are generally agreed that the activity of brain synapses does not take place at the quantum level, and so human freedom cannot be based on Heisenberg's uncertainty principle. See Barbour, *Issues*, 305–14.

61. *Confessions*, III, 6: *"intimior intimo meo."*

62. See text and reference for note 3 above.

63. James Jeans, *The Mysterious Universe* (Cambridge: Cambridge Univ. Press, 1930), 186. Quoted by Barbour, *Religion*, 114.

64. James Jeans, *Physics and Philosophy* (Cambridge: Cambridge Univ. Press, 1943), 216. Quoted by Hiebert, "Modern Physics," 430.

65. *Summa Contra Gentiles*, II, ch. 3: *"Errores namque qui circa creaturam sunt interdum a fidei veritate abducunt, secundum quod verae Dei cognitioni repugnant."*

66. Bernard Lonergan, *Insight* (New York: Longmans, 1957), 731. For a full development of natural theology's service of the faith, see John Polkinghorne, *Science and Providence* (Boston: Shambhala, 1989), 1–16.

67. Polkinghorne, *One World*, 69. Robert John Russell has dealt in length with the larger issues involved here in "Quantum Physics in Philosophical and Theological Perspective," in Russell, Stoeger, and Coyne, *Common Quest*, 343–74.

68. The phrase is that of philosopher Filmer Northrop, used in his introduction to Heisenberg, *Physics*, 11–15. See Barbour, *Issues*, 304, 429.

69. In the Christian tradition this aspect of God's creative power has gone by the name of creation *ex nihilo*, a phrase coined in patristic times as a way to deny pantheism, dualism, and Manichaeism. Although on its face it seems to be referring to an act at some point in the past, its coiners were really much less concerned with origins than with making a claim about the sovereignty of God's present relationship to the cosmos, namely the latter's absolute dependence on God for its very existence. See Arthur Peacocke, "Cosmos and Creation," in *Cosmology, History and Theology*, ed. Wolfgang Yourgrau and Allen D. Breck (New York: Plenum, 1977), 365–81.

70. The issue of divine causality in the biological area involves too large a number of issues and problems for this chapter to deal with.

71. See *Summa Theologica*, 1, q. 105, a. 5: "Since God is personally the cause in all things of their whole very existence, than which nothing is more intimate

or interior, it follows that God acts innermostly in all things." For primary and secondary causality see ibid., 1, q. 19, a. 4 and 8; q. 45, a. 5; q. 83, a. 1, ad 3. See also Barbour, *Religion*, 181, 245–48, 268.

72. Aquinas treats the mystery of evil and its reconciliation with God's providential design in *Summa Theologica*, 1, q. 19, a. 9; q. 48, a. 1, 3–4; q. 49, a. 1–2.

73. See John Polkinghorne, "God's Action in the World," *Cross Currents* 41 (1991): 293–307. The scholastics usually referred to such intentions and purposes as 'final causality', in contrast to the 'efficient causality' of actions. The complexity of the issues involved here can be seen in the collection of essays edited by Owen C. Thomas, *God's Activity in the World* (Chico, Calif.: Scholars Press, 1983).

74. The classic text is Romans 8:19–23, especially verse 22: "From the beginning until now the entire creation, as we know, has been groaning in one great act of giving birth."

75. Philippians 2:6–11. The literature on this famous hymn is extensive. See the magisterial treatment by Paul Henry, "Kénose," *Dictionnaire de la Bible, Supplément*, vol. 5, cols. 7–161. The words of Dietrich Bonhoeffer are often quoted in this context: "God lets himself be pushed out of the world on to the cross. He is weak and powerless in the world, and that is precisely the way, the only way, in which he is with us and helps us" (*Letters and Papers from Prison* [New York: Macmillan, 1967], 188).

76. 1 Corinthians 1:24–25. The reader will notice that I have incorporated into Section 3 a number of insights from the process thought of Whitehead, although I cannot share his strictly philosophical concern to find a place for the temporal and contingent in God. For Whitehead, God's kenotic self-limitation through creation is integral to God's nature, demanded by the structure of being itself, not something voluntary on God's part. God thus appears to be ultimately powerless in the face of evil, and so differs radically from the God of Hebrew and Christian Scriptures. Because divine action is limited to that of being a "lure," of seeking to entice creatures in a certain direction, God inevitably seems to be standing at the sidelines, "the poet of the world," as Whitehead says, "with tender patience leading it by his vision of truth, beauty, and goodness" *(Process and Reality* [New York: Macmillan, 1929], 526). An extensive summary of process thought, both philosophical and theological, will be found in Barbour, *Religion*, 218–42, 260–67.

77. John Polkinghorne, *Science and Creation* (Boston: Shambhala, 1988), 49; *One World*, 81.

78. Arthur Peacocke, *Intimations of Reality* (Notre Dame, Ind.: Univ. of Notre Dame Press, 1984), 73.

79. Romans 5:21.

80. Whitehead, *Process and Reality*, 523.

81. Freeman Dyson, *Infinite in All Directions* (New York: Harper & Row, 1988), 8.

82. Sallie McFague, *Models of God* (Philadelphia: Fortress, 1987). The author gives a succinct summary of her insights in "Models of God for an Ecological, Evolutionary Era: God as Mother of the Universe," in *Common Quest*, ed. Russell, Stoeger, and Coyne, 249–71. This model of the world as God's body is one way to illumine the concept of 'panentheism', a word used by process theologian Charles Hartshorne to emphasize that the world is neither identified with God nor separated from God, but is *in* God. However, this concept can also be understood to refer to God's immanent presence *in the world*, which is the approach developed in these pages. According to the *Oxford Dictionary of the Christian Church* (Oxford: Oxford Univ. Press, 1957), 1010, the word itself, along with its twofold meaning, apparently was coined by K. C. F. Krause in the nineteenth century.

83. Peacocke, *Intimations*, 72. He develops this model further in *Creation and the World of Science* (New York: Oxford Univ. Press, 1979), 105–11; *God and the New Biology* (San Francisco: Harper & Row, 1986), 97–100.

84. Alfred North Whitehead, *The Concept of Nature* (Cambridge: Cambridge Univ. Press, 1964), 163.

85. Holmes Rolston III, *Science and Religion* (New York: Random House, 1987), 334.

4. Theology and Evolution

The discovery of biological evolution in the last century has come to touch every aspect of human living. No other area of science has done so much to shape the way we view ourselves and our relationship to the world around us. This is because the concept of evolution has symbolic force: it claims to explain how we humans were made, where we came from, and how we developed into the highly complex organisms we are today. It thus intersects with public consciousness and impinges upon religion in ways that discoveries in physics and chemistry do not. Evolution can also be easily sensationalized. When this happens, as philosopher Mary Midgley has noted, its story becomes melodrama, with the same strong imaginative appeal as the creation mythology of Genesis, as well as with the capacity to distort in religiously harmful ways the concept of evolution itself.[1] Hence, it is incumbent upon theologians to know as best they can what science is now saying about the evolutionary process, and to evaluate as accurately as possible the implications of such knowledge for Christian anthropology and the doctrine of God.

The root religious problem here is that efforts to come to terms with biological data tend to generate two very different responses. On the one hand there is astonishment and awe at the staggering proliferation and complexity of life: hundreds of millions of species coming into existence over some three and a half billion years, most of them now long extinct, with anywhere from ten to a hundred million still alive on earth but with only about 1.82 million actually identified, of which more than half are insects. On the other hand there is a certain discomfort and even alarm: this process is apparently so random and aimless that Darwin himself could say of it: "What a book a Devil's Chaplain might write on the clumsy, wasteful, blundering low, & horribly cruel works of nature!"[2] "Nature, red in tooth and law" is the sad line of Tennyson's *In Memoriam*. The current findings of biology are thus far more troublesome for theology than the more rational and generally predictable world of physics: a universe finely tuned from the beginning for the eventual appearance of life produces in the end a nature awash over time in conflict and disruption. And when humans finally appear on the scene, all this disorder is simply compounded by their acute reflective consciousness of physical disease, psychic suffering, and tragic death. What could God's providence and care possibly be doing in bringing such life into existence?

In what follows we shall seek first an understanding of what the biological sciences have to say about the phenomenon of life in general, then what they have to say about human life in particular. This will then enable us, thirdly, better to appreciate why Christian theologians are finding it so difficult today to integrate these findings into some coherent whole with the data and experience of Christian faith.

—— Evolution and Life ——

Let us begin with some significant differences between the biological and physical sciences. It is important to start here because, in contrast to physics and chemistry whose progress has been charted for centuries, biology as a discipline is both recent and at the same time so extensive that it is sometimes difficult to see where it begins in physics and ends in psychology. Francis Crick, the codiscoverer of the structure of the DNA molecule (about which more will be discussed presently), has written that "eventually one may hope to have the whole of biology 'explained' in terms of the level below it, and so right on down to the atomic level. . . . The knowledge we already have makes it highly unlikely that there is anything that cannot be explained by physics and chemistry."[3] Such reductionism is obviously quite valid as a research strategy: all living organisms can indeed be reduced to physico-chemical constituents and described in terms that strictly obey physico-chemical laws. But knowing these laws is not the same as knowing life; explaining how living organisms function is another matter entirely, and this for two reasons.

First, the biological sciences deal with an additional level of reality. As we shall see later at greater length, every living organism possesses an information system inherited from each parent and stored in the genes (called its "genotype"), that directly or indirectly controls all its physiological behavior. Biological systems are thus able to respond to external stimuli, to grow, differentiate, and reproduce. No such coded information-controlling activity is to be found in nonliving matter. This "genotype" control then results in the formation of an extended "body plan" for the particular organism, with a certain appearance and behavior, known as its "phenotype."

This means that, unlike the physical sciences, which search out single causes for phenomena, biological sciences are involved with a double causality, proximate causes altering the phenotype at the macrolevel and ultimate explanatory causes altering the "genotype" of organisms at their microlevel. Geneticists, biochemists, and molecular biologists focus on this second type of causality; paleontologists, zoologists, and comparative anatomists focus on the first type. While these two sets of causal phenomena are consistent with physical laws, they can neither be reduced to these laws nor deduced from them.[4] Life may be no less material and physical than nonlife, but it is incomparably more complicated. Biology is thus logically distinct from the physical sciences insofar as it focuses on the results of cell activity, namely whole organisms, rather than on the cell's physical and chemical structure.

Not only are the levels of reality different in the physical and biological sciences, the role of laws in these two areas is different too. In physics, laws are intended to be universal, while in biology any high-level generalizations are usually not called laws but theories, coherent sets of statements that provide explanations for certain phenomena. This usually means that the problem of testing is more acute in the biological than in the physical sciences. There is, for example, no general theory of bodily form that will tell us beforehand what organisms ought to look like, but only the experience accumulated over time of what they actually do look like. In the case of evolutionary biology, unlike functional biology, this will in turn depend on fossils embedded and preserved in rocks and earth.[5] Understood in this way, evolutionary biology is a plausible account of past events based on inferences from present-day observations. These observations must therefore be judged by the proper criteria. For we are dealing here with a historical science of the singular and the unrepeatable, the reconstruction of what has happened to living organisms over long periods of time, in the same way that geology and cosmology try to reconstruct what has been happening from their beginnings to earth, galaxies, and solar system.

ORIGIN FROM A COMMON ANCESTOR. This brings us now to the two most important biological theories regarding evolution. These differ greatly from each other and it is important for us to understand why. The first of these theories is that all organisms, whether current or extinct, are interconnected through common descent from one primordial life form. Originally this theory spoke only of the transformation of organisms over time. Such a formulation was already in place when Darwin arrived on the scene, and it owed much to another naturalist, Jean-Baptiste Antoine de Monet, who went by the name of Chevalier de Lamarck. A botanist of high repute who had in the late 1700s expanded his interests into zoology, Lamarck became fascinated with the apparent family relationships among animals and plants. Since the mid-eighteenth century evidence had been accumulating that species might not be immutable: a larger and larger number of very different plant and animal fossils were being found embedded in precisely dated rock strata uncovered by pioneering geologists like Charles Lyell. Lamarck finally concluded from this research that species had indeed changed over time and that all organisms were somehow related. His 1809 book, *Philosophie Zoologique,* contained what was really the first explicit recognition of organic evolution.[6]

Darwin's contribution to this theory, beginning in 1859, was to emphasize that this evolutionary change must have taken place by way of descent from one common ancestor, one original life-form. He argued to this not from the fossil record, but from an enormous amount of circumstantial evidence that he had gathered over many years on "homologies," remarkable similarities between the limbs of the most diverse living animals. How would such similarities have come into existence except through common descent? For the rest of the nineteenth century and well into the twentieth, naturalists were preoccupied with proofs for this first evolutionary theory. The evidence that has now accumulated in its favor is so consistent and massive that it is regarded today as a fact in all biological sciences, so well established that its degree of certainty is beyond reasonable doubt, just as countless numbers of astronomical observations corroborate the Copernican rather than the Ptolemaic view of the solar system. Let us briefly summarize this evidence, which is constituted by an extraordinary correlation of data from three separate and very diverse areas of biological investigation.

The first evidence is from the fossil record, an accumulation of millions of fragments of early life preserved in beds of rock and earth whose dating is both accurate and reliable. The closer paleontologists get to the present in geological time, the more modern are the fossils they find. There is thus a rather orderly history to life. Different groups seem to have arisen at different times, not all at once. We do not find the fossils of plants in billion-year-old Precambrian rocks, nor mammals in strata before the

end of the Triassic period about 200 million years ago. Could plants or
horses have existed for hundreds of millions of years without leaving a
trace and then suddenly leave abundant remains?

Obviously one cannot read this record like a book from one end to the
other; its contents depend on what happens to have been found. Nor can
one open up the record at will and look up dates and particular historical
forms. Fossils from different ages usually cannot be connected in a linear
sequence, but rather represent small samples from a lot of parallel lines.
The fossil record is thus more like a series of bushes than the orderly
branching of an evolutionary tree, "more like a library that has been hit by
a typhoon, pages and bits of book everywhere. It can be pieced together,
but inevitably there will be gaps."[7]

The most striking feature of these gaps is that they are always to be
found between species, which inevitably appear suddenly in the record
without any transitional links to earlier species. Contrary to what Darwin
envisioned,[8] fossil sequences do not show that species multiply through
a gradual accumulation of small changes, with an eventual branching of
a single species into two. How then do species multiply? At present this is
one of the chief unresolved controversies of evolutionary history. Ernst
Mayr, generally regarded as the world's most distinguished living evolu-
tionist, working not from the fossil record but from his observations of
bird populations, postulated in 1954 that a numerous and widespread species may evolve when a small and geographically isolated population of
that species undergoes very rapid genetic change at the microevolutionary level.

Following Mayr, Stephen Jay Gould and Niles Eldridge proposed in
the early 1970s their concept of "punctuated equilibria": such transitional
forms are unlikely to be picked up by the fossil record at the macroevolutionary level, which will generally tend to show an equilibrium of
established species over long periods (five to ten million years), punctuated by short bursts of rapid change (over about fifty thousand years)
during which new species will suddenly be encountered in the fossil
record. Evolutionary change would thus not be continuous but episodic.
However, neither geneticists nor paleontologists seem to be in agreement
as yet on the more fundamental question of whether what happens at the
macroevolutionary level of species can in principle be shown to be a de-
ductive consequence of happenings at the microevolutionary level of
genetic change.[9]

The second category of evidence supporting common descent is that from "homologies," which, as we saw, were Darwin's main preoccupation. Such similarities between the bodily characteristics of organisms (both living and fossilized) go far today toward dispelling our ignorance about life's history resulting from the incompleteness of the fossil record. Single ancestry is the only reasonable explanation that has been proposed for such similarities. The forelimbs of all four-footed vertebrates, for example, are always found to have a similar bone structure. These similarities are the domain of comparative anatomy, which studies the configuration of organisms. Through such homologies, anatomists work out what might be the most reasonable links between species. Organisms sharing a more recent common ancestor are likely to be more similar than organisms whose common ancestor is remote. Degrees of similarity are thus used to infer the relative position of a particular species in evolutionary branching.[10]

Finally there is a third category of evidence that comes from molecular biology. But to appreciate its highly probative force we shall first have to have some understanding of modern genetics, and this will require a rather long digression into one of the great achievements of modern science.[11] The origins of this achievement go back to the mid-nineteenth century, when an Austrian monk, Gregor Mendel, published in 1866 the results of his experiments on garden peas. While the heredity of parental characteristics by offspring had been assumed since antiquity, it was Mendel who first discovered the reason. By patiently crossing several generations of garden peas he found that every specific trait inherited by offspring was determined by what he called "factors of heredity," one set of factors coming from each parent. All such factors, moreover, passed discrete and unchanged from generation to generation and, under the right circumstances, could once again produce the same trait in some subsequent generation. Mendel's paper detailing these hereditary laws went unnoticed until 1900, when it was discovered by three European botanists who had independently reached similar conclusions.

In 1904 an American, Walter Sutton, concluded that these mysterious hereditary units were contained in sausage-shaped structures in the nucleus of every cell, which is the unit of all organic life. These structures he called "chromosomes" ("color bodies") because early geneticists had to color them with dyes to see them under a microscope. In 1909 a Danish biologist, Wilhelm Johannsen, named these hereditary units "genes," from the Greek "giving birth to." At the same time both genes and their chromosome carriers were found to come in pairs, with one half of each pair inherited from one parent, the other half from the other parent. Then in 1941 two Americans, George Beadle and Edward Tatum, showed that the function of genes was to produce the twenty amino acids constituting proteins, large molecules that are the building blocks of the cell's life and metabolism. Certain forms of these proteins, called enzymes, act as the machine tools of the cell, carrying out those second-to-second chemical reactions that make life possible.

No one yet knew the nature of genes, however, not until a series of discoveries in the 1940s, by the American physician Oswald Avery, began to suggest that they were composed of a previously ignored acid in the cell nucleus, a large molecule rich in a sugar called deoxyribose and hence known as deoxyribonucleic acid (or DNA). Finally in 1953 British physicist Francis Crick and American biologist James Watson determined that DNA's physical structure resembled a spiral or helix of two incredibly long strands of sugars and phosphates linked together at regular intervals by rungs of hydrogen, like a ladder, each rung connecting pairs of very tiny opposing molecules called "base nucleotides," or simply "bases."

These bases are only four in number, but they are dotted along each strand by the hundreds of millions. Their sequence varies so widely, moreover, that they constitute an almost limitless information storage system, resembling the memory bank of a computer, their information written like tickertape in a linear code. A gene is thus an instructional segment of DNA, made up of a specific sequence of about ten thousand of these nucleotide bases.[12] The bases themselves are all stretched out along this double stranded ladder of nucleic acid, which in turn is tightly twisted inside the chromosomes of every living cell.[13] It was this discovery of Crick and Watson that won them the Nobel Prize and laid the foundation of modern molecular biology.

A further question was not answered until 1961: how does the cell go about transferring these instructions, written on nucleic acids with one chemical structure, into the very different chemical structure of the twenty amino acids in each of its proteins? In other words, how does the cell machinery manufacture its multiple proteins by "reading" the DNA locked in its nucleus? The answer was found to reside in the four DNA bases, which act like an alphabet of a four-character language. When these letters combine into triplets, they constitute a vocabulary of sixty-four possible words, which are then translated by the cell's enzymes into the twenty-character language of its amino acids, one triplet of bases specifying one kind of amino acid. This translation process takes place by way of another nucleic acid (RNA), which the cell uses as a messenger to carry information written on the DNA bases to those places outside the cell nucleus where protein molecules are being synthesized. There the enzymes read the coded RNA instructions and hook together specific amino acids to form specific protein strands. An average protein with five hundred amino acids thus corresponds to fifteen thousand DNA nucleotide bases in triplet form.[14]

Moreover, while proteins are the essential components of a cell's activity or metabolism, which is the first basic function of life, the cell's nucleic acids are the essential components of life's second function, replication. This capacity for replication is based on the structure of DNA. For the pairs of its nucleotide bases are chemically complementary, one side of the double spiral strand being in effect a genetic mirror of the other, like a photograph and its negative. Hence whenever a cell divides, its DNA is also able to divide, the two strands unwinding from inside their chromosomes and unzipping right down the middle. The nucleotides of these two separated strands then link up with "free floating" nucleotides in both cells to give the proper match in pairing the bases. Each separated strand of DNA now has a new complementary other half, with which it zips together, rewinding back inside the chromosomes of the two cells. The end result is two new double-stranded lengths of DNA, identical in base sequence with the original, carrying exactly the same hereditary information.

This long digression on genetics has been necessary in order to appreciate the probative force of the third category of evidence for common descent derived today from molecular biology. Before we begin we should note that data regarding the large molecules we have been discussing (nucleic acids and proteins) have two notable advantages over data from paleontology and comparative anatomy, which, as we saw, constitute the first two categories of evidence. First, the number of nucleotides or amino acids involved in these molecules is readily established once their sequence is known, which is hardly the case with the fossil record. Second, similar macromolecules in organisms as diverse as yeasts, pine trees, and humans can easily be compared, whereas sciences whose focus is "homologies" have almost nothing to say when confronted with such diverse entities.[15] The information contained in these macromolecules is thus the dominant theme of molecular biology.

What do we learn about common ancestry from all this genetic information? First, the genetic code that translates the information from the
nucleotide bases in DNA (via messenger RNA) to the amino acids in
protein is exactly the same in all living organisms from viruses to humans.
That is to say, any particular triplet of bases in DNA will always translate
into the same amino acid in all protein chains in anything alive. This
coding relationship is quite arbitrary, however, since there has yet been
found no clear chemical reason why it could not be otherwise. Its universality would thus seem to be comprehensible only as a result of evolution:
all living organisms have come from some original living matter that
became self-producing, and happened to have the particular coding relationship now imprinted on all subsequent organisms.[16]

The second thing molecular biology tells us about common ancestry
has to do with discoveries regarding the different sequence of the amino
acids in any particular cell protein, as this protein is now found in the cells
of widely different species. It turns out that these amino acids can vary
from species to species without at all affecting the ability of the protein in
question to perform its assigned function. For example, a protein involved
in cell respiration (cytochrome c) contains 104 amino acids in a sequence
that remains unchanged within any one species but differs in different species. Thus for humans and chimpanzees this sequence differs in only one
amino acid position, as it does also for horses and donkeys. But humans
and horses differ in twelve of the 104 positions, while chimpanzees and
horses differ in eleven, and so on down the line as proteins with the same
function are found in all other species. These amino acid substitutions are
considered to be one of the best measurements of genetic difference
among species.[17]

Much more importantly, however, determining such substitutions for
a given class of protein in different species has enabled molecular biologists to construct a "molecular clock" that can be calibrated to tell us how
long it has been since any particular pair of species diverged from a
common ancestor. The procedure followed was to select a number of species whose time of evolutionary divergence was clearly known from
geological dating of their fossil remains. The number of substitutions in
their amino acid sequencing was then counted and compared in order to
estimate the rate at which changes in sequencing occurred as generations
succeeded one another. Because this rate of substitution turned out to be
quite uniform, it was then possible to apply it to estimate the branching
points of other species whose present amino acid sequences were known

but for which there was no fossil record.[18] This allowed an approximation both of the time and of the order of branching: the greater the difference in amino acid sequencing between any two species, the more widely they are likely to be separated in evolutionary chronology. While such calibration can never yield more than probability, this probability has nevertheless been shown to be constant, thus making the molecular clock fairly accurate and generally reliable. Using this method, geneticists estimate that humans, chimpanzees, and gorillas diverged from a common ancestor between five and seven million years ago.

Most important of all, as knowledge of more and more of these sequences accumulated, the differences between species at the molecular level began to correspond more and more with differences in their classification based on the fossil record. In other words, their fossil dates and their molecular dates began to converge; evolutionary data regarding their genotype began to mesh experimentally with an entirely different type of evolutionary data regarding their phenotype. This truly remarkable coincidence thus managed to correlate the findings of three very diverse biological disciplines: paleontology, comparative anatomy, and molecular biology. This correlation convinced scientists that the only rational basis to explain such an extraordinary coherence is the supposition of a common descent for all forms of life. The almost total consistency of the data constitutes, they believe, the strongest of arguments that evolution from a common ancestor is no longer a theory, as it was in the last century, but a fact beyond any reasonable doubt.

THE MECHANISM OF NATURAL SELECTION. Constructing a plausible explanation for this fact of evolution from a common ancestor, however, has turned out to be a different matter entirely. This brings us now to the realm of Darwinism in the strict sense and to the second major theory of evolutionary biology; the mechanism of natural selection. This was Charles Darwin's insight in the last century into how the evolutionary process actually works. What must be studied in evolution, he was convinced, was not the classification of different types of species, which had preoccupied biologists up to then, but rather the variation that existed among organisms of the same species. For it was these differences in individuals that would eventually accumulate into differences between species. Why was it, he asked, that these individuals did not all undergo the same changes? There were instead different rhythms in the life process—some organisms surviving reasonably well in their environments, others quickly dying out. Darwin referred to this harmonious character of the organic world as "that perfection of structure and coadaptation which most justly excites our admiration."[19] What accounts for it? His answer was formulated in 1859 in *The Origin of Species:* "This preservation of favourable variations and the rejection of injurious variations, I call Natural Selection."[20]

By "natural selection" Darwin was referring not to a process that brings about variation in individual organisms, but rather to a process whereby variations already there and favorable to survival in a particular environment are preserved in organisms that adapt and reproduce. The first step of the process is thus the variation, a phenomenon whose causal chain is totally independent of the selection process, which is in turn a distinct causal chain that totally depends on the variation. Darwin readily acknowledged his ignorance of the laws governing such variations, but their inheritance, he insisted, was not the exception but the rule. His explanation relied on his personal experience of the animal breeding industry so widespread in England at the time. Sheep breeders and pigeon fanciers both sought some type of artificial selection to eliminate or to perpetuate certain characteristics. Darwin believed that an analogous selection process was going on in nature, channeling its seemingly inexhaustible supply of variations into evolutionary change within and between species.[21]

All such adaptation and change, Darwin argued, comes about through an intense struggle for existence among organisms, which may or may not respond to the challenges of their environment by altering their hereditary endowment. He relied here on another analogy, this time the doctrine of English economist Thomas Robert Malthus regarding the imbalance between population growth and food supply. Organisms will tend to increase geometrically, said Malthus, while the increase of the food supply tends to be linear and arithmetical. Darwin applied this doctrine to the growth of all biological populations. Because all living creatures tend to produce more offspring than their environment's limited resources can support, only organisms having some advantage in the struggle will adapt to these environments and so survive and reproduce. Given enough time, this interaction of predator and prey, of parasite and victim, as well as the frequency of species extinction, eventually adds up to evolution. In Darwin's words:

> Owing to this struggle for life, any variation, however slight and from whatever cause proceeding, if it be in any degree profitable to an individual of any

species, in its infinitely complex relations to other organic beings and to external nature, will tend to the preservation of that individual, and will generally be inherited by its offspring. The offspring, also, will thus have a better chance of surviving, for, of the many individuals of any species which are periodically born, but a small number can survive. I have called this principle, by which each slight variation, if useful, is preserved, by the term Natural Selection, in order to mark its relation to man's power of selection.[22]

Darwin did not believe that his theory was without flaws, and this is why he dealt so openly in his book with the theory's problems, especially those arising from the very large gaps in the fossil record that existed in the 1850s.[23] But he could hardly have anticipated the major objection of subsequent generations. This arose because, beginning with the *Origin's* fifth edition, Darwin began using as a synonym for natural selection the unfortunate phrase "survival of the fittest," coined seven years before the first edition by British philosopher Herbert Spencer.[24] Spencer had only a casual acquaintance with biology and did not use the phrase in a biological context at all. He was rather concerned about promoting his notion of the ideal society, in which cooperation and altruism must always yield to self-interest. Much later this approach was designated as "social Darwinism," in which natural selection was applied to human affairs to justify the elimination of the weak and the perpetuation of the strong. Spencer was enjoying an enormous popularity when the *Origin* appeared, especially in the United States, where his writings outsold those of all other philosophers.

The difficulty with Spencer's phrase is that if the fittest are understood to be those best capable of survival, then we have an untestable tautology, true by definition but containing no new information: "the survival of those who survive." If we grant this supposition, namely that survival is the criterion of fitness, the objection is logically quite valid. But such a supposition ignores Darwin's larger argument that natural selection depends upon an analogy with the artificial selection of animal breeders, who identify certain traits as superior *before* breeding begins, not subsequent to their survival. In like manner, said Darwin, nature also determines an organism's fitness, not by its subsequent survival and spread but by the fact that variations beyond its control (whether these be physical, psychological, or behavioral traits) enable it beforehand to fit more snugly into some environmental niche. Variations from whatever source thus supply the raw material for evolution, while natural selection directs its course by fitting organisms to their environment long enough for them to propagate.[25]

"Survival of the best fitting" would be the proper phrasing. For all his talk of struggle, what Darwin ultimately describes is thus a positive, not a negative, natural force.

The triumph of *The Origin of Species* was that it convinced a whole generation that evolution had actually occurred. But it succeeded in convincing very few in that generation that evolution's mechanism was natural selection. The difficulties, all of which Darwin publicly agonized over, were simply too many and too complex. "Darwin's work," admits a present-day authority, "is filled with ambiguities, contradictions and theoretical revisions."[26] One problem in particular not even Darwin could address, namely the fact that no one knew where the variations came from on which natural selection was supposed to work. While his theory was based on some form of heredity, Darwin himself had no idea what was being inherited, and was faced with the fact that everyone at the time believed inheritance to mean the passage of *similarities* between parents and offspring. How then could heredity be related to variation?

It was not until 1900, almost twenty years after Darwin's death, that Mendel's early experiments on "factors of heredity" were discovered and a totally new branch of biology was born to study the transmission of "genes." The mutation of these genes, as well as their recombination in bisexual reproduction, eventually came to be seen by geneticists as the two main sources of variation in nature, as observed in a wide variety of plant, insect, and animal populations. The upshot was that heredity and variation were finally understood to be two aspects of the same phenomenon. Actual variation in organisms of the same generation, in other words, is precisely what is responsible for the passage of similarity across generations. Harvard's Richard Lewontin believes that this synthesis of the antithetical properties of heredity and variation "represents as difficult and subtle an insight into nature as any in the history of science."[27]

Early in the century, however, geneticists actually believed that they had found a rival mechanism for evolutionary change, and as a result natural selection began to fall into disrepute. For over thirty years the biological focus remained fixed on these mutations in the genes and chromosomes. Through tightly controlled laboratory observations, it was discovered that whenever a cell divided it copied itself exactly, except that once in a few hundred thousand times there was a mistake, due to some error in the code or some damage to DNA nucleotides. (A specific gene in any human set, for example, will mutate probably once in every hundred thousand generations as a result of such a mistake. But since individual humans get at least ten thousand genes from their parents, the chances are high that about one in every five persons will pass on a mutant gene that was not originally inherited.)

These mistakes were found to arise, moreover, regardless of whether they were useful or harmful to the particular organism. Almost all in fact were harmful, producing hereditary defects and diseases, and some of the mistakes were lethal. An incredibly small number, however, turned out to be useful, making the cell more adapted to its environment and so more able to survive and reproduce. Mutant genes not useful to one environment were still found to be quite adaptive in another. Evidence from the genetic bases of different species also showed that the same processes responsible for these microevolutionary changes were relevant for understanding the differences between species at the macroevolutionary level. Eventually these and other developments made it possible in the late 1930s and early 1940s for conflicts between Mendelians and Darwinians to resolve themselves into a neo-Darwinism known today as "the modern synthesis" of Mendelian genetics and natural selection through the impact of the environment.[28]

The catalyst for this synthesis was a general realization on both sides that each needed the other. The Mendelians needed natural selection in order to avoid the chaos that gene mutation alone would cause. Most of these Mendelians were highly reductionistic population geneticists, however, and so accepted natural selection as a mechanism only in so far as it provided some organizing influence that could modify the random character of gene frequencies, since incessant mutability would make maintenance of life unlikely. The Darwinians, on the other hand, were keenly aware that their mechanism depended critically on Mendel's achievement. For if superior types are destined more and more to characterize a species, as Darwin claimed, then selection should gradually cause a population to lose the very variation that is the basis for the whole mechanism. An absolute fidelity to self-reproduction would develop that would make evolution impossible. Mendel's discovery solved this dilemma. For it was now clear that genes passing from parents to offspring maintain their individuality even when mixed with other genes, and that they are held together in groups until sooner or later they too are passed along to progeny in new sperm and egg cells. New variations will thus never be diluted by mating, but will always be available for selection.[29]

Since the 1940s this neo-Darwinist synthesis has established its hegemony not only in genetics but in all other areas of biology. It is important to emphasize, however, as does Ernst Mayr, that this "is not a simple theory that is either true or false, but is rather a highly complex

research program that is being continuously modified and improved."[30]
The strongly reductionistic version of the synthesis, represented by the
early population geneticists, has been largely relegated today to biology's
fringe, yielding dominance to a more holistic version representing an al-
liance of naturalists and molecular biologists. All of these emphasize that
natural selection works not with genes but with individuals having whole
genetic endowments. What survives and reproduces is not the gene but a
living organism (or phenotype), whose genetic endowment (or genotype)
accumulates information about the environment and then adapts to it by
generating a creative response. In other words, mutant genes are integrated
into the total system, and only if they are then beneficial are they preserved by natural selection. Hence the "genetic program does not by itself
supply the building material of new organisms, but only the blueprint for
the making of the phenotype."[31]

A most important recent modification of the neo–Darwinist synthesis
(besides the "punctuated equilibria" issue discussed earlier[32]), has been the
recognition that not all genetic change involves an improved adaptation to
environment. Some of this change, in other words, is *not* due to the directional force of natural selection impinging upon an abundant variation. It
can simply be the result of one of several nonadaptive phenomena. We
already saw one example when we discussed the molecular clock: substitutions over time in the amino acid sequencing of proteins for different
species occur independent of natural selection for specific adaptation.[33]
But the most important nonadaptive phenomenon has turned out to be
"genetic drift."

To understand such drift, the reader should recall[34] that only three nucleotide bases of DNA are needed to specify any single amino acid in
proteins. But since there are four base "letters" in DNA's language, it is
possible to have a vocabulary of sixty-four such triplets and, since proteins
have only twenty amino acids, some of these acids can be coded by any
number of triplets. Because of this redundancy in the genetic code, then,
a mutation that alters one of these triplets at the DNA or genotype level
need not necessarily produce any effect on amino acids at the protein or
phenotype level. While such mutated genes can propagate indefinitely
down through generations, they would be no better or worse than the
genes they replaced but simply "neutral," unrelated to survival and confer-
ring neither advantage nor disadvantage on the organism.

When this happens there can obviously be some evolution in a population, but it would not be influenced by natural selection, which simply

cannot deal with mutations that are neither beneficial nor detrimental. Such nonadaptive evolution is still controversial and its ultimate influence and significance disputed. But it has resulted in a growing pluralism in neo-Darwinism that is now firmly entrenched. There is now general recognition that all aspects of the shape, function, and behavior of organisms are not molded in detail by the mechanism of natural selection, which cannot of itself explain a certain experimental drift in the life process. Freeman Dyson, relying on the work of mathematical geneticist Motoo Kimura, proposes that genetic drift was probably more dominant in the earliest phase of biological evolution, before the mechanism of heredity had become exact. "Darwinian selection will begin its work after the process of genetic drift has given it something to work on. . . . Darwinian selection is unavoidable as inheritance begins, no matter how sloppy the mechanism of inheritance may be."[35]

Before we end we should note another large modification that the neo-Darwinist synthesis has made in Darwin's original theory. The element of struggle was, as we saw, essential for Darwin. But this element is rarely mentioned today because biological populations are known to be more often cooperative than competitive, increasing rather than diminishing each other. This is especially true when one species or several species are in some equilibrium, with births approximately equal to deaths. One of the architects of the modern synthesis, George Gaylord Simpson, was convinced that struggle is, in fact, very rare and on the whole is a source mostly of minor disturbances in nature that often work against natural selection. What matters for survival, he said, are births and deaths, and these can be very peaceful and unnoticed. The emphasis today is thus on the rates with which species produce progeny, as well as on the different rates of survival of progeny in the course of adapting to their environments. Such survival no longer implies a conqueror and a conquered, but simply a parent producing the largest number of progeny who will themselves reach parenthood.[36]

It should be clear at this point that this second theory we have been discussing regarding the "how" of evolution is vastly different from the first theory, which concerns the historical transformation of organisms from a common ancestor over some three and a half billion years. Biologists accept the first as a fact proven beyond reasonable doubt; the second continues today to be the subject of vigorous disagreement, continuous debate, and constant modification. As originally proposed by Darwin, the mechanism of natural selection was so strange to his contemporaries that only a handful adopted it, and almost three generations passed before it was generally accepted even by biologists. Proponents of its "modern synthesis" formulation freely admit their ignorance on how to apply the theory in a great many areas. They also recognize how often it has been reshaped since 1900, and acknowledge that it will inevitably be recast again, because as an explanatory mechanism it is still incomplete. It cannot yet fully account for gaps in the fossil record, nor for the origin of complex organs like the eye, nor can it provide any detailed explanation of how precisely macroevolution is related to what is known today about microevolutionary processes at the genetic level.

Why then do almost all practicing biologists adhere to it so strongly?[37] There are two reasons. The first is one that we saw at the start: unlike the physical sciences and functional biology, evolutionary biology is a historical discipline, dealing with currently available data regarding singular and unrepeatable events in an inaccessible past. Evolutionists thus do not expect their explanations to be complete, which is why a theory as complex as the neo-Darwinist synthesis can never be regarded as any more than plausible. But the more important reason is that this plausibility is perceived by most biologists to be extremely high. This theory, they say, manages to integrate an unusually wide range of well-understood processes in genetics, molecular biology, paleontology, and comparative anatomy. No other mechanism is available that can even remotely rival its consistency and explanatory power, especially in view of what we know today of DNA's role as carrier of hereditary information. Why should a theory that explains so much be rejected simply because it cannot as yet explain everything?[38] Evolutionary biology is, after all, a very young discipline, whose data is sometimes bafflingly complex and in many of whose areas our ignorance is still vast. An observation of Holmes Rolston thus serves well as our conclusion:

> The main theory has not been found yet, and natural selection is only a fraction of some bigger truth. . . . Biology in its Darwinian stage stands where physics once stood in the Newtonian stage, and its Einstein has yet to appear. . . . Every big step that science has so far taken teaches that present theories are approximate and valid under limiting conditions, telling less than the whole truth, and evolutionary biology is no exception.[39]

——— EVOLUTION AND HUMAN LIFE ———

Darwin's primary purpose in his writings and research was not to look into the ancestry of human beings, but rather to set forth a coherent explanation for the evolutionary development of species. But reaction to his extraordinary contribution to biology has always centered on its dramatic conclusion that humans evolved from some lower form of life. This conclusion disturbed so many in Darwin's time and continues to do so today because it implies that there is nothing special about the human species, an implication that especially offends Western religious sensibilities. While it is true that the repeated demonstration of common ancestry inevitably relativizes all anthropocentrism, it is nevertheless clear today that biologically there is something quite exceptional about the presence of humans in the world of nature. This "something" is an unusually large and immensely complex brain.

A NEW BIOLOGICAL REALITY. We noted earlier that it is now generally agreed that the genus *homo* diverged, along with chimpanzees and gorillas, from a common ancestor between five and seven million years ago. The earliest hominid fossils that have been discovered go back almost four million years and bear the name *australopithecus,* with species that are called *afarensis, robustus,* and *africanus,* many discovered in southern Africa by Louis and Richard Leakey. These all walked upright, along with other hominid features, but still had an ape-sized brain of about 440 cubic centimeters. Another one and a half to two million years had to pass before hominid fossils appeared that were given the name *homo,* mainly because of an increasingly larger brain size. This went from 600 cubic centimeters in *homo habilis* (who chipped stones for tools two million years ago) to 930 cubic centimeters in *homo erectus* (who probably used fire about 1.6 million years ago) to 1,400 and 1,600 cubic centimeters when *homo sapiens* finally arrived on the scene in the form of Neanderthals about one hundred thousand years ago and Cro-Magnons about sixty thousand years later.[40] These latter, who were anatomically fully modern and crafted the most sophisticated stone and bone tools, diversified subsequently into races, invented agriculture (ten thousand years ago) and writing (six thousand years ago), and eventually took over all other *homo* species.[41]

Just what the forces were that directed this brain evolution is unknown, as is the time these larger brains became capable of thought in our modern sense. One crucial event in the process was surely the modification of the larynx and the capacity for language, used both as a tool for communication and as a system for sorting out information and drawing inferences. Biologically this was a tiny development, but socially it was a momentous leap, enabling humans eventually to change their environment to suit their

needs. Soon there was to come the mastery of sophisticated tools and art-
work, which suddenly appear in the archeological record about forty
thousand years ago. In any case, the evolution of the human brain is acknowledged to be a feat of fantastic difficulty, the most spectacular
enterprise of life since its origin, a unique instrument of as many as one
hundred billion nerve cells or neurons, each putting out between ten
thousand and a hundred thousand fibers or synapses connecting it to other
neurons. It is a network of incredibly complex neural circuits, part of the
complexity being the real possibility that each neuron is unique, unlike
cells in the rest of the body, and so not interchangeable with other neurons.[42] The human brain is thus an almost incomprehensible magic box,
enabling persons to contemplate themselves, their world, and the inevitability of their death.

According to the late British immunologist Peter Medawar, among
others, the biological significance of the brain is that it is responsible for
what is most distinctive about the species, namely the development of a
wholly new and nongenetic system of heredity. As the brains of humans
became larger and more complex, they passed from the stage in which
they could merely receive instructions, like the brains of most other
higher animals, to the stage in which they could hand these instructions
on from one generation to the next, a phenomenon that became their
defining character. Adaptive behavior in humans thus no longer required
either genetic input or Darwinian selection for its origin and maintenance. For in human societies self-consciousness, intentionality, purpose,
creativity, and freedom became operative for the first time.[43] This change
in the nature of heredity is, moreover, a clear example of evolution's acceleration. Cosmic evolution took billions and billions of years before the
coming of life, which in turn needed about three billion years to produce
humans, but in just a few million years this species has changed the
nature of the instructions transmitted to posterity.

Anthropologists emphasize the importance of social life and values for
this transmission, which took the form of human learning and culture.
Peter Wilson points out that *homo sapiens* is the only primate whose sexual
activity is not limited to rather narrow time periods. This has colored the
whole of human social existence, because it does not dictate a single pathway of cultural change but opens the way to the many pathways actually
taken over time. Moreover, bipedalism (requiring changes in the pelvis
that lead to less flexibility in birthing) and large head size (demanding that
infants be born less mature or smaller headed) required prolonged infant

care and a lengthy childhood, thereby giving the brain time to mature and learn. Not only was this primary bonding of mother and infant longer, it was also responsible for a male-female bonding that gave rise to father-hood, the recognition by the male adult that the child was his. This in turn created kinship systems, which then led to social systems, all of which represents, says Wilson, cultural, not genetic evolution.[44]

During the last two hundred years this change in human culture, language, and learning has obviously speeded up, leaving the enormously slow genetic evolution far behind. Genetic changes in human mental abilities, for example, probably peaked some tens of thousands of years ago, although there continue to be genetic adaptations to such things as diseases and air pollution, and humans still differ genetically in things like skin color and blood. But by and large they have overthrown the tyranny of the genes that lasted over three billion years, imposing on all species the rigid demands of the replicating process.[45] Humans now solve most of their adaptive problems as well as influence posterity by other than genetic means. If they wish, they can choose to keep a defective gene in circulation simply because their culture tells them not to let hemophiliac children die.

While chemically and genetically, humanity remains all of a piece with the cosmos, human social evolution has turned out to be inconceivably more rapid than any specific adaptations from chemical or genetic evolution could ever be. Natural selection probably continues at its characteristically slow rate of change in large and fairly stable populations, but cultural change has dwarfed its influence. Through technology humans have taken control of the ecologies of all other life systems, deciding in effect which will live and which will die. Their political revolutions can profoundly and all at once alter the traits of whole cultures. Such acceleration is also responsible today for the "generation gap" phenomenon, something unknown even in the last century. Harvard paleontologist George Gaylord Simpson summarizes well this new biological reality of *homo sapiens*:

> It is false to conclude that man is *nothing but* the highest animal or the most progressive product of organic evolution. He is fundamentally a new sort of animal and one in which, although organic evolution continues on its way, a fundamentally new sort of evolution has also appeared. The basis of this new sort of evolution is a new sort of heredity, the inheritance of learning. This sort of heredity . . . combines with man's other characteristics unique in

degree with a result that cannot be considered unique only in degree but must also be considered unique in kind.[46]

This new biological reality found in *homo sapiens* has provoked two very different reactions, known respectively as sociobiology and neo-Lamarckism. The first is a generally pessimistic understanding of the human condition verging on a genetic determinism, the second a more optimistic approach emphasizing evolution's directionality and progress. It will repay us to study both these interpretations more closely, since each has very significant theological implications.

THE INTERPRETATION OF SOCIOBIOLOGY. Sociobiology is a branch of neo-Darwinism that originated in the early 1970s to counteract the belief, widely held at the time, that genetically transmitted factors had only a very insignificant effect on the course of human affairs. This discipline was defined in 1975 by its chief representative, Harvard entomologist Edward O. Wilson, as "the systematic study of the biological bases of all social behavior."[47] Wilson's 1971 work, *The Insect Society*, had already established him as the world's foremost authority on insect behavior. But his true focus was much larger, on animal societies in general, "their population structure, castes, and communication, together with all of the physiology underlying the social adaptations." These areas became the subject of the first twenty-seven chapters of Wilson's impressive 1975 work, *Sociobiology*. Controversy erupted, however, over the last chapter, which was "concerned with the social behavior of early man and the adaptive features of organization in the more primitive contemporary human societies."[48] It was in this chapter that Wilson stated his ultimate objective:

> It may not be too much to say that sociology and the other social sciences, as well as the humanities, are the last branches of biology waiting to be included in the Modern Synthesis. One of the functions of sociobiology, then, is to reformulate the foundations of the social sciences in a way that draws these subjects into the Modern Synthesis.[49]

This objective, and the intellectual imperialism it seemed to reflect, provoked a strong reaction from mainstream sociologists, who resented Wilson's suggestion that genetic inheritance plays so strong a role in such areas of human behavior as altruism, ethics, aesthetics, romance, and religion. Wilson did not help matters by asking his readers to look at humans as if they were zoologists from another planet. "In this macroscopic view the humanities and social sciences shrink to specialized branches of biology; history, biography, and fiction are the research protocols of human ethology; and anthropology and sociology together constitute the sociobiology of a single primate species."[50] Among Wilson's proposals in this last chapter were that people might be genetically predisposed to enter certain social classes, that interbreeding among the races might lead to a proliferation of selfish people, and that genetic factors were probably responsible for many of the differences in custom and tradition between one society and another.

Critics were quick to point out that reasoning from behavioral tendencies to genetic factors may be quite valid for insect societies, where behavior is simple and may well be controlled by genetic materials, but the behavior of humans represents a quantum leap in the direction of complexity. The human brain is what controls social behavior, they insisted, not human genes, even though genetic factors may affect how the brain constructs itself in organic growth and development. Some critics even argued that Wilson's theories could be used like social Darwinism to justify racism, sexism, and oppression.[51] Wilson replied to these critics in 1978 with *On Human Nature,* in which he insisted that he was not claiming that genes control human behavior like that of lower animals, but only that they constrain it. They create biases or predispositions, founded in adaptive strategies from our evolutionary past, not only toward territoriality, bonding with the young and suspicion of strangers, but also toward religion, morals, and ethics. These cultural choices of the past are then reinforced by genetic recoding. "The genes hold culture on a leash. The leash is very long, but inevitably values will be constrained in accordance with their effects on the human gene pool."[52]

The problem here is that for Wilson the proper study of humans is "through the front end of a telescope, at a greater than usual distance and temporarily diminished in size," so that we can see ourselves in zoological relationship with other species.[53] But persons as we know them are not visible in such a way, and so an ultimate reductionism permeates *On Human Nature,* humans appearing to be much less than they actually are. No biologist would question, of course, that genes supply the necessary conditions for the development of human social life, along with the limits to such development. But since even Wilson would agree that this genetic explanation is not a sufficient one, the key issue is assessing how large a genetic base there actually is in complex behavioral factors like human motivation, purpose, and the capacity for agency. As a materialist, Wilson was clearly not disposed in *On Human Nature* to rate these complex factors very highly. This is undoubtedly why he says little about human interiority and intentionality, and almost nothing about cultural inventiveness and achievement.

Hence the questions of his critics: If genes really exercise such constraint over human behavior, why are human cultures so different when the underlying gene pools are so similar? How is it that cultures have changed so completely and so quickly over time when substantial genetic change is admittedly so slow? In 1981 Wilson responded to this gene-culture challenge with *Genes, Mind and Culture,* a book coauthored with a physicist, Charles Lumsden, which came closer than ever to genetic determinism. They argued that how fast natural selection works depends on the rate of relevant environment changes, and that human culture changes the relevant environment rather quickly. They included an elaborate mathematical analysis to show that gene-culture coevolution could conceivably bring about substantial changes in gene frequencies in a very short time, perhaps a thousand years.

While this "thousand-year rule" might well have worked for small prehistoric societies, however, we know of almost no historical population isolated for anywhere near a thousand years, something required for such a cumulative effect of natural selection. In more contemporary cultures, moreover, the lightning speed and spread of technological change would seem to render the "thousand-year rule" meaningless. Also, noted some critics, there is the problem of the obvious persistence of maladaptive cultural traits, which by definition could not be genetically based. Could not this same mathematical analysis be used, then, to show that all such traits got diffused in a population primarily as a result, not of genetic control, but of human social invention?[54]

Wilson recognized in all these books that religion was sociobiology's greatest challenge, both because it is a uniquely human phenomenon and because it "is above all a process by which individuals are persuaded to subordinate their immediate self-interest to the interests of the group."[55] This conviction led him into an analysis of altruism, "the central theoretical problem of sociobiology,"[56] because altruistic symbols are so prominent in all world religions. Can altruism be genetically selected for in the evolutionary process? Wilson acknowledged that genetic evolution can only account for what we think of as animal altruism, by which an individual sacrifices or risks its life or reproductive potential for the benefit of its closest kin, the most common example being that of a bird who gives a warning call to its kin-group when it sees a hawk, at the risk of calling the hawk's attention to itself. In this case, as well as in the case of humans doing the same for family members, the explanation is always in terms of results for the group, not of individual motivation. Such behavior is really genetic selfishness: the altruistic action, even if suicidal, saves the largest number of shared genes and passes them on to the next generation.

Since no group awareness is necessary here, this argument obviously rests on the assumption that we can properly speak of a gene or complex of genes for a particular kind of behavior. The gene or genes for altruism would thus transmit information by some causal chain, which affects the development of an organism's nervous system so as to make it more likely than not to behave altruistically. While this theory of "kin selection," first elaborated in the 1960s by Oxford biologist William Hamilton, is quite plausible for animal societies (experimental studies in this area are still in their infancy), its application to humans usually implies a biological determinism. It also involves sociobiologists like Wilson and Richard Dawkins in a curious attempt to personify the gene. "The argument of this book," writes Dawkins in *The Selfish Gene,* "is that we, and all other animals, are machines created by our genes. . . . I shall argue that a predominant quality to be expected in a successful gene is ruthless selfishness." Humans are merely "robot vehicles blindly programmed to preserve the selfish molecules known as genes."[57]

For sociobiologists, then, genes are much more than closely linked subordinate components of cells in the totality of a whole organism. They are treated as calculating agents, manipulating humans who may believe they have purposes of their own but really do not. Whereas classical Darwinians believe organisms to be the units of selection, sociobiologists insist that natural selection works exclusively at the level of genes, which compete to leave more copies of themselves in future generations. For Wilson, "the individual organism is only their vehicle, part of an elaborate device to preserve and spread them. . . . [T]he organism is only DNA's way of making more DNA."[58] Dawkins elaborates: "By dictating the way survival machines and their nervous systems are built, genes exert ultimate power over behavior. . . . Genes are the primary policy-makers; brains are the executives."[59] But, we may ask, is the situation not just the opposite, namely that we humans with our brains know all about DNA and DNA knows nothing? The reason for such a strange personification eventually becomes clear, however, if we realize that both authors believe that gene selfishness gets transferred to human selfishness, which in turn is the only possible explanation of altruistic behavior. Wilson is explicit:

The "altruist" expects reciprocation from society for himself or his closest relative. His good behavior is calculating, often in a wholly conscious way. . . . The capacity for soft-core [selfish] altruism can be expected to have evolved primarily by selection of individuals and to be deeply influenced by the vagaries of cultural evolution. Its psychological vehicles are lying, pretense and deceit, including self-deceit, because the actor is most convincing who believes that his performance is real.[60]

In an effort to explain why this biological selfishness still has such influence at the social level, Dawkins postulates that selfish genes must have had successors in the case of humans, other selfish replicating units capable of "achieving evolutionary change at a rate which leaves the old gene panting far behind." These units he calls "memes," living ideas spawned in brains that survive by actively exploiting their environment. The more rapidly a meme spreads from one brain to another, the greater its chance of survival. Memes are not metaphors for Dawkins; even though they are cultural traits, they obey the laws of natural selection exactly. "Just as genes propagate themselves in the gene pool by leaping from body to body via sperms and eggs, so memes propagate themselves in the memo pool by leaping from brain to brain via a process which, in the broad sense, can be called imitation."[61] To paraphrase Wilson, brains are therefore only the memes' way of making more memes.

Once again, then, we are left with an impression not only that true altruism is a rare human aberration, but that humans as personal agents really do little either to plan or to innovate their cultural evolution. Calculating memes do most of the work, manipulating the human brain for no other reason than to propagate for their own selfish advantage. What Wilson calls "hard-core altruism" (overcoming selfish genes by genuine self-sacrifice) is indeed possible, but only rarely and with enormous effort, and when it actually happens it is really irrational, a mindless death wish and "the enemy of civilization." For Dawkins too it is possible to defy the "selfish memes of our indoctrination," thereby enabling us to change our world for the better. But biological inertia, he reminds us, renders all such hope very fragile indeed.[62]

Before leaving sociobiology we should note that the effect of its understanding of the origins of "kin altruism" need not be entirely fatalistic. Religious psychologists point out that such biological perspectives can help us understand better the natural springs of that human affection which unselfish love must necessarily build upon, as well as enable us to avoid a personalism disconnected from biology. For we now have genetic reasons for the special love relation between parents and children. Commenting on the rigid determinism of Wilson and Dawkins, Stephen Pope argues that the error here "lies not in its uninhibited recognition of biological causality, but in taking it to be a quasi-exclusive causal factor that minimizes the force of a multitude of other causal factors."[63] Emphasizing the importance of genetic influence would thus be to acknowledge one of many motivations in human behavior, namely that of self-preservation, in addition to personal, cultural, and economic motives, along with free moral reflection, which usually predominate among humans.

THE INTERPRETATION OF NEO-LAMARCKISM. In contrast to this perspective of sociobiology that we have been discussing, there is a second interpretation of human biological reality whose focus is on evolution's directionality and progress. It is frequently called neo-Lamarckism, and its chief exponent is the French paleontologist Pierre Teilhard de Chardin. Its name comes from Lamarck, second only to Darwin in the history of evolutionary theory because, as we saw earlier, he was the first to conclude that evolution is a general condition of life in all its forms. Long before Darwin, Lamarck also proposed, in 1802, a theory on how this historical process works through heredity. All the forms of life represent a progression, he said, with the human species as the most progressive. He based this conviction on his observation that limbs of bodies grow stronger with use and weaker with disuse, usually as a result of adapting to different environments. Any particular environment would require habits appropriate to it; these habits would produce structural changes from an organ's use or disuse, and these changes would then be inherited. The giraffe was often cited as an example: it was assumed to have been originally short-necked and to have developed a longer neck from its desire and effort to reach the leaves of tall trees.

Lamarck's understanding of evolution's mechanism was thus transformational: species evolve because of the striving of their individual members to meet the demands of the environment. The characteristics thereby acquired were then passed on to subsequent generations. Put in more modern biological language, this would mean that the environment can somehow issue genetic instructions to living organisms that, if duly assimilated, could be passed on to progeny.[64] Darwin's mechanism of natural selection, on the other hand, when combined with Mendelian genetics, says that the environment brings out the potentialities present in the organism by selecting among a large number of variables. Hence the instructions are already there; the environment just causes them to be carried out. In an environment of tall trees, therefore, giraffes who happened to be born with longer necks (and hearts strong enough to pump blood up to their brains) could browse better and be better able to survive and have progeny than giraffes with shorter necks.

Developments in molecular biology during the 1950s played a decisive role in finally discrediting Lamarck's original theory. In those years there took place a pooling of experimental data between those molecular biologists concerned with the general structure of molecules and those concerned with the transfer of specific genetic information. Their conclusion was that any such information flows in one direction only, from DNA to RNA to proteins to an organism's body, but never in the reverse direction. Eventually this conclusion became known as molecular biology's "Central Dogma." It said that changes in the genetic apparatus (the "genome") could come about only by errors in replication. Variation thus had to be accidental; there could be feedback only through the relative success or failure of variants before the selective forces of the environment. Hence the directionality of evolution, in so far as it is the result of the mechanism of natural selection, cannot be the result of any striving on the part of the organism itself, because DNA can be taught nothing. The environment chooses among the organism's variations, but the organism itself does not accept instructions from the environment.[65]

All this may be true, of course, but there is an exception for one living organism, the human brain. As we noted already, through the brain humans *do* accept instructions from their environment, because the brain acts as intermediary in a hereditary system of its own. Humans not only learn, they teach and hand on, and their cultural tradition accumulates in the information and wisdom they store in books and technology. Such social evolution is thus in a certain sense a continuation of biological evolution, but it is not Darwinian in nature. It is Lamarckian. The environment may not be able to imprint genetic evolution on the human species, but it can and does imprint nongenetic information, which humans can and do pass on cumulatively to future generations. Hence knowledge and skills acquired by persons in their lifetime can certainly be inherited, not through chromosomes and genes but through precept, example, and instruction.

In order to find an antidote to the mechanistic materialism of much neo-Darwinism, a handful of biologists, encouraged by this obviously

Lamarckian character of human social evolution, have recently sought in vain to show that ordinary genetic inheritance really works in some inner directed way too.[66] These are not nearly so foolish and dangerous, however, says Nobel laureate Peter Medawar, as those who have attempted to graft a Darwinian interpretation upon the cultural evolution of humankind. In an obvious reference to sociobiology, he says that we must "abandon any idea that the direction of social change is governed by laws other than laws which have at sometime been the subject of human decisions or acts of the mind." For it is a profound truth, he adds, "that Nature does *not* know best; that genetical evolution . . . is a story of waste, makeshift compromise and blunder." It is therefore of paramount importance to recognize that what happens in society does not occur in the style and under the pressures of genetic evolution.

> That competition between one man and another is a necessary part of the texture of society; that societies are organisms which grow and must inevitably die; that division of labor within a society is akin to what we can see in colonies of insects; that the laws of genetics have an overriding authority; that social evolution has a direction forcibly imposed upon it by agencies beyond man's control—all these are biological judgments; but, I do assure you, bad judgments based on bad biology.[67]

Hence contemporary neo-Lamarckism does not want to return to the original position of Lamarck that biological evolution is an "orthogenesis," that is to say, a predetermined and optimizing process, an unfolding of preexisting rudiments, like the development of an individual from a fertilized egg or of a flower from a bud.[68] What neo-Lamarckism *does* want to emphasize, however, along with neo-Darwinism, is that this process is not one of pure chance either. For the mechanism of natural selection is clearly of an antichance nature. Darwin himself made this point at the conclusion of the *Origin*: "And as natural selection works solely by and for the good of each being, all corporeal and mental endowments will tend to progress toward perfection."[69]

However, this progressive movement is not to be found in the genetic variations that initiate the evolutionary change, since these are completely random with respect to whether they are useful or harmful to the functioning of an organism. This functioning, in other words, has nothing to do with the mutational event itself or with any of its causes. (But such randomness is not pure chance either, since the possibility of any single mutation is obviously limited by the history and structure of a particular gene.) What natural selection does is to direct such mutations into adaptive channels, thereby promoting a harmonious ordering and adjustment of life to its environment. It thus becomes a true antichance agent but not a rigidly deterministic one, because it has no eye on the future. That is to say, there is no way to predict, as far as a particular species is concerned, whether the new environmental niche it enters will prove to be a dead end or a new adaptive zone. It is only *after* a species has been evolutionarily successful that it can be said to represent evolutionary progress.[70]

French paleontologist Pierre Teilhard de Chardin once spoke of natural selection in terms of "groping," a process that "proceeds step by step by dint of billion-fold trial and error." He referred to it as "directional chance" and "strokes of chance which are . . . selected," because it results in evolutionary stability as well as in progress for certain lineages.[71] Teilhard's friend and fellow paleontologist, George Gaylord Simpson, who was certainly no neo-Lamarckian, makes an important point about such progress. "Within the framework of the evolutionary history of life," he writes, "there have been not one but many different sorts of progress. Each sort appears not with one single line or even with one central but branching line throughout the course of evolution, but separately in many different lines."[72] Evolutionary progress does not mean, then, that lower organisms are always replaced by higher ones; higher and lower often co-exist, each in its separate ecological niche. Life is thus a ramifying bush with millions of branches, only one branch of which represents the single pathway leading in the direction of *homo sapiens*.[73]

Moreover, geneticist Theodosius Dobzhansky (with Mayr and Simpson, one of the architects of the modern synthesis) points out that events that in fact moved evolution in this direction were unique, their exact repetition having the probability of zero. Along this pathway were a vastly greater number of potentialities than were ever realized, because only a minuscule fraction of possible gene combinations can ever be actualized. Far from resembling a predetermined process, therefore, the lack of inevitability here is striking, in spite of the antichance character of the "groping" involved.[74] Even when such "groping" is successful and extinction here and now avoided, the fit of some species to their environments will inevitably be too tight, resulting in a loss of plasticity and rendering them helpless in the future if the environment suddenly changes. This means that the emergence of humans from perhaps hundreds of evolutionary branching points was a very contingent event, an example of evolutionary opportunism. If the whole process were replayed, starting from the bottom of the Cambrian period some half billion years ago, there could thus be no biological guarantee that the outcome would be the same. In principle a completely different set of organisms could arise.[75]

Hence the neo-Lamarckian emphasis of Teilhard de Chardin on the directionality of evolution can only be understood as a focus upon the extraordinary outcome of this contingent life process. Its antichance "groping" has finally achieved, in and through the human species, a genuine interiorization of matter. Even someone as unconcerned about directionality as Simpson acknowledges that humans represent an "absolute difference in kind, . . . a unique degree and direction of progress in evolution."[76] Teilhard would go much further: the coming of thought created a psychological abyss between humans and other higher animals, "a mutation from zero to everything," for which in 1940 he coined the term "hominization."[77] Teilhard quotes zoologist Julian Huxley: humans are "*nothing else than evolution become conscious of itself. . . . The consciousness of each of us is evolution looking at itself and reflecting upon itself*."[78] Life was thus carried forward into thought and thought is simply life interiorized. Humans are consequently "the arrow pointing the way to the final unification of the world in terms of life."[79]

> The being who is the object of his own reflection, in consequence of that very doubling back upon himself, becomes in a flash able to raise himself to a new sphere. In reality, another world is born. Abstraction, logic, reasoned choice and inventions, mathematics, art, calculation of space and time, anxieties and dreams of love—all these activities of *inner life* are nothing else than the effervescence of the newly-formed center as it explodes onto itself.[80]

This explosion takes place for humans at the species level, where an enlarged nervous system and a more complex brain structure are capable of inheritance in the true Lamarckian sense. "Under the free and ingenious effort of successive intelligences," says Teilhard, "*something* (even in the absence of any measurable variation of brain or cranium) irreversibly accumulates, according to all the evidence, and is transmitted, at least collectively by means of education, down the course of ages."[81] This accumulation takes place not so much in the sphere of life, the "biosphere," as in the sphere of thought, the "noosphere," the "thinking layer," which since its germination at the end of the tertiary period has spread over and above the world of plants and animals. Thought is thus the criterion for Teilhard's claim of privileged status for human directionality (even though the human line was brought about by the same biological causes involved in unprivileged lines). For with their intelligence, humans are able to know that they know. They can thereby control their environments and reach a very high degree of biological security, capable of choosing for themselves evolution's future direction and goals, "because we are evolution."[82] Teilhard's insight is repeated often:

> This sudden deluge of cerebralization, this biological invasion of a new animal type which gradually eliminates or subjects all forms of life that are not human, this irresistible tide of fields and factories, this immense and growing edifice of matter and ideas—all these signs that we look at for days on end—seem to proclaim that there has been a change on the earth and a change of planetary magnitude. . . . The greatest revelation open to science today is to perceive that everything precious, active and progressive originally contained in that cosmic fragment from which our world emerged, is now concentrated in a "crowning" noosphere.[83]

THE ENIGMA OF THE HUMAN. This overview of neo-Lamarckian optimism regarding human directionality and progress shows it to be the polar opposite of sociobiology's pessimistic determinism. But neither enslavement to the selfish gene nor liberation from its control in the noosphere seem able adequately to deal with what is perhaps the most curious biological phenomenon of the human condition. Humans cannot avoid evidence of a certain misfit between themselves and their environment, something found in no other species. Their "consciousness of consciousness" and their rational distancing from their animal instincts apparently come at a high psychological price. While this prehuman animality and genetic programming cannot be left behind, efforts to integrate it into the rational and the cultural continually get frustrated, causing mental and emotional disturbances that render humans strangely ill at ease in their world.

The rest of nature may be vastly inferior in achievement, but it possesses a harmony and rhythm of life that mocks the restlessness and depression that characterize the human. Humans alone in the biological world commit suicide. They alone go through their biological lives with a sense of incomplete fulfillment, frustrated in their quests for "self-realization" and "personal growth." Their aspirations and needs go far beyond the basic biological necessities of food, rest, shelter, and procreation. Alienation of every type permeates contemporary society, set in bold relief by the brutal power of psychology to clarify but not to explain. Self-awareness, reason and imagination, says one eminent psychoanalyst, have "made man into an anomaly, into the freak of the universe. He is part of nature, subject to her physical laws and unable to change them, yet he transcends the rest of nature. He is set apart while being a part.... Reason, man's blessing, is also his curse; it forces him to cope everlastingly with the task of solving an insoluble dichotomy. Human existence is different in this respect from all other organisms; it is in a state of constant and unavoidable disequilibrium."[84]

Normal instincts are thus compounded by the heightening of self-consciousness and freedom, which transform the common animal experience of physical pain into reflective psychological suffering. For humans are acutely aware of nature's crazy indifference—the inheritance of physical defect, the brutality of accident, the stealth of disease, the tyranny of moral and intellectual makeup—all rendering humans rebellious and impotent, and ruthlessly limiting their field of action and choice. Nor is such pain simply the result of biological inevitability. Often it is gratuitously inflicted by one member of the species on another or by one group on other groups, producing acute trauma at both individual and social levels. The most emotionally unacceptable form of such psychological suffering is, of course, the contemplation of death. The anguish caused by this thought is in stark contrast to its quiet existence in the rest of nature, where new forms of life arise only from the demise of old forms, where death is essential for the release of food for new arrivals, and where species routinely become extinct by losing their ecological niches. Humans, in contrast, generally regard death as an affront that renders their lives absurd, although they claim no such thing for any other animal.

This self-consciousness of humans is rightly regarded today as one of the most difficult problems in nature, giving rise to the burgeoning field of research centered on the biochemistry of the human brain. How precisely are mental events caused by the firing of the brain's thousand billion neurons and their synapses?[85] The deeper the insights achieved into this mind-body problem, the more baffling things seem to become. For it is generally agreed that what the brain does by way of abstract reflection and the experience of emotions like fear, pain, wonder, and love—whatever makes one's intelligent life meaningful—cannot be described by the physics and chemistry of the organ itself, whose mechanics and electronics are daily being charted with greater and greater precision by the discoveries of neuroscience. In other words, while consciousness is obviously implemented by the brain's neurobiology, the language of neurobiology cannot convey what it is like to be conscious.

One's own consciousness may indeed be self-evident through introspection (itself a form of consciousness), but someone else's consciousness is simply not an observable property of living matter. No amount of outside analysis can possibly tell us what this person's experience is in itself, and what it consists of, as distinct from its causes and effects. Because reality has this subjective dimension along with all its objective dimensions, two totally different methods of inquiry seem to be required, making the connection between brain and consciousness extremely difficult for neuroscientists to pinpoint. Their present approach seems to be to keep pressing the experimental side without worrying too much about aspects of the problem that cannot be solved at present by existing scientific tools.[86] The one thing they are all agreed upon, however, is that the answer, when and if it ever comes, will be monist and not dualist. That is to say, human self-consciousness represents the total state of the brain at any given moment, not the functioning of some nonphysical "mind" interacting with the brain but distinct from it.

In this monist view, now held by almost all biologists, neuroscientists, and philosophers, it is the *total state* of the brain, not the functioning of any particular set of neurons, that constitutes human consciousness. In the form of self-awareness this is one's capacity to be present to oneself, to experience one's subjectivity, that basic characteristic which constitutes human "spirit" and the distinctive mode of human existence. Such self-consciousness is obviously causal, with the brain controlling bodily movements as well as continually probing the environment. In any given instance, moreover, the precise direction of such control and probing may be undetermined and unpredictable, something corresponding to the common human experience of inner freedom, the awareness that we are somehow responsible for ourselves. While the incredible complexity of the source of these experiences places them as of now beyond description in purely neurological terms, we nevertheless seem able to speak of them quite easily with the language of reasons, intentions, and emotions. Needless to say, however, this whole question remains today enormously difficult and highly disputed, involving a great variety of arguments and data from philosophy and mathematics as well as from the physical and psychological sciences.[87]

As we come to the end of this biological survey of the evolution of human life, therefore, we are faced with a puzzle: why should this process have produced such a highly unusual species? That such enormously complex beings have arisen is perfectly consistent with what is known of the process, but if the process had resulted in far less complex beings, this would have been equally consistent. While evolution thus allows for growing complexity, it does not require it. In other words, the biological sciences can explain reasonably well the "how" question of human presence in the world of nature, but this "why" question is one for which they ultimately have no response. This is because, as we said at the start, evolutionary biology, unlike functional biology, deals with the unrepeatable and largely nonexperimental; while it can describe and explain phenomena with considerable precision, it cannot make reliable predictions.[88]

The real problem in the case of *homo sapiens*, therefore, as Holmes Rolston has noted, is not ongoing *survival* but oncoming *arrival*. Because it can in no way be predicted, the ascent of the process toward the human necessarily appears as an anomaly, an outcome wholly fortuitous and unexpected. *Why* should this particular species have appeared in the life process after billions of years when myriad other potentialities in this radically contingent process were never realized? No biological theory has the resources to deal with this question. "Some of the movements here are causal to be sure, but the movements we most desire to have an explanation for are *casual*, not *causal*. They happen without sufficient cause in the shuffling of materials. The seminal principle is missing entirely, and randomness stands in the gap. And randomness is noise, not explanation."[89]

Peter Medawar acknowledges that here science reaches the limits of its knowledge. While he sets no limit on the power of science to answer the kind of questions science *can* answer, he insists that "ultimate" questions about human origin, destiny, and purpose are logically outside its competence. "[These] questions make sense to those who ask them, and the answers, to those who try to give them; but whatever else may be in dispute, it would be universally agreed that it is not to science that we must look for answers."[90] He cautions, however, that any such answers, though outside the domain of actual or possible empirical sense experience, should not be outrageously incongruent with such experience or with common sense. "I do not believe—indeed, I deem it a comic blunder to believe—that the exercise of reason is *sufficient* to explain our condition and where necessary to remedy it, but I do believe that the exercise of reason is at all times unconditionally *necessary* and that we disregard it at our peril."[91]

—— EVOLUTION AND GOD ——

It has been clear for some time now that, to be credible, contemporary Christian theology must recognize the religious significance of the biological data with which we have been dealing. Traditionally theology has emphasized answers to "why" questions, without taking much account of answers to the "how" questions asked by science. Today, however, the very formulation of these "why" questions can no longer be done in isolation, because the answers scientists are giving to many of their "how" questions frequently carry the implication that religious answers to "why" questions should really be irrelevant for any thinking person. Hence it is important that Christians discern at least some correspondence, some connection between what their theology says about the meaning of the cosmos and the arrival of humans, and of Jesus in particular, and what science has discovered about the survival and development of life over billions of years. Otherwise, as Karl Rahner has said, theological statements on these matters risk being regarded as so many irrelevant mythologies.

I believe there is such congruity, and that it can be found by reflecting anew on the basic Christian doctrines of creation, Incarnation, and redemption. For these teachings all deal with something done to matter, which in turn must mean for Christians that God is not to be found in some sacred sphere, separated from the biological world. Rather, God is to be known and God's designs are to be discovered in and through matter, and more specifically in self-reflecting human matter as it has emerged from the evolutionary process. The role of Christian faith is to give ultimate significance and worth to this human phenomenon, first by pointing to God as the true and only fulfillment of human aspirations and hope, and second by making more bearable the scandal of chance, waste, suffering, and death. But this can be done only if this faith recognizes the full impact of the biological sciences on these three fundamental Christian beliefs. Such recognition will be our aim in what follows.

THE PUZZLE OF LIFE'S ORIGINS. What can it mean for Christians to say that God created life and human life? Let us start with what biologists can tell us about life's origins. Earlier we spoke of evolution from a "common ancestor" but did not say what this ancestor was nor how it came into existence. Later we spoke of the living cell as the unit of all organic life, with the dual function of metabolism (or growth capacity) and replication, its proteins being the essential component of the first function, and its nucleic acids, containing the genetic code, being the essential component of the second. However, as we also saw, the code contained in these nucleic acids is meaningless until translated into the twenty amino acids of proteins by enzymes, which are themselves a form of protein and so owe their existence to DNA coding.[92] Hence the riddle of life's origins: the code cannot be translated except by the products of coded instructions. How did this circle first get closed? For the first living cell would have been our "common ancestor," with the replicative coding structure now shared by all species from viruses to human. Is it possible to get some idea of how this first cell might have come into existence?

Yes, it is possible. But no one can explain how it actually happened, both because the crucial transition left no evidence and because the chasm is still too vast between the simplest of living cells and the most highly ordered nonliving matter like crystals and snowflakes. (This chasm is the reason that a handful of scientists like Francis Crick believe that the seeds of life must have drifted to earth from interstellar space, which of course just pushes the question of origins further back.) There is not even a theory as yet, in the sense of a detailed description of postulated events, but only two hypotheses, both fragile for lack of experiment.

The first, that of a single origin, says that life began once, that its replicative function is primary, and that this took the form of the very simple RNA molecule to which metabolism was linked from the start. The second hypothesis says that the present dual structure of all organisms into proteins and nucleic acids points rather to a dual origin. There were first protein molecules capable of growth but without genetic apparatus, followed after some time by RNA molecules that acted as parasites on the former's metabolism to replicate themselves; as soon as the protein-based life learned to tolerate the RNA parasite, the first primitive cell was born. But as yet there are no experimental clues to support either of these hypotheses.[93]

Now it is important to emphasize at this point that, however gigantic the evolutionary step taken by this first primitive cell, the probability of its happening is today believed to be high. The reason is not, as one might presume, that we suddenly know more than in the recent past about conditions on the earth at this first moment of life, approximately 3.5 billion years ago.[94] Chemists have actually known for a long time that high concentrations of water, methane, and ammonia must have been present in the primordial "soup," since these are so essential for the existence of proteins and nucleic acids. Breathable air, from oxygen spun off from ancient algae, also had to have formed the ozone layer to protect the myriad cells that ramified. The reason for believing in the probability of life is thus not new knowledge of the past but rather new knowledge of the present: the merging interdisciplinary field known as complexity theory or chaos theory.

This theory began with the work of Belgian Nobel laureate Ilya Prigogine, who showed that in complex chemical systems a very small input of energy from the outside environment can be amplified, leading first to instability and rapid fluctuation and then to a new and more complex ordered state that resists fluctuation and maintains equilibrium in its newly structured form. In other words, new states of highly ordered regularity can occur spontaneously out of the random open processes of low-ordered states. "Order of chaos" Prigogine called it.[95] This propensity of matter for self-organization into increasingly complex systems is now seen to be a principle so basic as to constitute, when applied to biological systems, a plausible explanation of how life began. For the initial conditions envisioned demand that all the systems involved (water, gases, air) be wholly open to the inflow of heat energy from the sun, which could in principle so destabilize them that the emergence of new, highly structured and self-replicating molecules could well have been the result.

These newly ordered life forms would then also feed on energy from the outside, but we should note that they would be doing so from within a closed universe governed by the First and Second Laws of Thermodynamics. These laws describe any system isolated from its environment, in which heat energy is always conserved but degraded by use. Such use transforms it from one form into another and dissipates it into the system, which as a whole gradually runs down and tends toward greater disorder as its entropy, the measure of its unusable energy, slowly increases. Part of the reason for such inevitable entropy increase in the universe, however, is precisely the fact that large amounts of its energy are continually being sucked up by living matter in the form of greater complexity and order. The upward movement of life is thus totally dependent for its birth and nourishment on matter's overall entropic movement downward in the course of time.[96] "Weird" is physicist Freeman Dyson's word to describe this extraordinary phenomenon; a process of "inexhaustible queerness" is the phrase of biologist J. B. S. Haldane.[97]

CREATION AND THE POTENTIALITIES OF MATTER. How is a Christian to speak in this context of "creation"? The problem is that the word has been burdened in the popular mind with unfortunate connotations from the fourth century onward. At this time its religious link to the history of salvation began to be lost, and the doctrine came to be framed philosophically rather than narratively within the Christian story. The word became primarily a cosmological term used to oppose the Greek pantheistic conviction of the coeternity of God and matter, as well as the moral dualism of the Gnostics who believed material reality to be evil and only the spiritual to be good. Patristic theologians like Tertullian coined the phrase *"creatio ex nihilo,"* from nothing, but their primary concern was not with origins but with the absolute dependence of the cosmos on God for its very existence. As centuries passed, however, the focus shifted from this metaphysical claim to a specific historical claim, namely God's initial bringing of everything into existence as a result of a singular event in the past.

The problem in modern times is that such a singular event has been pushed back by science some fifteen billion years, resulting in the creative action of God becoming further and further removed from the natural causal workings of the world. Neither Augustine's reflection on the nature of time and divine conservation, nor Scholasticism's emphasis on the notion of participation, had much influence over the centuries on the popular mind.[98] Even today most religious people believe that creation is simply a single primordial act of God, who belongs to another world yet who periodically intervenes on planet Earth to bring into existence first life and then human life.

The literal reading of the creation story of Genesis, while quite understandable historically, simply compounded this problem. We know today that the creation narratives of primitive cultures were not addressing an intellectual problem of origins but an existential problem of humans threatened by their surroundings. Out of questions by threatened humans in a threatened world arose questions about the beginning as ground and support for their survival in their present. This type of questioning characterized all the ancient polytheistic societies, which explains the multiplicity of creation narratives throughout the ancient world. Israel's narrative was a late extension of the nation's original faith in Yahweh as

God of the Covenant and of history as well as of the promise of salvation. In very personal categories the first chapters of Genesis present us with a mythical reflection on this salvific work of Yahweh as it launches the beginnings of history. Scholars generally agree today that this book's authors had no intention of providing a description of *how* the world actually came to be; they were simply telling a story, the only way they could possibly speak about what happened. This is a story of origins—of the world, of human beings, of Israel. Its essential affirmation is that everything without exception owes its existence to the free and sovereign action of God, that everything is "good," and that its source is God's love for Israel and humankind.[99]

Creation was thus a story of total dependence long before it was a teaching about origins. As Thomas Aquinas said later, creation does not refer merely to an initial moment but is fundamentally an ongoing relationship between God and all that is not God. He used the term "conservation" (*conservatio*) to indicate that God holds in being contingent creatures who need not exist, and the term "concurrence" (*concursus*) to emphasize that God must therefore cooperate with all creature activity. In this sense creation is a continuous action of God as absolute being and primary cause of all finite beings. Hence God's action does not eliminate action that is proper to creatures but is ultimately responsible for it. Any particular behavior is therefore totally that of the creature or "secondary" cause, doing whatever it is inclined to do naturally in whatever way it naturally does it, but also totally that of God as "primary" cause, communicating existence to the creature and to its behavior. As Aquinas put it: "Since God is personally the cause in all things of their whole very existence, than which nothing is more intimate or interior, it follows that God acts innermostly in all things."[100]

Karl Rahner is the theologian who has done most to link Aquinas' understanding of God's creative action with the evolution discovered by science. This he does first by retrieving from Christian tradition the sense in which God is immanent in the creative process, and second by elucidating what we know today to be the effect of such immanence, namely matter's capacity for self-transcendence. Of course in attempting to speak of God's immanence there is always risk of slipping into some form of pantheism by making God simply identical with the world. Indeed, pantheism's perennial attraction is that it decisively overcomes the general tendency of theistic religion to emphasize God's transcendence, thereby distancing God from creation and fostering the kind of deism prevalent in the early days of science during the seventeenth and eighteenth centuries. Eventually this tendency made it relatively easy in the nineteenth century for science to isolate God altogether from the immediate functioning of organic evolution. Ironically, many scientists who speak today about belief in God are more than likely to be pantheists, like Albert Einstein, because they are convinced that the matter they see organizing itself with such staggering precision and complexity must somehow be self-creative.[101]

Rahner, on the other hand, understands immanence to be a corollary of transcendence. God's incomprehensible "otherness" is precisely the reason that God can be present as Creator to the action of all creatures, from that of the sparrow's fall of which Jesus spoke to that of the highest human intelligence. This conviction Rahner grounds in the most fundamental of Christian beliefs: God's loving self-bestowal in Jesus through the Incarnation, which is offered to all humankind through what Christians call "grace" or the divine "indwelling," alluded to in the Gospel of John 14:23. These central mysteries, Rahner insists, ought not be considered totally different from God's creative action in nature as a whole.

In other words, the divine *concursus* of Aquinas is really an analogical self-bestowal of God to all matter as such, by which God's own mysterious reality is communicated, and within which matter emerges in its evolutionary form. God's presence and causality would thus be veiled within the total process and matter's behavior on its own level would also be the hidden action of God on another level. The universe is consequently self-organizing because of the pressure within it from the loving omnipresence of God. Although this divine dynamism does not belong to finite creatures as finite but to God as sovereignly independent, it is nevertheless truly intrinsic to creatures. It becomes their own.

Secondly, such an approach to God's immanence enables Rahner to elucidate its effect. What cosmic and organic evolution shows is that the omnipresent divine self-bestowal is not simply a conserving power but a becoming, a divine collaboration with material energy, enabling creatures both to be rooted in what already is and yet to develop into the qualitatively different, not just the quantitatively more complex. That is to say, the natural evolutionary process has within itself the capacity of creatures to become, actively not passively, what they are not, namely something genuinely new and self-transcendent, without any divine intervention from the outside, but simply as a result of the radically immanent self-bestowal of the transcendence of God. Such active self-transcendence is obviously not operative in all evolutionary change in the same way, since much of the latter consists in mere temporal and spatial rearrangements of matter or the reproduction of the almost identical. But whenever there is a true becoming, says Rahner, there will also be a true surpassing of self, an intrinsic increase in being, a genuine activation of God's creative power.

> But on any showing the immanence of God in the world must be conceived as of so radical a kind that the process of self-transcendence inherent in beings in process of becoming genuinely is and remains an active process of *self-transcendence*. At the same time, however, the transcendence of God must be maintained for this reason too, not merely because of God's sovereign independence of the world, but in order to ensure that what emerges from this process is that which is genuinely new.[102]

The outcome of the biological process that is most "genuinely new" is obviously the arrival of the human species. In effect, says Rahner, echoing Sir Julian Huxley, humanity is the universe become conscious of itself. Matter, in other words, develops out of its inner being in the direction of spirit. This term "spirit" is for Rahner simply the human person in so far as she or he is self-conscious and so conscious of the mystery surrounding all human life.[103] To become spirit in the fullest sense is precisely to accept this mystery in freedom. At this evolutionary level, therefore, God's loving self-bestowal can be received through "grace" and returned through love and surrender. It is in this sense that one can speak of humans as the goal of creation, since when this acceptance of God is manifested over time and objectified in words and deeds, human cultural history, as the culmination of biological history, becomes what Christians call salvation history, for salvation is not so much a gift from and by God as the gift of God's very self. In the words of Goethe, "Man is the first conversation which nature holds with God."[104]

All three histories (biological, cultural, salvific) constitute, moreover, a single process of self-transcendence, which can reach its climax only if a total and irrevocable acceptance of God's absolute self-bestowal actually takes place in human history. Christians believe that such an event has indeed taken place in the life, death, and resurrection of Jesus of Nazareth, and theologically this is what "Incarnation" really means. This total acceptance by Jesus of God's self-bestowal thus constitutes, says Rahner, "the supreme and unsurpassable apogee of the dynamic immanence of God."[105] This last statement requires treatment of evolution's impact on current Christology, which we shall come to presently. First, however, we must ask about chance and its place in the theology of creation we have just sketched.

CHANCE AND PROVIDENCE. Providence is God's immanent creative action insofar as this is conceived as guiding the course of matter and human life according to God's all-loving plan for the cosmos. Belief in such a plan and its execution has been one of the essentials of Christian faith since biblical times. In the last section of Part 3 we shall consider how such guidance might encompass the mystery of evil in the world. Just now, however, our focus is on the phenomenon of chance. How might we conceive God intelligently caring with foresight and purpose for an evolving world of nature in which chance plays a role at all levels? I have elsewhere discussed God's involvement in the radical indeterminacy of the microworld, as this is now known to us through quantum theory and the Heisenberg uncertainty principle, as well as how this might be related to the indeterminacy of human freedom.[106] Our inquiry here is thus limited to God's relationship to indeterminism in the biological processes, an indeterminism we documented at length in Part 1. Does not the presence of such randomness imply the lack of any divine plan in the realm of life?

No one in recent years has challenged the existence of such a plan more eloquently than the French microbiologist and Nobel laureate Jacques Monod. His widely read *Chance and Necessity*, published in English in 1971, bases its case on a lucid scientific exposition of the two independent causal chains involved in natural selection, both of which we discussed earlier.[107] Rare genetic mutations, due ultimately to quantum fluctuations at the submolecular level, are copied invariably by the first causal mechanism. But these are totally random with respect to their interaction with the second causal mechanism, involving an organism's biological drive to survive and reproduce under pressures from its various environments. That is to say, most mutations are harmful to this survival capacity and many are lethal; only an incredibly small number turn out to be useful. Environmental success of an organism thus depends upon the rare and fortuitous influence of favorable genetic mutations which are themselves rare and fortuitous.

"Randomness caught on the wing," Monod calls these events, "preserved, reproduced by the machinery of invariance and thus converted into order, rule, necessity."[108] While he would acknowledge, of course, that humans act with deliberative purpose, his point is that the evolution of living organisms can have no such teleology. Individual organisms have only what he calls "teleonomy," meaning that each has its own structure within which is a capacity and drive for invariable self-reproduction. Since all living things are the result of the randomness in evolution's two causal chains, no one of them individually can be anything other than a chance reproduction preserved by an invariance mechanism.

Hence the line of development actually taken by evolution is only one of an enormous number of potential developments, each of which would have resulted in a totally different world. Talk of divine providence is thus patently absurd, because we now have biological proof of the absence of any master plan. "Pure chance, absolutely free but blind, at the very root of the stupendous edifice of evolution: this central concept of modern biology is no longer one among other possible or even conceivable hypotheses. It is today the *sole* conceivable hypothesis, the only one compatible with observed and tested fact." What then is to be said of the arrival of *homo sapiens*? "Our number came up in the Monte Carlo game."[109]

One eminent geneticist, Theodosius Dobzhansky, believes that Monod is using his categories too loosely. "Natural selection does not fit in the category of 'necessity,'" he writes, "nor does mutation fit in that of pure 'chance,' under any reasonable definition of these terms (which Monod leaves rather vague). Evolution was from time to time, and in some lineage, progressive; at other times and in other lineages it was neutral or even regressive."[110] Hence natural selection, while indeed an antichance agent, is not rigidly deterministic; it knows nothing of the future needs of the organisms on which it acts, which explains why there have been so many more extinctions than improvements in the history of matter. The whole process is thus unpredictable in the long run, opportunistic and creative rather than necessary, restraining the turmoil of mutations and gene recombination by guiding organisms into a multiplicity of channels that are as a rule adaptive. In this way "ingredients of chance and antichance are blended in a way which makes the dichotomy meaningless."[111]

Interestingly enough, centuries before anyone knew about evolution, Thomas Aquinas did not seem to have any theological problem with randomness. Asking whether providence excluded chance, he said that "it would be inconsistent with divine providence if all things happened of necessity.... Therefore it would be contrary to the nature of providence and to the perfection of the world if nothing happened by chance."[112] Otherwise, he continued, there would be no contingency; everything would be necessary, taking place in one particular way because it had to. The result would leave God no room to maneuver in matter's guidance. At the human level, for example, we know that our intentions can never extend to all the contingencies in a given situation, and if something happens that we did not intend, we often call this chance. It is precisely because such human choices are open that they can allow for both divine guidance and human freedom. At a lower level also, says Aquinas, "there may be chance in the making of things produced from matter."[113]

Convinced that randomness in evolution is not only consistent with providence but somehow required by it, and utilizing all the scientific data Aquinas lacked, British biochemist and theologian Arthur Peacocke has written at length on the role of chance in a world of purpose. Chance is the biological tool used by the immanent creative action of God to explore and activate the rich potentialities of matter. "Instead of being daunted by the role of chance in genetic mutations as being the manifestation of irrationality in the universe, it would be more consistent with the observations to assert that the full gamut of the potentialities of living matter could be explored only through the agency of the rapid and frequent randomization which is possible at the molecular level of DNA." The enormous number of mutations thus elicited provide, in other words, the raw material which the environment then selects via the independent second causal chain operating at the higher macrolevel.

This combination of chance mutation and environmental pressure, leading to more complex structured forms, constitutes for the Christian mind "the search radar of God, sweeping through all the possible targets available to its probing."[114] Far from contradicting God's providence, chance rather illuminates it. For as Prigogine has demonstrated,[115] the universe is in fact creative over time. Looked at theologically, it is this biological exploration of matter's potentialities, allowing more complex form to emerge from the less complex which transforms chance and randomness into the creative agents of God's immanent power and love. Without denying creation the freedom to be itself, God's intentions can be actualized precisely in and through this flexible process that is structurally open.

Humans eventually arrive on the earth precisely as the result of this open-ended trial and error exploration of possibilities, where there is even more room for God to maneuver, because of the unpredictable openness of free persons to persuasion.[116] Physicist Paul Davies points to a great surprise here, what he calls the biosphere's "ordered contingency," in which organisms are all antecedently unpredictable in their particular forms, yet in fact are found not to be haphazard but conspicuously ordered, an orderliness whose structures are actually intelligible to the human mind.[117] This mutual interplay of chance and order, contingency and necessity, chaos and complexity, is thus extremely subtle. John Polkinghorne makes this point well:

> Theology has always been in danger of a double bind in relation to physical causation. A tightly deterministic universe, evolving along predestined lines, seems to leave little room for freedom and responsibility. It is congenial only to a deistic indifference or to the iron grip of Calvinistic predestination. On the other hand, too loose a structure dissolves significance. Meaning can drown in the rising tide of chaos. A world capable of sustaining freedom and order requires an equilibrium between these rigidifying and dissolving tendencies. The actual balance . . . we perceive seems to me to be consistent with the will of a patient and subtle Creator, content to achieve his purposes through the unfolding process, and accepting thereby a measure of the vulnerability and precariousness which always characterizes the gift of freedom by love.[118]

Seen from the theological perspective, then, biological processes are interactions between the creative presence of God in matter and matter's own evolutionary dynamisms. There are thus no interventions of God from the outside; the natural processes as observed by science are themselves the creative action of God. Arthur Peacocke suggests two analogies for this divine presence, both tentative because of God's total otherness and incomprehensibility. The first is with the psychosomatic unity of every mind/brain/body event. A personal agent chooses to move an arm, for example, thereby provoking a series of muscular changes that do not interfere with any laws of biochemistry but do influence the way these laws act. So also we can say that the transcendent God, immanently present to all that is, communicates purpose and direction to the physical world without disturbing any of its physical energies as described by science. The second analogy is with a composer of genius who expands and elaborates the notes of a simple tune into those of an extremely complex and harmonious orchestral symphony. So God, "an improvisor of unsurpassed ingenuity," unfolds the potentialities of creation, selecting and shaping with providential care all those that are to be realized in the course of evolving time.[119]

INCARNATION AND PAROUSIA. At the end of Part 2 we saw that the advent of humans has proved to be the most puzzling of all the outcomes of evolution. We are the only species capable of knowing and reflecting upon the process that produced us, and whose freedom for personal relationships and cultural control has totally transformed the animal instincts we inherit from other species. We saw just now that the chance and randomness laced through evolution are not incompatible with the Christian conviction of a divine providence that lovingly cares for the dynamisms of life. But what in the concrete are the purposes of such a plan, and how are they related to matter's potential to produce the human? The Christian answer has always been that these purposes can be seen in the birth, life, death, and resurrection of Jesus of Nazareth, the one human being who has realized to the fullest God's design for the human. So we must ask now why this is so. How is it possible for this very particular and, for the Christian, decisive event in human history to illumine the meaning of the evolutionary process as a whole?

Two theologians have elaborated answers in depth to these questions. The first is Karl Rahner. We saw earlier that, for Rahner, God's immanent creative presence in matter is a loving self-bestowal, pressuring matter from within to transcend itself into the genuinely new and ultimately into the human. At this human level, however, the potential for self-transcendence differs from that present in other species, because it consists in the capacity consciously to receive and freely to return God's self-gift as a constitutive principle of human existence, an offer which permeates every aspect of human existence and pervades all of human history. What "Incarnation" must mean for the Christian, then, is that in Jesus of Nazareth such acceptance was total and irrevocable, thus constituting in history the ultimate self-transcendence of the human, the unique inner moment in the universal bestowal of grace, as well as the unsurpassable climax of God's creative immanence in the world.[120]

Hence for Rahner, Christology really ought to be seen as an anthropology pointing to the ultimate purpose of the evolutionary process. For the human is not "one factor in a cosmos of things . . . but the subject on whose freedom as subject hangs the fate of the whole cosmos: otherwise salvation history and profane history could have no cosmological significance, and Christological cosmology would be infantile concept-poetry."[121] In this sense Christology is the culmination of a self-transcendent anthropology. The reason is that in Jesus God became enfleshed in living matter as an act of self-expression, as John says in verse 14 of his Gospel's prologue: "The Word was made flesh and lived among us. We saw his glory, the glory that is his as the only Son of the Father, full

of grace and truth." This is an echo of Paul's doctrine of the divine self-
emptying in Philippians 2:7, in which divinity stripped itself of power and
glory "to assume the condition of a slave."

This body of Jesus, however, was constituted by the same chemical
elements common to the cosmos as a whole and by the same genetic elements common to all humans. Hence what God was doing in Jesus must
somehow be related to what God was doing throughout the universe. This
is why Christians believe Jesus to be the goal of creation, the full "Yes" of
the human to God that Paul speaks of in II Corinthians 1:20, as well as the
final "Yes" of God to creation. Nor does Rahner conceive this Christ
event as something static in the past. It is rather a historical event with
cosmic consequences, transcending the cultural limitations of its historical expression, an event in process from Jesus' birth to his Second Coming
at the Parousia when his fullness will be achieved at the end of time. "Jesus'
resurrection . . . is the beginning of the transfiguration of the world as an
ontologically interconnected occurrence. In this beginning the destiny of
the world is already in principle decided and has already begun."[122]

Creating matter that evolves over billions of years and becoming enfleshed in that matter are consequently two interrelated dimensions of
God's self-bestowal, "two moments and phases in the real world of the
one process of God's self-expression into what is other."[123] This means,
as William Dych has noted, that from the very beginning the intrinsic
dynamism and goal of evolution has been not just the transcendence of
matter beyond itself into human knowledge, freedom, and love, but also
the transcendence of this human life into God's own life. "Hence the Incarnation is not an abrupt interruption or aberration in the 'normal'
course of history, but the fullness of time, the culmination of a movement that began with creation itself."[124] The historical Jesus is thus the
beginning of the end, independently either of how long evolution lasts
or how much it produces by way of history and culture. Here is Rahner's
brief summary:

> The Incarnation . . . appears *ontologically* (not merely morally or as an after-
> thought) as the unambiguous goal of the movement of creation as a whole, in
> relation to which everything prior is merely a preparation of the scene . . .
> Here we must remember that the world is a unity in which everything is
> linked together with everything else. When anyone grasps a portion of the
> world for his own life's history, at one and the same time he takes upon him-
> self the world as a whole for his personal environment. Thus it would not be

extravagant, as long as it is done with prudence, to conceive the evolution of the world as an orientation *towards* Christ, and to represent the various stages of this ascending movement as culminating in him as their apex. . . . If what St. Paul says in Colossians 1:15 is true and not softened by some moralistic interpretation; if furthermore the world as a whole, including therefore its physical reality, is actually in process of reaching in and through Christ that final state in which God is all in all, then the line of thought we are developing here cannot be entirely false.[125]

This reference to a verse from Colossians (Christ is the "first-born of all creation") brings us now to our second theologian, who relied heavily on St. Paul to elucidate the goal of evolution. He is Pierre Teilhard de Chardin, whose neo-Lamarckian interpretation of human biology we outlined in Part 2. Like Rahner, Teilhard was reacting against an extrinsecist view of God vis-à-vis the world of nature. Far more than Rahner, however, he was concerned with understanding the meaning of the so-called cosmic texts in the Pauline letters, assertions of God's presence in Christ and of Christ's physical relationship to humankind, a relationship which in turn extends through the human to the whole of the cosmos. It was clear to him, for example, from a text he cited often, Romans 8:19–23, that for Paul the whole of material creation is the object of redemption, mediated by the bodily resurrection of human persons.

It is important to note at the outset that Teilhard explicitly rejected pantheism.[126] Yet he nevertheless had from childhood what he calls a "cosmic sense," an intuition of universal wholeness, that was teleological in character and was confirmed for him by Paul's statement in I Corinthians 15:28 that "when all things will have been placed under Christ's rule, then the Son will place himself under God . . . so that God may be all in all." In another of Teilhard's favorite texts, the famous two-strophed hymn of Colossians 1:15–20, the author declares that it is Christ who effects this unity. The Greek term *pleroma* ("plenitude," "fullness") is here stripped of its Stoic pantheism and given a content familiar to the Hebrew scriptures, that of the cosmos filled with the creative presence of God. This "fullness" now resides in Christ, who has both fullness of divinity and fullness of the universe. Because "he holds all things in unity" (vs. 17), everything finding its stability in him, what God does for humans, namely Christ's work of redemption, is done for the whole of creation. In this text, as well as in verses from the first chapter of Ephesians, where the word *pleroma* also appears, the author obviously had no desire to elaborate a cosmology, and hence no intention of explaining *how* Christ is Lord of the Universe, but Teilhard appeals to these texts precisely in order to explain this "how."[127]

Like Rahner, Teilhard was convinced that a Christology that could not easily be integrated into the evolution of matter as we know it might easily be dismissed as mythology. Hence Christology's central assertion that in Jesus God became matter, "flesh," must mean, Teilhard insisted, that the question of *how* Christ is the Lord of the universe is capable of being answered in evolutionary categories. Teilhard's key category is "genesis," by which he means that evolutionary change can be seen phenomenologically as directional (though not necessarily as "directed"), insofar as it has, *a posteriori*, manifested a double movement from less complex to more complex matter, and from less to greater interiority. This movement over billions of years has now culminated in the human, where the most complex organic structure, the human brain, corresponds to the most sophisticated interiority we know, namely self-consciousness or reflective thought. We are thus entitled to speak successively of a cosmogenesis moving toward a biogenesis and emerging eventually into an anthropogenesis or noogenesis.

But Christians are also entitled, says Teilhard, to identify a religious concept with these secular concepts: "Christogenesis." In coining this term he was, of course, utilizing and reconciling two sources of knowledge, on the one hand the data of Christian revelation regarding the enfleshment of God and Christ's fulfillment of creation, and on the other hand scientific data regarding the evolutionary movement of matter. Teilhard thus sees Jesus of Nazareth as the means whereby God becomes united with God's ongoing work of creation. For "being" in his metaphysics is a processive concept, meaning not "to be" but "to unite." He was led to this conviction after coupling evolution's discovery that matter is not static with Christian belief that all things tend toward God through Christ. Continuing creation thus has to mean that God is continually uniting with matter. While God remains free to create or not, God is not free to create in any way other than evolutively. A nonbecoming, perfectly ordered, totally immobile universe would be a contradiction in terms, like a square circle.[128]

In this way, created matter and uncreated divinity complement each other and have a need to be combined because of this drive toward unification in God's triune nature. Teilhard insists that "God is entirely self-sufficient; yet the universe contributes *something that is vitally necessary to him*."[129] In this process of unification Christ becomes the divine "milieu," the physical center of evolution as well as its environment. Christ is the divine atmosphere, the divine redemptive omnipresence, the evolver ceaselessly at work in creation, whose mediatorial role is fully creative, transforming cosmogenesis into a Christogenesis oriented toward Christ's Second Coming at the Parousia.

This event at the end of time is for Teilhard the final critical point of evolution, like the critical transitions to life and reflective consciousness and like the Incarnation itself. At critical points in the evolutionary process there is always a change of state, a sudden jump in the course of development. Just as the Incarnation could not take place until humanity had undergone a certain anatomical evolution and social organization, so too the coming of the Parousia requires, as a physically necessary albeit insufficient condition, that humanity have reached the critical point of its planetary maturation. Hence in the Parousia, Teilhard sees the world as both evolved to maturity through the creative immanence of God and received gratuitously by God through Christ.[130]

While science knows only that evolution may be somehow directional, then, Christian faith believes that evolution is being directed toward an ultimate goal. The spiritual is thus not a derogation of the material but its transformation.[131] "Fundamentally," says Teilhard, "one single thing is always and forever being made in creation: the Body of Christ."[132] God's redemptive presence in matter through Christ is thus "a prodigious biological operation," that will enable creation eventually to reach its completion at the Parousia in a universal divine incarnation, the "pleroma," which is being built up in the course of time. Teilhard's understanding of this "pleroma" is therefore cellular, but with the Christian qualification that all the cells of this divine organism preserve their full individuality as incorporated elements. Hence creation, Incarnation and Christ's work of redemption are not separable actions only loosely connected. Since to create is for God to unite with creation, which is in turn to share in suffering and death, these three are in fact three aspects of a single unifying act of "pleromizing," a Christification that is at work everywhere, in nature as well as in history.[133]

REDEMPTION AND THE MYSTERY OF EVIL. "There are no short-cuts; there is no gnostic possession of eternally pre-packaged truths," writes Irish theologian Gabriel Daly. "The great soteriological truth that Christ died to save us from sin has to be constantly grappled with if it is to reveal its meaning and effectiveness in successive ages."[134] In II Corinthians 5:19 St. Paul states with admirable terseness Christian belief in both the Incar-

nation and the work of Jesus: "God was in Christ, reconciling the world
to himself." But, as Daly points out, while the first belief was subjected
to the most rigorous intellectual analysis in the early Christian centuries, the second was not. Instead of conflicting theories, what we find
are a number of compressed narrative models and metaphors, like "salvation" and "redemption," which seek to convey by analogy what Jesus
achieved through his suffering and death. But metaphors are the products of culture, and cultures change. We cannot simply repeat them today
as if they resonate with us in the way they did in the past. We must study
how they functioned in ages that found them credible, and then "ask
whether we in our age can create vehicles of expression which function
in a comparable way and with a comparable effect on the Christian imagination."[135]

How then is belief in Jesus' work of redemption to be understood in
the context of evolution? We must start with what is absolutely clear to
Christian faith: Jesus of Nazareth, who lived and taught in first-century
Palestine and who was executed as a criminal under Pontius Pilate, accomplished by his death and resurrection the redemption of the world.
"He was put to death for our sins and raised to life to justify us," says Paul
in Romans 4:25. The first Christians thus proclaimed Jesus to be not
merely risen but saving.

"Salvation" means "to make safe" and "redemption" means "to rescue."
But from what precisely? Surely that cannot be only personal sinfulness
and guilt, large as these may be in individual lives, since humans yearn for
deliverance from much more than these. What oppresses humans most is
the ambiguity, suffering, and sheer sense of incompleteness in human existence, all that unavoidable alienation and frustration that, as we saw at
the end of Part 2, characterize the human species and result in its curious
misfit with its environment.[136] Is it possible to relate these two fundamental experiences, the Christian and the human, to God's creative immanence in matter and the culmination of that immanence in Jesus?

In humans the ongoing evolutionary process clearly reaches a point of
complexity and consciousness where it needs some kind of healing and
reconciling, and some of this need surely arises from moral failure. But
from a theological point of view, this humanity we know to be so enigmatic and ambiguous has to have been built into the very concept of a
creation capable of flowering into intelligence and freedom. To have the
awesome power of saying yes or no to God's creative offer of self-bestowal
is thus what it means to be human and to be in need of rescue. Hence sal-

vation is not to be seen as an afterthought on God's part, but as a piece with creation. To create is precisely to prepare the way for salvation and salvation is God's ultimate creative achievement. As such, salvation is bound up with both the continuities and the discontinuities of the evolutionary process. Redemption is consequently not a new offer but the original offer colored by the capacity for refusal.[137]

The historical crucifixion of Jesus, his acceptance of the lowliness of human death in loving obedience, must therefore have significance for matter as such, and have been implicit in the primordial energy of God's creative act. This is why Irenaeus of Lyons in the second century could see the Incarnation as an intrinsic constituent of the redemptive event. For by becoming human, the Word of God "recapitulated" in himself all men and women of every age, so that the whole history of humanity stands under God's forgiving love in Christ. Later in the fourth century Gregory of Nyssa and Gregory of Nazianzus said that what was not assumed could not be healed.[138] In this sense Jesus' death and resurrection are the historically visible culmination of God's gratuitous creative love first shown in the Incarnation, as the First Letter of John says in 4:9–10: "God's love for us was revealed when God sent into the world his only Son . . . to be the sacrifice that takes away our sins." In modern times Pierre Teilhard de Chardin has more than anyone emphasized this evolutionary significance of the crucifixion:

> Jesus on the Cross is both symbol and reality of the immense labor of the centuries which has, little by little, raised up created spirit to restore it to the depths of the divine Milieu. He represents and, in a true sense, he is creation, as it re-ascends the slopes of being, supported by the hand of God, sometimes clinging to things for support, sometimes tearing itself from them in order to transcend them, and always compensating by physical suffering for setbacks caused by its moral failures.[139]

There is one great advantage from this linking of Christ's work of salvation with God's creative design for evolution, namely that we are able to deal more reasonably with the presence of sin, suffering, and death in God's world insofar as these constitute a purely intellectual problem. As we saw earlier,[140] God's presence in all matter as "primary" cause at the level of existence does not interfere with the actions of a particular creature as "secondary" cause doing whatever it is inclined to do naturally in whatever way it naturally does it. In other words, earthquakes, hurricanes, and floods are the result of what nature does naturally, with small-scale versions appearing in the lives of individuals as heart attacks, cancer, strokes, and debilitating disease. These are designated as "evils" only insofar as they bring misery to self-conscious humans; in themselves they simply represent the normal workings of physical and biological processes and are therefore unavoidable. To be religiously scandalized at this is to presume that God's creation of matter over billions of years is wholly anthropocentric in character, with purposes for no other creature but the human.

Teilhard de Chardin spoke often of the inevitability of a certain amount of waste in an evolutionary world. Physical decomposition among the pre-living, suffering among the living, sin in the domain of freedom: there is no order under formation, he said, which does not at every stage imply disorder. In a vase of flowers it would be surprising to find broken or sickly blossoms, since these have all been picked with care and assembled with art. But on a tree, which has to fight the hazards of growth, climate, and time, broken branches and bruised blossoms are all in the right place.[141] Death, of course, is the sum and consummation of all these diminishments, but it appears to have a simple function as part of the evolutionary process: to make room for new life. If nothing ever decayed and died, nothing much would ever have lived, since new organisms require the death of old ones and all forms of life prey on other forms. At the human level, for example, the good of the species demands there to be more new people in the world. For without the constant arrival of youth, there would be nothing to safeguard the species from lapsing into boredom and routine, and from losing that diversity and spontaneity of life essential to evolution at the cultural level.

From this point of view, classic belief in the reality of "original sin" can also be clarified. This is not the calamity that for centuries Christians believed they found in their literal reading of the biblical creation story. We know today that the authors of Genesis knew nothing of such an aboriginal "fall" from a state of perfection. We also know that Paul's interpretation of the Adam verses in Romans 5 follows an understanding of them in late Judaism and has no foundation in the Genesis narrative. It was Augustine, in his opposition to Pelagianism, who developed the first full-blown theology of what he misnamed "original sin." This was, he said, a human predisposition toward evil and away from God, called "concupiscence," inherited by all at birth because of their solidarity with a historical and sinful Adam.

Yet there is general scholarly agreement today that "Adam" was never intended as a historical figure, and that the Genesis narrative is not really answering the question of human origins as much as that of human ambivalence arising from the possession of freedom. "The account of the origins," writes one Genesis scholar, "shows with great depth and with great clarity that it belongs to man's very state as a creature that he is defective. And this defectiveness does not show itself in one single act in history, but in a variety of ways."[142] And another writes: "Genesis does not contrast the way things are with the way they once were, but the way they are and ever have been with how they ought to be."[143] A theological understanding of "original sin" in the context of evolution must focus, then, as Gabriel Daly insists, not on ontology but on anthropology, not on some *a priori* theory of human nature but on a simple description of how humans behave in their culture, where human evolution most dramatically continues.

What we find is that humans are wounded and despoiled, in the sense that they have lost that level of peace appropriate to their animal ancestors who lived by instinct. There is a pluralism in their impulses which in practice is incapable of being integrated into any unity. With large brains, self-awareness, and above all conscience, humans have become capable of freely choosing the right and wrong use of these animal drives and passions. When such choice becomes sin in the proper sense of freely and personally rejecting God's offer of self-communication, then a negative vector is introduced into cultural evolution, often referred to today as the "sin of the world." Christians have always believed, however, that this force of sin, both "original" and personal, has been embraced from the very beginning by the gift of God's self-bestowal and offer of forgiveness, and so is radically unequal to the power of God's redeeming love in Christ. The Incarnation, death, and resurrection of Jesus is thus the center and measure of the human, and sin in all its aspects is a derivative. "Sin is located along a graced horizon that humans are struggling toward. It is less lost innocence than incompleteness."[144]

This clarification of the intellectual problem of situating human sin and suffering into the evolutionary process nevertheless leaves Christians with a deep and irreducible mystery. On the one hand, they are secure in affirming that in Jesus' crucifixion we see God actually submit to the evil produced by the world's evolutionary process. And they are convinced too that God would never have permitted such evil to exist if

God's absolute love for the world, manifested in the crucifixion, were not able somehow to overcome evil by bringing out of it a greater good. For this is what Paul says in Romans 5:21: "where sin increased, grace abounded all the more."

On the other hand, they know that the real mystery of evil, whether natural or moral, is not its existence but its enormous scope and the gross inequality of its impact. The terror of Auschwitz as a *fact* is what appalls us, as Gabriel Daly notes, independent of the moral guilt of those responsible. And what is to be said of the cruelty experienced every day by innocent children throughout the world, from the ravages of war or famine or disease? Is there any response to the inexorable pain and loss in the lives of those victimized by disasters like hurricanes and floods, which can in an instant totally wipe out the savings of a lifetime? Even when we take into ample account the inevitable waste of organic process and the malice of freedom, we still have to ask why evolution has taken a course which allows *this* degree of suffering to exist. Can any purpose which God might have justify it? "The fact that God in Christ shares the horror of innocent suffering does not remove the scandal of the fact that innocent suffering actually exists in a world created by a good God."[145]

The most Christians can do here is to make this mystery livable by accepting in faith and hope that there really is some explanation, but that it cannot be understood because ultimately it is rooted in the incomprehensibility of God. This was in the end the experience of Job, as well as that of Paul in Romans 11:33: "O the depth of the riches and wisdom and knowledge of God! How unsearchable are his judgments and how inscrutable his ways." Karl Rahner says that suffering is precisely the form in which this incomprehensibility of God appears in human lives, and our acceptance of its unanswerability is the concrete form in which we allow God to be God. Yet "this answer can be heard only if we surrender ourselves in unconditionally adoring love as answer to God. If we do not achieve this love, forgetting itself for God, or, better, if we do not accept it as given to us, there is nothing left but naked despair at the absurdity of our suffering, a despair which is really the only form of atheism that must be taken seriously. There is no blessed light to illumine the dark abyss of suffering other than God himself."[146]

The need to assuage this dark abyss has given rise in recent years to the conviction of a mysterious divine vulnerability in God's very self. That is to say, in creating and in being immanently present to all creatures, God incurs risk, not only because pain, suffering, and death are inevitable in life, but especially because, when evolution reaches the human, there is the awesome power of freedom to frustrate God's purposes. God thus suffers universally with the suffering of creation. God is still God and is still present uniquely and decisively in the sufferings of Jesus, but must somehow, throughout time, have the same kind of experience of death and forsakenness that Jesus had on the cross.[147] Creation is consequently seen to be the self-emptying of God as well as God's self-bestowal, an extension of the self-emptying of Jesus on the cross that Paul speaks of in Philippians 2:6–11. Teilhard de Chardin saw this suffering of God in and with creation to be the only way to support the darkness of faith in human life, and we may end with his words:

> In my opinion, the obscurity of faith is simply a special instance of the problem of evil. I see only one possible way to avoid being seriously scandalized by it, and that is to recognize that if God allows us to suffer, to sin, to doubt, it is because he is *unable*, now and at a single stroke, to heal us and to show himself. And if he is unable, the sole reason is that we are still *incapable*, at this present stage of the universe, of receiving higher organization and thus more light. . . .
>
> No, God does not hide himself to make us search for him, of that I am sure,—much less to let us suffer in order to increase our merits. On the contrary, bent down over his creation which moves upwards to him, he works with all his power to give us happiness and light. Like a mother he watches over his newly born child. But our eyes are unable to see him yet. Is not precisely the whole course of centuries needed in order for our gaze to accustom itself to the light?
>
> Our doubts, just like our suffering, are the price and conditions for the perfection of the universe. Under these conditions I consent to walk right to the end along a road of which I am more and more certain, towards an horizon more and more shrouded in mist.[148]

—— CONCLUSION ——

The discoveries within the last century of biological evolution and genetic mutation surely constitute one of the great achievements of the human mind. In Part 1 we surveyed these discoveries in their broad outline and in Part 2 we situated humans within this extraordinary potentiality of matter. We noted how curious and puzzling a species humans appear to be from a biological point of view, and how very differently their biological existence has been interpreted. The Christian anthropology we developed in Part 3 asked how this discovery of evolution and the appearance of humans as its outcome could be related to the fundamental Christian beliefs in creation, Incarnation, and redemption, and we saw the remarkable congruence that theologians now find between what science has discovered and what Christians believe. The relative success thus far of this Christian endeavor is a true measure of contemporary biology's impact on theology when the latter is carried out within an evolutionary view of the world.

Let us close with a brief word about the Gaia hypothesis. Gaia is a theory that all of earth's life systems, from microorganisms through plants, animals, and humans, are linked by means of the atmosphere into a single delicately interactive and self-sustaining organism named after the Greek goddess Earth. All of these systems, in other words, are part of a giant feedback loop by which the earth, as a self-regulating whole, operates by its own laws to preserve life. The chief proponents of this hypothesis, British naturalist James Lovelock and American biologist Lynn Margulis,[149] have marshaled large amounts of scientific data to show that the biosphere, hydrosphere, and atmosphere are in fact all dependent on each other in intimate interchange. Their main point is that as yet we barely understand any of these delicate interrelationships. Consequently, humans, as one life form, have no warrant to threaten, much less destroy, any of the subtle connections among other life forms, especially since humans are not in possession of any fail-safe mechanism to prevent possible disasters.

The obvious problem here is that speaking of a nonreproductive entity as a purposive organism, but without any past adaptation through natural selection, is hardly consistent with contemporary biology and has understandably brought the Gaia hypothesis into conflict with the scientific community. It is legitimate therefore to demand a careful evaluation of the validity of such assertions of organic harmony. I want to suggest, however, that the Gaia hypothesis can function at a deeper level, that of myth, pointing to something in nature beyond the realities of physics, chemistry, and biology, something the methodologies of these disciplines are unable to deal with.

Christian theology would call this something the creative omnipresence of God in every part of nature, continually imparting existence at the level of being to all forms of life and nonlife. The widespread appeal of Gaia to a growing number of persons outside the scientific community is an indication that this myth has a certain power today to motivate people to reverence life in its totality and to hope for some eventual harmony of creation. Christians would call such harmony "salvation." Gaia is thus the secular equivalent of a theological emphasis upon the immanence of God, whose self-bestowal on all matter nonetheless grants it freedom to be itself, whether at the level of subatomic particles, molecules, organisms, animals, or free human beings. In Romans 8:22–23 Paul likened this exercise of freedom to matter's effort to give birth, which is an apt closing image: "From the beginning until now the entire creation, as we know, has been groaning in one great act of giving birth; and not only creation, but all of us who possess the first-fruits of the Spirit, we too groan inwardly as we wait for our bodies to be set free."

— NOTES —

1. Mary Midgley, *Evolution as a Religion* (New York: Methuen, 1985), 1–4.

2. Letter of July 13, 1856, to Joseph Dalton Hooker, quoted by Adrian Desmond and James Moore, *Darwin* (New York: Warner Books, 1991), 449. For the estimate of numbers of species, see Edward O. Wilson, *The Diversity of Life* (Cambridge: Harvard Univ. Press, 1992), 132–34. The vast differences in current estimates by skilled professionals of the number of living species are an indication of how much is yet to be learned about life on earth.

3. Francis Crick, *Of Molecules and Men* (Seattle: Univ. of Washington Press, 1966), 14, 98. This strong reductionism is somewhat softened in Crick's recent *What Mad Pursuit* (New York: Basic Books, 1988), 137–42.

4. Ernst Mayr, *Toward a New Philosophy of Biology* (Cambridge: Harvard Univ. Press, 1988), 2–3, 8–14, 402–3.

5. Ibid., 14–21. Mayr points out, for example (70–71), that for the first two billion years of life only single-cell algae and bacteria filled the planet's seas and swamps. Then some extraordinary symbiosis apparently took place between some of these cells, and life as we know it today suddenly exploded into existence across the planet, all its cells thereafter having chromosomes and a well-organized nucleus. By the end of the Cambrian period, about 500 million years ago, there were at least fifty different phyla or animal body plans, most of which quickly became extinct. No new type of anatomical structure has been found since that time.

6. Mayr, *New Philosophy,* 198–99. Geneticist Christopher Wills observes, however, that when Lamarck began to describe the evolutionary process he "seemed perversely to fall into every logical trap he could find, like a kind of eighteenth century Keystone Kop. As a result his name is now synonymous with every incorrect idea about evolution—including some for which he cannot even be blamed" (*Wisdom of the Genes* [New York: Basic Books, 1989], 65–68).

7. Ibid., 87.

8. In spite of the title of his famous book, Darwin never really tried to explain the origin of new species. He was concerned not with "speciation" (the branching of one species into two or more) but mostly with how single species might change over time. Like everyone else in the nineteenth century, Darwin tended to classify different species by how different they *looked*. But "species" has turned out to be a much more complex concept. Only in recent years, mainly through the pioneering work of Ernst Mayr, has it been possible to define species biologically: two forms, whether they differ much in appearance or not, are different species if they develop differences on the genetic level as a result of reproductive isolation. Because they do not interbreed, these new species are free to move in different evolutionary directions, which interbreeding would prevent by immediately mixing together any new genetic differences between them. The number of genetic mutations involved in producing a new species is vast, however, and so geneticists usually focus on individual organisms as members of a population with a specific gene pool, one inherited over millions of years and existing in the totality of individuals. See Mayr, *New Philosophy,* 313–31, and text for note 28 below.

9. Ibid., 402–22, 457–88; Stephen Jay Gould, "Darwinism and the Expansion of Evolutionary Theory," and Francisco J. Ayala, "Beyond Darwinism? The Challenge of Macroevolution to the Synthetic Theory of Evolution," in *Philosophy of Biology,* ed. Michael Ruse (New York: Macmillan, 1989), 100–33.

10. On homologies see Douglas J. Futuyma, *Science on Trial* (New York: Pantheon Books, 1983), 44–67.

11. For this digression on genetics I am indebted to the following sources: Mayr, *New Philosophy,* 402–38; Wills, *Wisdom,* 16–44; Futuyma, *Science on Trial,* 102–37; R. C. Lewontin, "The Dream of the Human Genome," *New York Review,* May 26, 1992, 31–40; Jerry E. Bishop and Michael Waldholz, *Genome* (New York: Simon & Schuster, 1990), 15–27; Freeman Dyson, *Infinite in All Directions* (New York: Harper & Row, 1988), 74–96; Ian Barbour, *Issues in Science and Religion* (New York: Harper & Row Torchbook, 1971), 318–24.

12. Since there are four nucleotide possibilities for each position on the double strand, the number of possible kinds of genes is astronomically large: a 1 followed by 6,020 zeros. The arrangements in messages of these four bases are thus of infinite variety. See Lewontin, "Dream," 32.

13. Most human body cells have twenty-three matched pairs of chromosomes, forty-six in all, in the form of these long DNA strands, with about 6 billion nucleotide bases in the complete chromosome set, an average of about 130 to 150 million for each chromosome. All the DNA of any single cell would extend about three yards if stretched out, but is in fact twisted up and compacted a hundred thousand-fold into chromosomes in the nucleus of the cell, which is about two billionth of the volume of a pinhead. See Wills, *Wisdom,* 24.

Parents give only half of their forty-six chromosomes to their offspring, one of each pair of twenty-three, but the three thousand to four thousand genes in any one of these twenty-three chromosomes could have come from either of their own parents. Hence they themselves pass on an overlapping but partially different set of genes to each offspring. This blending of parental DNA is called its "recombination," and explains why offspring of the same parents can all be so different from each other, except of course for twins or triplets.

14. This translation of the genetic program into growth processes is at present the most challenging problem of developmental biology. For if the DNA in every body cell is identical, why are nerve cells, muscle cells, blood cells, bone cells, and reproductive cells all so different from each other? There are over a billion of such qualitatively different cells in any higher organism, but it is now known that genes constitute less than 10 percent of the DNA in these cells. While the function of these genes is to carry information to be translated into protein, the function of the remaining 90 percent of a cell's DNA is still unknown. Some have called it "junk DNA," nucleic acid containing no instructions and doing neither good nor harm, but merely taking a free ride in a cell and benefiting from the cell's efficient replicative apparatus.

Only 2 percent or less of the genes codes for any specific protein. Genes thus seem to be turned off by protein repressors, thereby preventing certain sections of the DNA from transferring their coded information to messenger RNA. There also seem to be protein inducers that do exactly the opposite. This switching on and off of DNA has proved to be bafflingly difficult for geneticists. "It hardly needs stressing," says Mayr, "how complex the genetic program must be, to be able to give the appropriate signals to each cell lineage in order to provide it with the mixture of molecules which it needs to carry out its assigned tasks" (*New Philosophy*, 50). These tasks of the average cell, it should be noted, include about five hundred metabolic processes involving some ten thousand proteins.

15. Francisco J. Ayala, "The Theory of Evolution: Recent Successes and Challenges," in *Evolution and Creation,* ed. Ernan McMullin (Notre Dame, Ind.: Univ. of Notre Dame Press, 1985), 62–63.

16. Arthur Peacocke, *God and the New Biology* (San Francisco: Harper & Row, 1986), 36–37.

17. Ayala, "Theory of Evolution," 61–70.

18. Peacocke, *New Biology*, 37–38: Ayala, "Theory of Evolution," 68–70. Many paleontologists are still skeptical about the molecular clock, and most would date human origins no later than eight million years ago. On molecular biology, see Kenneth F. Schaffner, "Chemical Systems and Chemical Evolution: The Philosophy of Molecular Biology," and John Beatty, "The Insights and Oversights of Molecular Genetics: The Place of the Evolutionary Perspective," in *Philosophy of Biology,* ed. Ruse, 198–220. See also the critique by Ruth Hubbard and Elijah Ward of the notion that there is a gene for almost every disease and behavior: *Exploding the Gene Myth* (Boston: Beacon, 1992).

19. Charles Darwin, *The Origin of Species,* 1st ed., published in 1859 by J. Murray, London (New York: Avenel Books, 1979), 66.

20. Ibid., 131.

21. Ibid., 71–113.

22. Ibid., 115. See the lengthy analyses of natural selection by Mayr, *New Philosophy,* 93–125, 133–47, 215–32, as well as his study of Darwin's intellectual history, 168–84.

23. Speaking of extremely intricate organs like the eye, Darwin writes in the *Origin* (217, 219): "To suppose that the eye . . . could have been formed by natural selection, seems, I freely confess, absurd in the highest possible degree." While suggesting that even in its transitional forms, the eye was most probably of some advantage to some animal under changing conditions of life, he nevertheless acknowledges that he has "felt the difficulty far too keenly to be surprised at any degree of hesitation in extending the principle of natural selection to such startling lengths." Two years later, in 1861, he is more explicit in a letter to an American biologist, Asa Gray: "The eye to this day gives me a cold shudder" (*Life and Letters of Charles Darwin,* vol. 2 [London: John Murray, 1888], 273). The issue is still neuralgic. Mayr (*New Philosophy,* 72, 240) reports of recent work by several eminent biologists showing the convergent evolution of eyes in forty different lineages of animals, but critics continue to ask how any variation can be beneficial except in its fully developed form. And if it is not beneficial, how can it be selected? See Gertrude Himmelfarb's study of Darwin's impact on the nineteenth century, *Darwin and the Darwinian Revolution* (New York: Norton, 1968), 268–309.

24. Spencer also coined the term "evolution," but Darwin never used it, preferring to call the process "descent with modification" because he deeply distrusted the meaning that Spencer gave to "evolution," namely that of Lamarck's vast escalator, proceeding steadily upward from lifeless matter through plants and animals to humans and eventually on to higher things. See Midgely, *Evolution as a Religion,* 34–35. Regarding the ongoing influence of Darwinism in American social thought, see Carl N. Degler, *In Search of Human Nature* (New York: Oxford Univ. Press, 1991).

25. The tighter the fit, of course, the less adaptable the organism would immediately become, and so the greater chance of its extinction if the environment were suddenly to change. This standard objection and its standard answer are both well formulated, respectively, by Tom Bethell, "Darwin's Mistake" and by Stephen Jay Gould, "Darwin's Untimely Burial," in *Philosophy of Biology,* ed. Ruse, 85–98.

26. R. C. Lewontin, "Darwin's Revolution," *New York Review,* June 16, 1983, 25. In *The Eclipse of Darwinism* (Baltimore: Johns Hopkins Univ. Press, 1983), Peter J. Bowler shows that at the turn of the century there were many theories of evolution that were anti-Darwinian and yet quite plausible given the state of biology at the time.

27. See R. C. Lewontin, "Darwin, Mendel and the Mind," *New York Review,* October 18, 1985, 18–20.

28. See note 8 above for Mayr's approach to the formation of species. Ronald Fisher and J. B. S. Haldane in England and Sewall Wright in the United States were the founders of the new theory, which was consolidated and expanded by Ernst Mayr, Theodosius Dobzhansky, George Gaylord Simpson, and Julian Huxley. That this path from Darwin to the synthetic theory was nothing like a straight line is well documented by Peter J. Bowler, *The Non-Darwinian Revolution* (Baltimore: Johns Hopkins Univ. Press, 1988).

29. Mayr, *New Philosophy*, 534–40; Lewontin, "Darwin, Mendel," 18–19.

30. Mayr, *New Philosophy*, 535.

31. Ibid., 538. See also Theodosius Dobzhansky, *The Biology of Ultimate Concern* (New York: New American Library, 1967), 118–22.

32. See text for note 9 above.

33. See text for note 18 above. Precisely because the tiny percentage of difference in molecular composition between humans and apes is nonadaptive in character, it cannot be converted into a percentage of difference in organism, which is profound in regard to brain size and function.

34. See text for note 14 above.

35. Freeman Dyson, *Origins of Life* (New York: Cambridge Univ. Press, 1985), 17–18. See note 5 above; also Mayr, *New Philosophy*, 136–41; Lewontin, "Darwin's Revolution," 23–24; Futuyma, *Science on Trial*, 40–42, 136–37. Another nonadaptive change is the random fixation of a positively detrimental trait. The antlers of the Irish elk, for example, evolved to such an enormous size that they resulted in its inability to function and its eventual extinction. Neo-Darwinians would say that these elks probably acquired this trait because the gene influencing it piggybacked on the same chromosome as some totally unrelated gene that was being selected.

36. George Gaylord Simpson, *The Meaning of Evolution* (New Haven: Yale Univ. Press, 1949), 201.

37. Australian molecular biologist Michael Denton has given the most wide-ranging critique of Darwin's original theory and its development into the modern synthesis in *Evolution: A Theory in Crisis* (Bethesda, Md.: Adler & Adler, 1985). Denton believes that problems with the theory are not puzzles which are in principle solvable but counterinstances that can never be adequately explained within current evolutionary orthodoxy. Denton's outlook is shared by Berkeley law professor Phillip E. Johnson, who carries on a similar polemic against evolution in an even sharper adversarial style in *Darwin on Trial* (Washington: Regnery Gateway, 1991). A more balanced critique is that by Robert Wesson, *Beyond Natural Selection* (Cambridge: MIT Press, 1991), who believes that the theory is quite valid but more limited in its application than its adherents claim.

38. See Peacocke, *New Biology*, 39–41; Ernan McMullin, "Evolution and Special Creation," *Zygon* 28(1993): 299–335.

39. Holmes Rolston III, *Science and Religion* (New York: Random House, 1987), 121.

40. Futuyma, *Science on Trial*, 106–12. Much controversy today centers on whether Neanderthals were really ancestral kin to modern humans or just an evolutionary dead end. Totally different interpretations of the same fossil record have been given by Erik Trinkhaus and Pat Shipman, *The Neanderthals* (New York: Knopf, 1993); Christopher Stringer and Clive Gamble, *In Search of the Neanderthals* (New York: Thames and Hudson, 1993).

41. In 1987 molecular biologist Allan C. Wilson advanced what was subsequently called the African Eve hypothesis. He and his colleagues at Berkeley analyzed, in people of various races on several continents, a genetic material, mitochondrial DNA, which is passed only from women to their offspring. (The mitochondrion is a small energy-producing unit outside the cell nucleus containing its own complement of very simple DNA, quite separate from the exceedingly complex DNA within the nucleus.) They concluded that all humans living today have mitochondria traceable to a common female ancestor, and that the first modern humans spread out of Africa fifty to one hundred thousand years ago to replace archaic humans throughout Europe and Asia. Wilson's hypothesis has been sharply criticized by geneticists, who found damaging flaws in the computer analysis leading to the hypothesis, as well as by paleontologists, who cite fossil evidence that modern humans evolved from ancient ones in many different parts of the world at different times. See Michael H. Brown, *The Search for Eve* (New York: Harper & Row, 1990). For another interpretation of the same data see Richard Leakey and Roger Lewin, *Origins Reconsidered* (New York: Doubleday, 1992).

42. See Gerald D. Fischbach, "Mind and Brain," *Scientific American,* September 1992, 48–57. On the language question see Derek Bickerton, *Language & Species* (Chicago: Univ. of Chicago Press, 1990). Neurobiologists note that this vast number of brain circuits offers many alternative paths for development, any one of which can be activated by living, a process not unlike Darwinian selection: fibers that successfully reach target cells survive, while others die out. From this perspective genes govern relatively little actual brain activity, although they obviously predispose the brain to act in certain ways. See Michael S. Gazzaniga, *Nature's Mind* (New York: Basic Books, 1993).

43. Peter Medawar, *The Threat and the Glory* (New York: Harper Collins, 1990), 144–77. See text for notes 86 and 87 below.

44. Peter J. Wilson, *Man, the Promising Primate* (New Haven: Yale Univ. Press, 1981).

45. Mayr applies to this situation the concept of "program" taken from information theory. The behavior of genes, he says, constitutes "closed" programs into which no new information can be introduced from outside. Higher animals, on the other hand, represent "open" systems, whose behavior can incorporate additional information through learning, conditioning, or other experiences. All such programs are goal-directed, though not necessarily purposive (*New Philosophy*, 48–53).

46. Simpson, *Meaning of Evolution,* 286.

47. Edward O. Wilson, *Sociobiology* (Cambridge: Harvard Univ. Press, 1975), 4.

48. Ibid.

49. Ibid.

50. Ibid., 547.

51. See Arthur L. Caplan, ed., *The Sociobiology Debate* (New York: Harper & Row, 1978).

52. Edward O. Wilson, *On Human Nature* (Cambridge: Harvard Univ. Press, 1978), 167.

53. Ibid., 17.

54. Edward O. Wilson and Charles J. Lumsden, *Genes, Mind and Culture* (Cambridge: Harvard Univ. Press, 1981). They subsequently published a popular version, *Promethean Fire* (Cambridge: Harvard Univ. Press, 1983). See the lengthy profile and critique of Wilson by Robert Wright, *Three Scientists and Their Gods* (New York: Times Books, 1988), 113–92.

55. Wilson, *Human Nature,* 176.

56. Wilson, *Sociobiology,* 3. On Darwin's approach to altruism see Helena Cronin, *The Aunt and the Peacock* (New York: Cambridge Univ. Press, 1991), 267–91, 325–53.

57. Richard Dawkins, *The Selfish Gene* (New York: Oxford Univ. Press, 1979), 2, ix.

58. Wilson, *Sociobiology,* 3.

59. Dawkins, *Selfish Gene,* 64. See the treatment of Wilson and Dawkins by Midgley, *Evolution as a Religion,* 122–31.

60. Wilson, *Human Nature,* 155–56.

61. Dawkins, *Selfish Gene,* 206.

62. Wilson, *Human Nature,* 157; Dawkins, *Selfish Gene,* 215.

63. Stephen Pope, "The Order of Love and Recent Catholic Ethics: A Constructive Proposal," *Theological Studies* 52 (1991): 273.

64. On Lamarck see L. J. Jordanova, *Past Masters: Lamarck* (New York: Oxford Univ. Press, 1984).

65. This Central Dogma still holds today, though not as tightly, because the structure of molecules and the functioning of genes have turned out to be infinitely more complicated than was first realized. Apparently part of the process of information flow from DNA to protein can be reversed, a finding that may be an important clue to the workings of cancer cells and of immune systems. See on this question the essays in John Maynard Smith, ed., *Evolution Now* (San Francisco: Freeman, 1982), 91–105.

66. See, for example, Denton, *Theory in Crisis;* Wesson, *Beyond Natural Selection;* Errol E. Harris, *Cosmos and Anthropos* (London: Humanities Press International, 1991).

67. Medawar, *Threat and Glory,* 174.

68. In biological terms, "phylogeny" (the evolution of a genetically related group of organisms) does not reproduce "ontogeny" (the development of an individual organism).

69. Darwin, *Origin,* 473.

70. Mayr, *New Philosophy,* 110–11, 251–54.

71. Pierre Teilhard de Chardin, *The Phenomenon of Man,* rev. ed. (New York: Harper & Row, 1965), 110, 302, 149, note 1. I have translated *hazard dirigé* by its more neutral meaning of "directional chance" rather than "directed chance," i.e., "being in a direction," whether teleologically directed or not. This translation is more consistent with Teilhard's aim in the first three parts of his book to analyze life phenomenologically, before his attempt in the last part to argue that the process must be seen as directed by a divine personal Omega.

It is not clear whether Teilhard intended to characterize natural selection in this way. His original manuscript was completed in 1940 and a number of biologists believe that he had only a hazy idea of the neo-Darwinist synthesis completed during the 1930s while Teilhard was working in China. This is why, they say, he usually equated natural selection with purely chance mutation (Ibid., 140, note 1; 302, note 1), and why he was forced to invoke as a stabilizing factor what he called "orthogenesis." But he then described its workings in very un-Lamarckian language as "groping," or as "the manifest property of living matter to form a system in which 'terms *succeed each other* experimentally, following constantly increasing degrees of centro-complexity.'" (Ibid.,108, note 1)

This was in effect an acknowledgement that evolution's directionality could be seen biologically only *a posteriori* and in retrospect, after surveying the total process. His general conception of evolution's nature, therefore, harmonizes much better with the fundamentals of the modern synthesis than with the original meaning of "orthogenesis" as a process with a predetermined goal. See the critiques of Theodosius Dobzhansky, *Ultimate Concern,* 118–25, and "Teilhard de Chardin and the Orientation of Evolution," *Zygon* 3 (1968): 242–58. See also George A. Riggan, "Testing the Teilhardian Foundations," *Zygon* 3 (1968): 259–313; Lodovico Galleni, "Relationships between Scientific Analysis and the WorldView of Pierre Teilhard de Chardin," *Zygon* 27 (1992): 153–66; Edward O. Dodson, *The Phenomenon of Man Revisited* (New York: Columbia Univ. Press, 1984), 147–54; and George B. Murray, "Teilhard and Orthogenetic Evolution," *Harvard Theological Review* 60 (1967): 281–305.

72. Simpson, *Meaning of Evolution,* 261–62.

73. A more pessimistic metaphor for natural selection's "groping" was coined by French bacteriologist Francois Jacob. He says that, far from being like that of a sophisticated engineer working from a prepared and specific plan, the process is more like that of a home-workshop tinkerer. Jacob sees the human brain as the ultimate example of such "tinkering." The youngest part of the brain in evo-

lutionary terms, the neocortex controlling intellectual and cognitive abilities, seems to have been added by evolution to the earlier structure controlling emotional and visceral activities, an achievement Jacob compares to equipping an old horse carriage with a jet engine. See "Evolution and Tinkering," *Science* 196 (1977): 1161–66. Richard Lewontin comments: "The biologist is constantly confronted with a multiplicity of detailed mechanisms for particular functions, some of which are unbelievably simple, but others of which resemble the baroque creations of Rube Goldberg" ("Darwin, Mendel," 23).

74. Dobzhansky, *Ultimate Concern,* 124–26. See also Mayr, *New Philosophy,* 67–73.

75. This is one of the major conclusions of Stephen Jay Gould's study of the Burgess Shale fossils in *Wonderful Life* (New York: Norton, 1990). These weird invertebrate creatures lived in the Cambrian period about 530 million years ago, and their remains were discovered between 1910 and 1917 in a small quarry in Yoho National Park in British Columbia. These organisms contain all the body plans ("phyla") that exist today, as well as a great many never seen before, including some with five eyes. Because organisms now alive show only a small fraction of the diversity of organic forms produced in this early period, it is clear that subsequent evolution has reduced the number of body plans, not increased them. Gould insists that the extinction of most of the phyla in the Burgess Shale but the survival of some of them (including that one that eventually moved in the direction of vertebrates, amphibians, reptiles, mammals, primates, and humans) have no other biological explanation than the indeterminacy of evolutionary life. Humans are therefore contingent; they need not have come into existence at all. See on this question Mayr, *New Philosophy,* 70–72.

76. Simpson, *Meaning of Evolution,* 284.

77. Teilhard de Chardin, *Phenomenon,* 171.

78. Ibid., 221. This is a constant theme in Teilhard's writings. See, for example, *Human Energy* (New York: Harcourt Brace Jovanovich, 1969), 20–28; *The Future of Man* (New York: Harper & Row, 1964), 214–26.

79. Teilhard de Chardin, *Phenomenon,* 224.

80. Ibid., 165.

81. Ibid., 178. Teilhard was struck by the propensity toward increasing complexity in the evolution of living organisms, as well as by much empirical evidence of a relationship in higher animals between greater psychic consciousness and greater complexity of nervous system and brain. He concluded from this that there had to be a "law" governing this relationship throughout the evolutionary process, even before the coming of life. This "law of complexity-consciousness" says that the more developed consciousness will always correspond experimentally with the more complex organic structure. While this can be seen most clearly in the human person, Teilhard was convinced that if this law were not already operating even at the level of inorganic matter, the

appearance of reflective consciousness at the human level would be unintelligible. (Ibid., 71)

What could be responsible for such a law? Teilhard postulated the existence of what he called a "within" to all matter, inorganic as well as organic, where an energy called "radial" operates (to distinguish it from the "tangential" energy of physics). Radial energy tends to draw an element forward into structures of greater complexity; tangential energy tends to link an element to other elements on the same level of organization. "To make room for thought in the world," he said, "I have needed to 'interiorize' matter" (Ibid., 290). He admits, however, that there is no experimental evidence in biology to support this hypothesis: "In the present state of our knowledge, of course, we cannot dream of expressing the mechanism of evolution in this 'interiorized,' 'radial' form" (Ibid., 151).

Why then did he insist on doing so? One explanation (Dobzhansky, "Teilhard and Evolution," 253) is that he believed such panpsychic assumptions to be absolutely necessary to explain the pathway leading to *homo sapiens;* he simply could not accept evolutionary "groping" as a sufficient explanation, even though such "groping" actually accomplishes biologically what Teilhard envisions to be the task of radial energy. While this explanation may well be correct, there is also a religious explanation: given Teilhard's conviction as a Christian of God's creative omnipresence in matter (see *Phenomenon,* 293–94), his postulate of radial energy was simply an effort to find by natural reasoning the existence of something in the evolutionary process which he already believed to be present through Christian faith. See text for notes 128–33 below.

82. Ibid., 232.

83. Ibid., 83–84.

84. Erich Fromm, *Man for Himself* (New York: Rinehart, 1947), 40.

85. See text for notes 42 and 43 above.

86. Jonathan Miller, "Trouble in Mind," *Scientific American,* September 1992, 180; Francis Crick and Christof Koch, "The Problem of Consciousness," ibid., 153–54. A biologically plausible model of how consciousness could have emerged has been worked out by Gerald M. Edelman in explaining what he calls "neural Darwinism." See his *Bright Air, Brilliant Fire: On the Matter of Mind* (New York: Basic Books, 1992), 73–154.

87. On the current state of the discussion see, in addition to Edelman, Roger Penrose, *The Emperor's New Mind* (New York: Oxford Univ. Press, 1989); John R. Searle, *The Rediscovery of the Mind* (Cambridge: MIT Press, 1992); Colin McGinn, *The Problem of Consciousness* (Oxford: Blackwell, 1991); Daniel C. Dennett, *Consciousness Explained* (Boston: Little Brown, 1991).

88. See Mayr's incisive discussion of cause and effect in evolutionary biology in *New Philosophy,* 24–37.

89. Rolston, *Science and Religion,* 106.

90. Peter Medawar, *The Limits of Science* (New York: Oxford Univ. Press, 1986), 66.

91. Ibid., 98.

92. See text for notes 12, 13, and 14 above.

93. Dyson, *Origins of Life,* 4–15. Dyson notes that Göttingen chemist Manfred Eigen has been able to reproduce in a test tube RNA molecules that replicate themselves like DNA, but this is a far cry from producing DNA. Also, Eigen had to use a living protein enzyme in his experiment, which means that, to be produced in a laboratory, RNA requires a biologically derived substance. No experiment has yet succeeded in producing RNA with prebiotic materials such as methane, water, or ammonia. While using such prebiotic materials to synthesize amino acids, the constituent parts of protein, is apparently not all that difficult, no laboratory has thus far produced living protein molecules that have a true growth capacity. See Harold J. Morowitz, *Beginnings of Cellular Life* (New Haven: Yale Univ. Press, 1992).

94. The UCLA molecular biologist J. William Schopf recently discovered single-celled fossils of microorganisms, preserved in an unusual rock formation in northwest Australia, that go back this far in time. See "Microfossils of the Early Archean Apex Chert: New Evidence of the Antiquity of Life," *Science* 260 (1993): 640–46.

95. Ilya Prigogine and Isabelle Stengers, *Order Out of Chaos* (New York: Bantam, 1984); James Gleick, *Chaos* (New York: Penguin, 1987); M. Mitchell Waldrop, *Complexity* (New York: Simon & Schuster, 1992).

96. See the long discussion of thermodynamics and life by Peacocke, *New Biology,* 140–60.

97. Freeman Dyson, *Infinite in All Directions* (New York: Harper & Row, 1988), 8; J. B. S. Haldane, *The Causes of Evolution* (Princeton: Princeton Univ. Press, 1990), 91.

98. See Piet Smulders, "Creation," in *Sacramentum Mundi,* vol. 2 (New York: Herder and Herder, 1968), 23–28; Langdon Gilkey, *Maker of Heaven and Earth: The Christian Doctrine of Creation in the Light of Modern Knowledge* (New York: Doubleday, 1965).

99. On Genesis see Claus Westermann, *Creation* (Philadelphia: Fortress, 1974), and *Genesis 1–11: A Commentary* (Minneapolis: Augsburg, 1984); Henricus Renckens, *Israel's Concept of the Beginning* (New York: Herder and Herder, 1964).

100. *Summa Theologica,* I, ques. 105, art. 5. See ques. 19, arts. 4 and 8 and ques. 45, art. 5. Aquinas also speaks of this divine involvement with all the actions of creatures in his *Summa Contra Gentiles,* III, chaps. 66, 67, 70, and in the following from *De Potentia,* II, 7: "God causes the action of everything in as much as he gives to everything its power to act and conserves it in being. . . . If we add to this the fact that God is his own power, and that he is present in all things not as an essential part of them but as maintaining them in their being, we should conclude that he acts in every agent immediately, but without eliminating the action of the will and of nature."

101. Stephen Jay Gould's reverence for nature is a good example of this pantheistic inclination of many scientists. "I yearn to establish an appropriate notion of grandeur," he writes in "Modified Grandeur," *Natural History,* March 1993, 20. No longer can this be based on nature's production of the human, however, since we are merely "a tiny and unpredictable twig on a richly ramifying tree of life—a happy accident of the last geological moment." Rather, we must accept nature on its own terms, "as something so vast, so strange (yet comprehensible), and so majestic in pursuing its own ways without human interference, that grandeur becomes the best word of all for expressing our interest and our respect." He opts for "awesome grandeur" as the proper phrase, "the feeling of solemn and reverential wonder, tinged with latent fear, inspired by what is terribly sublime and majestic in nature." Gordon D. Kaufman comes very close to this way of thinking about God in *In Face of Mystery* (Cambridge: Harvard Univ. Press, 1993).

102. Karl Rahner, "Christology in the Setting of Modern Man's Understanding of Himself and His World," *Theological Investigations,* vol. 11 (New York: Seabury, 1974), 224. For this presentation of Rahner's thought I am indebted to Denis Edwards, *Jesus and the Cosmos* (New York: Paulist, 1991), and to William V. Dych, "Theology in a New Key," in *A World of Grace,* ed. Leo J. O'Donovan (New York: Crossroad, 1989), 1–16.

103. On this large issue of spirit/matter dualism and the shift today in Christian thinking to the spiritual potential in the dynamisms of matter, see "Theology and Science: A New Commitment to Dialogue," the first chapter in this volume. In "Science and Theology," *Theological Investigations,* vol. 21 (New York: Crossroad, 1988), 44, Rahner notes that one can still refer to this coming of self-conscious spirit to nature as "the special creation of the human soul," thereby giving a benign interpretation to the words of Pius XII in his 1950 encyclical *Humani generis:* "The Catholic faith obliges us to hold that souls are immediately created by God" (DS 3896). Rahner insists that the ancient teaching tradition of the Christian Church on the origin of the human soul did not in fact hold this clearly. Hence the Pope could have meant only "to emphasize that the transcendentality of the human subject cannot be derived simply from its material presuppositions with their material foundations, since one must still make a distinction between body and soul (even if it is now more difficult than before to affirm their unity and diversity ontologically)." See also his "Natural Science and Reasonable Faith," ibid., 45. Rahner treats this question at much greater length in *Hominisation* (New York: Herder and Herder, 1965), 45–101.

104. Cited by Gabriel Daly, *Creation and Redemption* (Wilmington, Del.: Glazier, 1988), 116.

105. Rahner, "Christology in the Setting," 227. I have also relied on the following essays by Rahner: "Christology Within an Evolutionary View of the World," *Theological Investigations,* vol. 5 (Baltimore: Helicon, 1966), 157–92; "On

the Theology of the Incarnation," ibid., vol. 4 (Baltimore: Helicon, 1966), 105–20; "Nature and Grace," ibid., 165–88; "The Theological Dimension of the Question About Man," ibid., vol. 17 (New York: Crossroad, 1981), 53–70.

106. "Theology and the Heisenberg Uncertainty Principle," chapter 3 in this volume.

107. See text for notes 21, 28, and 29 above.

108. Jacques Monod, *Chance and Necessity* (New York: Knopf, 1971), 98. Like many scientists, Monod believes that all convictions of purpose in the universe are simply the psychological projections of humans longing for some significance in the face of cosmic emptiness.

109. Ibid., 112–13, 146. It should be noted that Monod is not arguing against theism as such. His point is that, whether or not there is a God who initiates the process, there can be no purpose or design for it. Nor does Monod claim that his argument is strictly probative, since religious people can obviously still claim that what we call chance just represents our ignorance about what is going on in this world and how God is actually acting with power and purpose. This claim says that everything is really determined, that there is no randomness in nature at all, and that what science has discovered to be happening in the life processes is not really happening. This seems to be the view of Donald M. MacKay in replying to Monod in *Science, Chance and Providence* (Oxford: Oxford Univ. Press, 1978), as well as that of William G. Pollard, *Chance and Providence* (New York: Scribners, 1958).

110. Theodosius Dobzhansky, "Two Contrasting World Views," in *Beyond Chance and Necessity,* ed. John Lewis (London: Garnstone Press, 1974), 138. Besides the other essays in this volume, see the critiques of Monod by D. J. Bartholomew, *God of Chance* (London: SCM Press, 1984); Midgley, *Evolution as a Religion,* 75–90; Arthur Peacocke, *Creation and the World of Science* (Oxford: Oxford Univ. Press, 1979), 92–104, and *Theology for a Scientific Age* (London: Blackwell, 1990), 115–21.

111. Dobzhansky, "Contrasting World Views," 132. See text for notes 68, 69, and 70 above.

112. *Summa Contra Gentiles,* III, chap. 74.

113. Ibid., II, chap. 39.

114. Peacocke, *Creation,* 94–95.

115. See text for note 95 above.

116. On God's ability to act on the subatomic level and at the level of human freedom, see the reference in note 106 above.

117. Paul Davies, *The Mind of God* (New York: Simon & Schuster, 1992), 170.

118. John Polkinghorne, *One World* (Princeton: Princeton Univ. Press, 1987), 69. This very concise statement is considerably amplified in his *Science and Providence* (Boston: Shambhala, 1989), 4–44.

119. Peacocke develops these analogies in *Creation,* 104–11, 131–39, and in his more recent *Theology,* 157–65, 173–77.

120. See text for notes 101 to 105 above. In traditional theology this self-gift of God is called "uncreated grace," to distinguish it from "created grace" or the diverse effects of this self-gift in the person to whom God is present, referred to as "actual graces" and "sanctifying grace." This self-gift is offered to all humans without exception, Rahner insists, antecedent to any human response. Such a rethinking of "grace" is one of the central undertakings of his theology. See, among many essays, "Nature and Grace," *Theological Investigations,* vol. 4 (Baltimore: Helicon, 1966), 165–88. See also the concise summary of Rahner's approach by John P. Galvin, "The Invitation to Grace," in *World of Grace,* ed. O'Donovan, 64–75.

121. Karl Rahner, "Theology and Anthropology," *Theological Investigations,* vol. 9 (New York: Herder and Herder, 1972), 39.

122. Karl Rahner, "Resurrection," *Sacramentum Mundi,* vol. 5 (New York: Herder and Herder, 1970), 333. It is important to note here that Rahner believes that other religious traditions can also mediate God's self-bestowal and so can be revelatory and truly salvific. He is simply stating the Christian claim that Jesus has significance for the salvation of all peoples as well as for the whole cosmos. See the multiple references cited by Edwards, *Jesus and the Cosmos,* 76–77.

123. Rahner, "Christology Within an Evolutionary View," 177–78. In "Theology and Anthropology," 28, and elsewhere Rahner says that "man is the *potentia oboedientialis* for the hypostatic union," using two very technical terms. "Hypostatic union" originated in the christological controversies of the fourth and fifth centuries and refers to the union of divine and human in a single person: the concrete reality of Jesus is the reality ("hypostasis") of the Word of God, who becomes matter in him as God's act of self-expression. "Oboediential potency" was used originally by Aquinas to denote a capacity open to fulfillment yet not meaningless if it is not fulfilled. Rahner's point is that, because God's self-bestowal is an intrinsic part of human existence, the divine enfleshment into this existence is an intrinsic possibility for the species. What determines its actually taking place is God's free initiative summoning a free human response, realized uniquely and definitively in history by Jesus of Nazareth.

124. William V. Dych, *Karl Rahner* (Collegeville, Minn.: Liturgical Press, 1992), 79.

125. Rahner, "Current Problems," 165.

126. Teilhard distinguished clearly between a pantheism of identification and a "Christian pantheism" of union. He actually preferred the term "pan-Christism," coined by Maurice Blondel, because of its closeness to 1 Corinthians 15:28. See among many texts, *The Divine Milieu* (New York: Harper & Row, 1965), 116. Teilhard's formula, "union differentiates," which he repeated constantly, emphasizes the Christian conviction that each person possesses an

inalienable individuality and that union with God is achieved not just without loss of self-identity but precisely through its maximization. See, for example, *Phenomenon of Man*, 259–63. I have given an extensive analysis of Teilhard's *Christology in Teilhard de Chardin and the Mystery of Christ* (New York: Harper & Row, 1966).

127. On the exegesis of these texts see ibid., 87–103.

128. For the development of Teilhard's theory of "creative union" see *Writings in Time of War* (New York: Harper & Row, 1967), 151–76; *Toward the Future* (New York: Harcourt Brace Jovanovich, 1975), 192–99. See also the comprehensive analysis of the theory by Donald P. Gray, *The One and the Many* (New York: Herder and Herder, 1969).

129. Pierre Teilhard de Chardin, *Christianity and Evolution* (New York: Harcourt Brace Jovanovich, 1971), 177. Teilhard's italics. This 1945 insight of Teilhard has recently been given theological depth in two studies. Catherine Mowry LaCugna's *God for Us: The Trinity in Christian Life* (San Francisco: Harper, 1992) begins with Karl Rahner's axiom that the immanent Trinity is the economic Trinity and vice versa. LaCugna insists that there is but one life of the triune God and that life includes God's relation to the human species. In other words, God's way of being in relationship with humans, as revealed in Christ and the Spirit, is precisely who God is as God. Because the course of temporal events thus somehow becomes constitutive of the divine life, the proper subject matter of the doctrine of the Trinity is the encounter between divine and human persons in the economy of redemption. Writing along the same lines, Paul S. Fiddes elucidates the consequences which must be accepted for the doctrine of God if we are to believe in a God who suffers change as a result of loving human persons in a truly personal way. See his *The Creative Suffering of God* (Oxford: Oxford Univ. Press, 1988), 46–76.

130. Teilhard discusses the Parousia often. See, for example, *Divine Milieu*, 150–55; *Toward the Future*, 149–56, 188–92; *Future of Man*, 236–37, 266–69, 306–8.

131. "It is astonishing," says Teilhard, "that so few minds should succeed, in this as other cases, in grasping the notion of transformation. Sometimes the thing transformed seems to them to be the old thing unchanged; at other times they see in it only the entirely new. In the first case it is the spirit that eludes them; in the second case, it is the matter. Though not so crude as the first excess, the second is shown by experience to be no less destructive of the equilibrium of mankind." *Divine Milieu*, 110, note 1.

132. Teilhard de Chardin, *Christianity and Evolution*, 74. See the discussion of radial energy in note 81 above.

133. Ibid., 181–83. On the implication for Teilhard of this cellular model of the *pleroma*, see note 126 above on differentiating union and also *Phenomenon of Man*, 291–99.

134. Daly, *Creation and Redemption,* 197.

135. Ibid., 169–73.

136. See text for note 84 above.

137. See Karl Rahner, "The Christian Understanding of Redemption," in *Theological Investigations,* vol. 21, 239–54; Daly, *Creation and Redemption,* 24, 33, 195–96.

138. Besides the metaphors of salvation and redemption, the early Christian tradition used others to speak of what Christ accomplished: ransom, expiation, propitiation, purification. These were later used in the eleventh century by Anselm of Canterbury to develop the "satisfaction theory" of redemption, which focused exclusively and in a purely juridical way on Jesus' death. The sinful disobedience of humans, said the theory, could be remedied only by a satisfaction which was greater than the offense. But only the God-man could make such satisfaction, and this Jesus did through his crucifixion, which was then "credited" to sinners. In this penal theory an angry God needed to be appeased by Christ's suffering and death, which was then seen as cause of God's love for sinners rather than being the effect of that love. Daly deals with this history in ibid., 169–93.

139. Teilhard de Chardin, *Divine Milieu,* 104.

140. See text for note 100 above.

141. Teilhard's example is developed in *Human Energy* (New York: Harcourt Brace Jovanovich, 1969), 49.

142. Westermann, *Creation,* 121.

143. Stephen J. Duffy, "Our Hearts of Darkness: Original Sin Revisited," *Theological Studies,* 49 (1988): 619.

144. Ibid., 618. See Daly's masterful treatment in *Creation and Redemption,* 114–47, where the whole biblical and Christian tradition is surveyed. See also Karl Rahner, "Original Sin," *Sacramentum Mundi,* vol. 4 (New York: Herder and Herder, 1969), 328–34. On original sin understood as "sin of the world," see Piet Schoonenberg, *Man and Sin* (Notre Dame, Ind.: Univ. of Notre Dame Press, 1965), 98–191.

145. Daly, *Creation and Redemption,* 25.

146. Karl Rahner, "Why Does God Allow Us to Suffer?" *Theological Investigations,* vol. 19 (New York: Crossroad, 1983), 208.

147. These themes have been developed by, among others, Jürgen Moltmann, *The Crucified God* (New York: Harper & Row, 1974), and Dorothee Sölle, *Suffering* (Philadelphia: Fortress, 1975), and have been lucidly synthesized and critiqued by Paul Fiddes, in *Creative Suffering,* passim.

148. Teilhard de Chardin, *Christianity and Evolution,* 131–32.

149. James Lovelock, *The Ages of Gaia* (New York: Norton, 1988).

5. Cybernation, Responsibility, and Providential Design

To know anything at all about divine providence, Augustine and Thomas Aquinas both insisted, we must first understand human providence. Human governance is the clue to understanding divine governance.[1] This is also the tradition of the Greek Fathers, whose concept of divine government, moving creatures toward the realization of cosmic order and redemption, was called *dioikesis* and *oikonomia*, words used more broadly for the government of a republic and more narrowly for the administration of a household. The crucial issue is thus not the abstract question of whether or not God is provident, but the very concrete question of what it means to say that God is provident. What might we expect a provident God to be doing in the human sphere, and how might we go about knowing what God does?

The answer is inseparable from a study of human history and an analysis of the dynamics of human freedom, responsibility, and choice. It is also inseparable from what modern science has discovered about the energies inherent in matter and the structures inherent in life, all those complex phenomena traditionally grouped together in former times under the theological rubric of "creation." Hence, to discover what God's providence is seeking to achieve for the human species, we must first ask what that species is seeking to achieve for itself, for it is in and through what the species is doing that divine providence works to accomplish its purpose and plan.

This classic interrelationship between God's providential design and human prudential decision has been severely strained in our modern age. The Judeo-Christian concept of human persons continually being drawn into coactivity with God has ceased to capture our imaginations, because human freedom has come to be equated with autonomy. Autonomy and self-sufficiency tend to be revered as absolutes. We moderns desperately want to eliminate the element of surprise in our lives, to receive no gifts, and to determine everything for ourselves. As we shall see, however, the malaise of contemporary culture is due in no small part to the general awareness that as a species we can no longer claim to have such an insurance policy against all things unforeseen.

In the following pages I shall (1) explore this new awareness as it has been articulated by several astute observers; (2) sketch a model for God's providential design that can be more easily translated into the categories of modern science and technology, i.e., the model elaborated by Pierre Teilhard de Chardin; (3) examine the cybernetic model of society so widespread today, and ask how, within this model as well as within an evolutionary understanding of providence, we can intelligently discuss the parameters of political responsibility and choice.

—— Facing a Technological Future ——

There seems to be general agreement in our time that something unusual is taking place in human consciousness. One clear symptom is what Robert Jay Lifton calls "psycho-historical dislocation" and what Alvin Toffler terms "future shock."[2] There is a kind of mass neurosis in the contemporary human psyche, an acute sense of stress and disorientation induced by the experience of too much change in too short a time. We are being asked to adapt psychologically to phenomena we do not yet fully understand, and our ability to do so is being taxed beyond healthy limits. Above all, there is the fear that we may not be able to adapt at all: the premature arrival of the future frightens us precisely because it is premature and we are unprepared. Accustomed for centuries to measure change in terms of the slow development of traditional institutions, we are being forced for the first time to evaluate our history in terms of the rapid adjustments required by our psychic experience.

"The process of change in the modern era," wrote Princeton historian C. E. Black over twenty years ago, "is of the same magnitude as that from prehuman to human life and from primitive to civilized societies." And Nobel Prize physicist Sir George Thompson has said that to understand the extraordinary cultural upheaval of the twentieth century we have to think in terms of an event such as the invention of agriculture in the neolithic age.[3] Erik Erikson calls this modern experience of the human psyche an identity crisis. "The traditional sources of identity strength—

economic, racial, national, religious, occupational—are all in the process of allying themselves with a new world-image in which the vision of an anticipated future and, in fact, of a future in a permanent state of planning will take over much of the power of tradition."[4] Erikson sees two principal ideological orientations as basic to the formation of future identities, the technological and the humanist, and even the great politico-economic alternatives will, he believes, be subordinated to these.

The cultural conditioning along technological and scientific lines has already been taking place for some time, according to Erikson, but is being opposed more and more by a humanist orientation, which insists that beyond the technological there is a much wider range of human values and possibilities now in danger of being lost. The technologists and the humanists seem to live in separate ecologies and almost to belong to different species: they oppose and repel each other; the acceptance of even part of one orientation could result in an ideological slide in the other's whole cluster of images, aspirations, hopes, fears, and hates. Erikson sees this polarity as most important in fostering a dynamic interplay between the technological and humanist identity, leading to radically new modes of thought and daring innovations in both culture and society. But he makes a point of adding to his judgment an ominous condition: "provided we survive."

This question of survival hovers in the background of most discussions of the present crisis, whether it be described as one of identity or otherwise. Psychiatrists have argued that there is serious psychoanalytic evidence for saying that people today are suffering from an unconscious despair, arising on the one hand from fear of becoming an appendage to the machine, and on the other from the sense of having less and less to say about their own destiny. Beneath this unrest is a deep and well-justified fear: that the next step in technological progress may bring about the annihilation of the species. The terrorism prevalent in many areas of the globe today is so terrifying because we see these atrocities not only as a threat to people everywhere but as an ominous prelude to the whole future. In our unconscious, says Lewis Mumford, many of us are living in a postcatastrophic world, and our conduct is rational in terms of that world. We think of survival as problematic precisely because we do not seem able to control the technology we have created, and because the technological society we *thought* we were making is not being made at all.

Nothing illustrates this more vividly than the "imagery of extinction" that now dominates our corporate psyche. This is the term coined by psychiatrist Robert Jay Lifton to describe the long-delayed impact on our memories of Hiroshima and the Holocaust, as well as the Armageddon-like way we now think about our future. The slow destruction of our planet's environment is one potent source of this imagery: the thinning of the life-protecting ozone layer in the high atmosphere; the gradual global warming that creates the fearful greenhouse effect; air pollution from acid rain and the smog that drains the life of lakes and forests; the sewage poisoning of coastal waters and estuaries on which marine species depend; the inexorable erosion of tropical forests which constitute the world's richest nurseries of life. The sources of all these threats are numerous, complex, and not easily understood. Damage to the environment is usually indirect and invisible, and the inevitable impact on humans usually long-delayed. Will we as a species have the courage to heed these warnings? Will we find the money and global cooperation necessary to conquer these threats?

A second potent source of this imagery is the fear engendered by our technology of destruction. The message of the nuclear threat is so grim because it pictures for us the prospect of a nuclear winter; even a very modest use of nuclear weapons could so block the sun's rays with dirt and debris and so lower the planet's temperature that no human, animal, or plant life could survive. This prospect could gradually alter our whole focus on the future from how to prepare for to how to prevent nuclear war. But we face a formidable obstacle to this radical change of focus: the more immediate threat of "nuclearism." Lifton sees this as an almost pseudoreligious phenomenon by which dependency on nuclear weapons reaches the point of worship. We seek from them precisely what they cannot give, i.e., security and safety; "the very objects that could destroy human civilization and the human species are embraced as a basis for symbolizing the endless continuity—and immortality—of that species."[5]

There is, then, a certain sense of despair stalking human consciousness in our time, a suspicion that we may not be succeeding as a species, that somehow the human enterprise may turn out to be a totally hopeless undertaking. This is what the French geneticist Jacques Monod, winner of the Nobel Prize in medicine, actually said just over a decade ago. He wrote a best-seller then, *Chance and Necessity*, in which he tried to explain why science has finally shown human effort to be utterly meaningless, no more significant than the efforts of Sisyphus, who never ceased pushing his stone up the mountain only to have it immediately roll back down again into the valley. The human species, Monod insisted, was a freak, a product of pure chance, a quite accidental mutation in that otherwise fixed and invariable microscopic machine known as the genetic code. "If he accepts this message—accepts all it contains—then man must at last wake out of his millenary dream; and in doing so, wake to his total solitude, his fundamental isolation. Now does he at least realize that, like a gypsy, he lives on the boundary of an alien world. A world that is deaf to his music, just as indifferent to his hopes as it is to his suffering or his crimes."[6]

It is interesting to compare the diagnoses we have been discussing with that made by Pierre Teilhard de Chardin over fifty years ago.

> O man of the twentieth century, how does it happen that you are waking up to horizons and are susceptible to fears that your forefathers never knew? . . . Here at this turning point where the future substitutes itself for the present . . . do our perplexities inevitably begin. Tomorrow? But who can guarantee us a tomorrow anyway? And without this assurance that tomorrow exists, can we really go on living, we to whom has been given the terrible gift of foresight? Sickness of the dead end. . . . This time we have at last put our finger on the tender spot.

It is this tender spot, the growing suspicion that we may have nowhere to go in the universe, which is causing us to ask today whether or not we have been duped by life. An animal may rush headlong down a blind alley or toward a precipice, but human beings, precisely because they can *reflect* upon their condition, will no longer continue to take steps in a direction they know to be blocked. Despite their control of material energy, despite the pressures of their immediate needs and desires, without a taste for life human beings will simply stop inventing and constructing. The human species, in other words, is quite capable of going on strike. Indeed, it will surely do so unless, as Teilhard says, "we should be assured the space and the chances to fulfill ourselves, that is to say, to progress till we arrive (directly or indirectly, individually or collectively) at the utmost limits of ourselves."[7]

There is, then, a tension between our sense of belonging together in a communal planetary enterprise and the fear that whatever efforts we make as individuals may ultimately be pointless. While we sense that we can almost invent the future, this holding of human destiny in our hands nevertheless terrifies us, because the incredible power we have has not been matched by an equal degree of control. What assurance do we have that we can ever gain such control? And what precisely should be our objectives as we pursue such control? We thus face a double need as a species. We have to overcome the fear that our future may be hopeless, and we have to find some focus for the exercise of our responsibility in creating and controlling that future. Behind both needs lies their source: the knowledge we now possess of our world and our culture, and the consciousness we have of our freedom to choose. Is it possible for our knowledge also to give us hope? Is it possible for our sense of freedom also to generate responsibility?

——— A Teilhardian Response ———

The understanding of evolution elaborated by Teilhard gives us an answer to this first question that can in large measure satisfy our first need. This understanding also provides the religious person with a coherent model, from the physical world, of God's design for the species, as well as with indicators of how free human decision might mesh with this ultimate divine plan. For Teilhard believed that what most discourages contemporary men and women is the fear that what is happening to them in the twentieth century is neither intelligible nor capable of success. "In the great game being played, we are the players as well as being the cards and the stakes. Nothing can go on if we leave the table. Neither can any power force us to remain. Is the game worth the candle, or are we simply its dupes? We will never take a step in a direction which we know to be blocked. There lies precisely the ill that causes us disquiet."[8]

Teilhard responds to this anxiety by analyzing the relationship between the "two complementary expressions of the arrow of time." On the one hand there is the law of entropy, the second law of thermodynamics, discovered over a century ago by physics, which says that the quantity of unusable energy in the universe is constantly increasing. While the first law of thermodynamics says that, during any conversion of energy from one form into another in any closed system, the total energy remains constant, the second law says that as a result of this conversion a certain amount of that total energy becomes unavailable for future use. No energy is lost by burning coal, e.g., but its conversion of energy into gas involves an irreversible expansion of the gas into space, and the coal itself can never be reburned. This dissipation principle in the second law has been generalized to mean that order in the universe tends to give way to disorder and to equilibrium, and that it is more difficult to achieve organization and structure than it is to have chaos. For all matter of its nature tends to become more diffused, sliding irresistibly downward, so that eventually, at some point of time billions of years hence, there will be no more energy to use: all activity will have stopped, except that of atoms vibrating in perfect equilibrium in the icy darkness of space.

In biology, on the other hand, we have an analysis of the phenomenon of life, revealing a long chain of composites extending from the electron to the human by way of proteins, viruses, and bacteria, which clearly seems to be moving in the opposite direction, i.e., toward an extraordinary degree of complexity and arrangement. This phenomenon of life, Teilhard says, though a relative newcomer to the universe and occupying an incredibly small volume of space, manifests itself nevertheless as having developed in the very heart of the flow of entropy precisely as an eddy, as a countercurrent. In other words, while the behavior of matter is totally predictable, the behavior of life in the midst of matter has, over millions of years, been totally unpredictable. Entropy and life, two properties of matter as we have come to know it, the one pulling backward, the other forward, the one a dissipation of energy, an unfolding or granulating of matter, the other an increase of energy, a complexification of matter, a tendency in matter to arrange or center itself around growth in consciousness. In entropy we have a descent toward ever more probable zones of disintegration, whereas in life we discover an ascent toward ever more improbable zones of interiority, and, in the case of the human species, personality.[9]

> No one doubts any longer that the world of living forms is the outcome of increasingly complex associations between the material corpuscles of which the universe is composed. But how are we to envision the generative mechanism of this "complexification"? It is very certain that matter on earth is involved in a process which causes it to *arrange itself*, starting with relatively simple elements, in ever larger and more complex units. But how are we to account for the origin and growth of this process of arrangement?[10]

For this growth itself is most extraordinary: eventually we see matter so organizing itself into nervous systems and brains that it becomes interiorized in the phenomenon of consciousness, and this consciousness so increasing in intensity in the human species that it becomes reflective.

In the human person, therefore, we see most clearly the undisputed fact that there is a certain pattern in the past: in all known forms of life the more developed consciousness always corresponds experimentally with the more complex organic structure. The human brain thus corresponds with the most sophisticated consciousness we know: the capacity for reflection. For Teilhard this scientific fact showed not simply that there has been change over millions of years, but that there has been "genesis," from the French word *genèse*, which means change in successive stages, change which is oriented toward some goal—more simply, directional change. This scientific fact also accounts for his coining the term "cosmogenesis," directional change in the universe. More importantly, however, he believed that this scientific fact showed that the goal of the evolutionary process is the human species, which at the present time has both the highest organic complexity and the highest degree of consciousness. This human consciousness, this power of reflection, was for Teilhard the key to the evolutionary process. In a world where change is directional, where it is a genesis, clearly the movement of evolution has been in the direction of the human person, and therefore in the direction of human consciousness, of spirit, mind, thought, and love.

The movement of evolution is consequently taking place no longer in the sphere of life, the "biosphere," so much as in the sphere of mind and spirit, the "noosphere." It is thus not primarily a "biogenesis" but a "noogenesis." Hence "the social phenomenon is the culmination and not the attenuation of the biological phenomenon." Teilhard finds this trend toward complexity-consciousness to be like the thread of Ariadne. If we keep following this thread, it eventually lights up the meaning of the whole process. Assurance that the process will continue, therefore, comes first from that human experience of being part of an evolutionary movement which has come from prelife to life and then to human life. "To bring us into existence it has from the beginning juggled with too many improbabilities for there to be any risk whatever in committing ourselves further and following it right to the end. . . . Life, by its very structure, having once been lifted to its stage of thought, cannot go on at all without ascending higher."[11]

It is at this point, however, that Teilhard makes a most unusual analysis of that directional change in human history which he calls noogenesis. Let us imagine, he says, using the geometrical image of meridians on a globe, that a pulsation enters a sphere at its south pole and spreads out inside the sphere in the direction of the north pole. The movement of this wave is a converging movement from the start, since it is on a curved surface, but it has two very different phases, one of expansion from the south pole to the equator, the other of contraction from the equator to the north pole. Now no better image illustrates the crisis of growth through which humankind is passing at this very moment. In the first millions of years of its existence it has been expanding more or less freely, slowly covering more and more of the uninhabited earth. Because lack of space was no problem, the result was that, century after century, the socializing process was also extremely slow. There was a gradual branching out into the various races; civilizations were able to grow and rub shoulders on a sparsely inhabited planet without encountering any major difficulty. "But now," says Teilhard, "following the dramatic growth of industry, communications and populations in the course of a single century, we can discern the outline of a formidable event. The hitherto scattered fragments of humanity, being at length brought into close contact, are beginning to interpenetrate to the point of reacting economically and psychically upon each other."[12] Given the fundamental relationship between geographic compression and the heightening of consciousness, the result is an irresistible rise within us and around us of the level of reflection.

In other words, what we have been experiencing for some time now, without being aware of it, is in reality the beginning of the second phase of noogenesis, the phase of contraction. In our own time humankind has crossed the equatorial point and entered into a new stage in the development of the species. "From the first beginnings of history," wrote Teilhard in 1950,

> this principle of the compressive generation of consciousness has been cease-
> lessly at work in the human mass. But from the moment—we have just
> reached it!—when the compression of populations in the teeming continents
> gains a decided ascendancy over their movement of expansion upon the
> earth's surface, the process is speeded up to a staggering extent. We are today
> witnessing a truly explosive growth of technology and research, bringing an
> increasing mastery, both theoretical and practical, of the secrets and sources
> of cosmic energy at every level and in every form; and, correlative with this,
> the rapid heightening of what I have called the psychic temperature of the
> earth. A single glance at the overall picture of surface chaos is enough to
> assure us that this is so.[13]

Moreover, this overall converging movement of evolution, in which simpler subsystems unite into more complex systems centered upon themselves, takes on a wholly new element at the conscious level, the element of freedom. Evolution in the noosphere is not only conscious of itself but free to dispose of itself. Until the mid-twentieth century the vast majority of men and women were like passengers closed up in the hold of a ship distracting themselves as did the humans in Plato's Cave. When more and more of them climbed up to the bridge, however, they gradually became aware not only of the drift of the universe, but also of the risks and dangers in guiding the ship. To use Teilhard's phrase, the task before them now is "to seize the tiller of the world," to take hold of the energies by which they have reached their present position and use these energies to move ahead.[14] This is a fearful task, however, and to counteract their awesome power to refuse it, human persons must cultivate the moral sense of obligation to life. If they do not, then they face either ecological disaster or nuclear destruction. Thus the fundamental law of morality for Teilhard is to liberate that conscious energy which seeks further to unify the world. This energy is what he calls "the zest for life," that disposition of mind and heart that savors the experience of life, and manifests itself particularly in the relish we have for creative tasks undertaken from a sense of duty.

More specifically, this conscious energy is what Teilhard calls "love-energy." This is the energy which unifies, the same energy which unifies molecules, but which on the human level operates in the realm of interpersonal consciousness. Teilhard uses the phenomenon of electromagnetic waves to illustrate how his law of complexity-consciousness meshes with this concept of unifying love-energy. Through technology humans have made an enormously complex use of electromagnetic waves to enable them to share thoughts over vast distances. Someone with an idea in the remote mountains of Tibet can communicate that idea immediately to someone else in New York, provided there is the requisite technological complexity in the use of electromagnetic waves.

But is this not a terrifying prospect, human energy propelling us toward some mechanized, impersonal world, some vast technological complex, possibly blind to the needs of individual persons? Is this to be our social destiny, a destiny quite capable of stifling personalities rather than developing them? In Teilhard's mind this prospect is the reason for the world's present discouragement with any human aspiration toward unity. So far every effort toward unity seems to have ended by stifling the human person. What we miss, however, says Teilhard, is the fact that, monstrous though they are, modern totalitarianisms are examples of good energy gone awry, a distortion of something magnificent. The reason for the distortion is that these are unities based upon coercion or fear, not upon love and freedom. Love is the only energy in the world capable of personalizing by totalizing, of freely promoting synthesis without destroying the person. It alone unites human beings in such a way as to complete and fulfill them. For "in any domain—whether it be the cells of a body, the members of a society or the elements of a spiritual synthesis—*union differentiates*. In every organized whole the parts perfect themselves and fulfill themselves." This familiar evolutionary pattern of differentiating union is thus applied by Teilhard to the personalizing union of beings who relate to each other as persons. In this way "the grains of consciousness do not tend to lose their outlines and blend, but, on the contrary, to accentuate the depth and incommunicability of their *egos*. The more 'other' they become in conjunction, the more they find themselves as 'self.'"[15]

Hence the importance of the concept of "amorization" in Teilhard's work: the gradual release of the power of love, the response of truly free men and women to increased social pressure. It is only love which can turn increasing socialization from a threat to a promise. Human persons need not fear the contemporary drift toward unity as long as they can freely relate to each other through what is most intimate to themselves. This fostering of freedom through love is the one way to counteract the blind necessity which forces human persons to actualize technological achievement simply because they *can* do so. The question to be asked is whether they *should* do so, and it must be asked in the context of the primacy of the person and the need for more humane ways to manage change. It is thus through the growth of love that we can cope as a species with the tendency to turn in upon ourselves in isolation and allow our world to become more and more impersonal and mechanized.

Teilhard takes great pains at this point to underline his answer to the chief objection leveled against his understanding of evolution: If the species is moving by design toward greater complexity, consciousness, and unity through the activation of love energy, how are we to explain the presence in our world of so much disunity, disruption, hatred, and evil, the very antithesis of love? Teilhard replies that for him growth in consciousness means growth in the *capacity* for love and union among persons, not growth in love itself. Insofar as human progress means growth in our capacity for love, it also means that we are growing in our capacity to refuse love. Tensions and turmoil continue in the political order precisely because of this freedom inherent in all self-reflective consciousness. Human progress thus takes place not in a straight line but in a coiling movement. Unifying energy pushes up the coil by tightening it, each new crisis constituting the product and result of some previous achievement. But each new advance also increases the temptation to stop or to regress. The human species is now aware of this option, and this awareness is precisely what has generated our fear of the future.

"Hence it is," says Teilhard, "that there has finally emerged into our human consciousness in the twentieth century, *for the first time* since the awakening of life on earth, the fundamental problem of action."[16] This problem of action is preeminently the problem of men and women using their reflective capacity responsibly, as an ethical imperative to advance the process of complexification and consciousness. In the concrete, at any given point in the process, this inevitably involves political decisions in the public sphere. But is there any evidence in modern society of such growth in complexity related to growth in consciousness? Is something happening to the species that accounts for the increase of psychic tension we now experience in the global village? If so, can we find in that something a practical guide to the types of political decision demanded by our particular stage in the evolutionary process?

────── Information as Control ──────

H. Richard Niebuhr has reminded us that human beings grasp and shape reality, including the experience of their own existence, with the aid of great images, metaphors, and analogies. The symbols used in any given age will inevitably have profound ethical implications, since they shape the way humans perceive, understand, and organize their world.[17] There is good reason today, I think, to say that what humankind is involved in at present is one of its periodic redefinitions of the human. Its dominant image of itself for generations has been that of the machine, an image drawn from the mechanistic certainty of Newtonian physics, that has exerted such enormous influence upon science, technology, and general culture for over two centuries. This image has emphasized stability, order, uniformity, and equilibrium. Because it can be applied to any closed system with linear relationships, it has been useful in mirroring an industrial society based on heavy inputs of energy, capital, and labor.

The obvious danger of this image, however, is that people who use it to grasp reality will tend to think of themselves as efficiently functioning but isolated parts of some mechanized whole. There will be a corresponding de-emphasis in their lives of the social aspects of the human, as well as a narcotic blunting of moral and spiritual sensitivity. The fact that this has not happened to any large extent is due to a most unusual phenomenon: the late-twentieth century has suddenly produced a world of high technology characterized by accelerated social change, where innovation and imagination are the critical resources. Physics has introduced us to a subatomic world so volatile and apparently chaotic that almost nothing is predictable. We thus tend to have in our corporate psyche far more instability and disequilibrium than in our recent past. We no longer like to think of our society as a closed system that operates like a machine, but rather as an open system, like the biological species that have recently come to interest us so much. Such open systems are continually exchanging energy with their environment and are characterized by change, disorder, and process. We find little difficulty in applying to our lives the concept of evolution from biology and that of relativity from physics. This is why we have ceased describing ourselves in mechanistic terms and are searching today for some new symbol and image.

This search has been greatly if not decisively influenced by the phenomenon we have come to call "information." A new kind of machine has been created to deal with this phenomenon, i.e., the computer, and a new branch of science has evolved, cybernetics, whose object is precisely to study its control. Norbert Wiener named this science in his 1948 book *Cybernetics*, creating the term from the Greek word for "steersman" or "governor," by which he meant, as his subtitle suggested, "control and communication in the animal and the machine."[18] Information, said Wiener, can be considered to be a thing in itself, like matter, a fundamental building block of reality. The communication scientists who followed him have, over the last forty years, made considerable effort to apply this insight to various communications "systems," such as the human body and brain, the social and political order, civilization in general, and even to the universe.[19]

Perhaps the most startling discovery of an information process built into organic life has been the genetic code. In the language of cybernetics, biological organisms are examples of self-regulating "systems," requiring no direct internal control by any human consciousness. A "system" in this sense is any group or set of elements interacting according to some unified pattern. The "information" in such systems is the patterned data itself, which can be communicated from one entity to another within the system, prescinding from whether or not the data is consciously known. "Information" is thus a concept that can be verified analogically in all living cells and organisms, in nervous systems, in all human communication, and also in the artificial communication of computers. In the case of biological reproduction, genetic information is imprinted in DNA molecules, to be transmitted indefinitely through heredity as well as through altered-by-chance mutations.

The functioning of these genetic codes is now providing us with a model for the whole evolutionary process. The fact that in the biological world generations communicate with generations in the molecular language of DNA gives us a new perspective on entropy, for example. Since we know that all life manifests itself as a countercurrent to entropy, genetic information can also be seen as counterentropic, establishing order and ever-increasing complexity in a universe doomed to increasing divergence and random disorder. "Just as the amount of information in a system is a measure of its degree of organization," says Wiener, "so the entropy of a system is a measure of its degree of disorganization; and the one is simply the negative of the other."[20] Positive information and the reduction of uncertainty are thus all negatives of entropy. In another context Wiener says that "certain organisms, such as man, tend for a time to maintain and often to increase the level of their organization, as a local enclave in the general stream of increasing entropy, of increasing chaos and dedifferentiation."[21]

By analogy with living beings, therefore, all systems—in particular, complex social institutions—are information-driven and information-producing. The more information generated, the more coherent the system and the greater the energy available to it for the achievement of its goals. Indeed, society itself must now be considered an information system, in effect a suprasystem, a complex maze of interrelated subsystems among human persons, one more interiorized than the other. In *The World as a Total System*, social scientist Kenneth Boulding sees this phenomenon as a hierarchy of complexity, where the content and meaning of messages and value systems, as well as the symbolism of art, music, and poetry, are transferred as information for subsequent generations through various forms of education. Rather than looking at the world as a mosaic of national political systems, he says, we should rather think of it as a dense web of communications channels, constituting an energy force pushing the planet toward a single world culture.[22]

Hence in this era of information systems the metaphor of the machine obeying "laws" is being replaced by that of the biological organism in dynamic evolution. That is to say, the astonishing storage capacity of the DNA molecule is now being duplicated by information storage at the human level. "And once you begin that," says Harvard biologist Edward O. Wilson, author of *Sociobiology*, "the potential becomes almost unlimited. And that's essentially what the information age consists of— the stepwise improvement in information gathering, storage, retrieval and transfer. When you put it all together, you have a truly impressive super-organism."[23] This superorganism is clearly growing socially as well as conceptually. In 1900 only 13 percent of American workers made their living primarily by handling information; by 1960 the estimate was 42 percent; by 1980, 51.3 percent.[24] We may well wonder what the per-centage will be in the year 2000.

It is at this point that we experience in a most acute way what Hans Jonas has called "the imperative of responsibility." Jonas is "in search of an ethics for the technological age" in order to "ease the great burden of freedom in an information society." In the human person nature has "left herself an unsure substitute for the shattered sureness of her self-regulation."[25] For our human "system" appears to us now not unlike those open systems discovered on the subatomic level by quantum physics, fueled by a constant exchange of energy and matter with their environ-ment, where information and innovation are critical elements. Totally unlike the machine, the human system is clearly dominated by nonlinear behavior in which small inputs can trigger massive consequences. While the future must indeed be seen as *our* future, as an activation of human energy now available to us, such a future cannot be conceived as one without surprise, or as no more than a crass extrapolation from our past and present. For the human system has now been opened by the con-sciousness of freedom, and it can never again be thought of as closed.

But how, in such an open system, shall we go about making those responsible political decisions that determine how to manage these dynamisms of our "hominised" world? Jonas takes it as axiomatic that "responsibility is a correlate of power and must be commensurate with the latter's scope and that of its exercise." He continues: "What we must avoid at all cost is determined by what we must preserve at all cost, and this in turn is predicated on the 'image of man' we entertain . . . an understanding of man's duties toward himself, his distant posterity, and the plenitude of terrestrial life under his dominion."[26] Such ethical sen-sitivity on a planetary scale was underscored earlier by Niebuhr:

When we approach man's existence as self-administrative with the aid of the idea of responsibility, we are caught up in the same movement toward the

universal in which the other approaches to ethics, that is, teleology and de-
ontology, find themselves involved. . . . And . . . we find ourselves led to the
notion of universal responsibility, that is, of a life of responses to actions
which is always qualified by our interpretation of these actions as taking place
in a *universe,* and by the further understanding that there will be a response to
our actions by representatives of universal community. . . .[27]

Here, then, is where from a religious point of view a meshing takes
place between prudential human decision and God's providential design.
For the task of prudence in human governance is to order action toward
an end, in this case the larger common good of the community. God's
governance, so the tradition has always held, involves itself in this human
action "with gentleness," i.e., in a manner that corresponds to the particular mode of human activity demanded at any particular time. Both
Augustine and Aquinas, as well as biblical authors before them, developed at length this graciousness of divine influence upon human
decision: God moves humans from within, assisting them to choose freely
what will promote the good of the species in its historical movement
through time.[28] Because this gentleness of divine governance is a reflection of God's love, its human counterpart in prudential decision must
also participate in that unitive energy. On the societal level this meshing
will be reflected in human communities built through consensus and not
through coercion or fear.

Now we have seen that the cybernetic character of our culture means
precisely that our enterprise as a whole is concerned with control. As a
species we want to control not only mechanisms and structures but also
communication, which is the necessary mediator of control. But for what
purpose? In what direction is the "steersman" steering? What objectives
does the "governor" have? The answer to each of these questions will
depend upon how one thinks about the "input" and "output" of information. It is these two phenomena that hold the key to the question of
how we are to search today for the common good, and where we must
seek to mesh responsible human decision with God's providential design.

Let us consider the process of input first. Here the cybernetic concept
of "feedback" is crucial, an idea popularized originally by Wiener in *Cybernetics.* By "feedback" he meant channeling back into control centers a
flow of information concerning the present state of any system. Feedback
will thus operate analogically in computers, living cells, nervous systems,
and intelligent human communication, as well as in the societal macro-

system and its subsystems. In each case feedback will consist of information about any discrepancy between the present state of affairs and the state of affairs the system seeks to bring about. The feedback process thereby enables future operations of the system to be guided and corrected in terms of its present performance. Any system, from thermostats to persons to society, must thus employ feedback in order flexibly to pursue its goals.

The political issue, therefore, in a society conceived as superorganism is how we envision our society's goal: How organic do we want our society to become in future decades? For control of the human system is now clearly collective, open, and free, with machines acting simply as society's muscles, performing tasks without fatigue and on a superhuman scale. Increased socialization on a planetary scale is thus inevitable. But in what direction will such socialization move? What will be the role and importance of the individual in this planetary maturation? Will our reliance upon technology foster a technologism that blunts our psychological, moral, and spiritual sensibilities?

This relationship between individual autonomy and organic community growth has its parallel on the international scene. While nationalism was the dominant political movement, people found themselves bound together in unities which did not in fact tend to injure their loyalties to smaller subgroups like family and religion. In the future, however, as nations begin steadily to surrender more and more of their autonomy to a larger political society, will this movement toward global unification tend to multiply what Boulding calls "threat systems"? And if such threat systems do in fact multiply, will not fear and coercion become dominant on a planetary scale?[29]

In this context feedback has to be seen as an essential element in the elaboration of prudential moral decision in the political sphere. For any practical moral code depends not only upon ends to be achieved but upon evidence of what is actually happening in concrete human experience when a particular course of action is followed. All social morality, in other words, is a problem-solving process through feedback of information about the results of decisions that are made to achieve certain community values. For their part, these "values" do not really present themselves to us as "things," as the English language seems to imply, but rather as processes of evaluation and reevaluation of what we believe to be socially good. Behavior on the societal level is thus not linear; our larger systems contain subsystems, with everything connected to everything else and with all in constant flux. What feedback does is to reinforce certain fluctuations until one or another subsystem becomes dominant, thereby achieving temporary equilibrium on the social scene.[30]

What we are coming to realize, however, is that the lifetime of an individual is not long enough any more to test out the adequacy of a given line of conduct. Humankind as a species will achieve true moral maturity (and not endlessly repeat the same errors and mistakes) only if we can develop an adequate species memory bank, a center for the analysis of information where long-range consequences of conduct can be observed and evaluated over many lifetimes, and then handed down to posterity as a common moral code accepted by the community. But there is only one way to enlarge this species memory bank: through feedback. Without it, what is more than likely to arise in the course of time are human evaluation structures that are pathological, that move society toward situations destructive of human personality and freedom. For the same evolutionary process that produced the complexity of heightened human consciousness is now producing complexity in that evaluation process that determines political choice. The judgment of Kenneth Boulding is much to the point here:

> The greatest cause for pessimism at the moment is the apparent stability of the set of valuations that leads into violence, national defense, and the eventual destruction of the human race in historic time by nuclear war. The destruction of the human race by the present system of valuation would certainly indicate that it does not have much survival value, but that reflection is not particularly cheering. It is precisely the observation, however, of the evolutionary process in human valuations and the fact that these valuations do change—and often away from the pathological modes that do not lead to survival—that indicates that there is at least a reasonable hope that human evaluations will change toward a survival pattern and that this will happen in the world as a total system.[31]

If the concept of feedback is crucial for prudential political decisions governing the input of information, the concept of power is crucial in governing its output. "Knowledge is power," said Francis Bacon, by which in his time he envisioned the scientific control of nature. But what is at stake in our present age is the control of society and its future, and power now is information. Just as land and heavy industry were power in the past, and all societies eventually passed laws to control the use of both, so today political responsibility must focus on controlling the information society processes by setting technological goals that are relatively modest. Such political caution is essential precisely in order to avoid that excessive use of power that inevitably takes place when totalitarian states ally themselves with technological expertise. If such cautious control is not to become mindless bureaucratic meddling, however, it must be based on norms derived from government's duty to promote the common good. It is thus not simply a question of negatively restraining the use of power, but of taking steps positively to create an environment in which science and technology are accountable to larger community needs.

Science itself will not be of much help here, because progress in all its fields is in principle unending, rooted deep in the dynamics of human cognition. Both this progress and these dynamisms are ambivalent, however, capable of damaging as well as fostering the human, and demanding some prudential control from the outside. The danger is that those exercising such control will have no adequate vision of the common good, but simply have functionalist concerns, like raising the gross national product by whatever means computers and their information can provide. This contrast between the narrow technocrat and the cultural idealist comes through in a scene from John LeCarré's *The Spy Who Came in from the Cold*. The Communist agent Fiedler wants to find out from the captured English agent Leamas what philosophy motivates English agents in their fight against Communism.

> "What do you mean, a philosophy?" Leamas replied. "We're not Marxists, we're nothing. Just people."
>
> "Are you Christians then?"
>
> "Not many, I shouldn't think. I don't know many."
>
> "What makes them do it, then?" Fiedler persisted. "They must have a philosophy."
>
> "Why must they? Perhaps they don't know; don't even care. Not everyone has a philosophy," Leamas answered, a little helplessly.
>
> "Then tell me what is your philosophy?"
>
> "Oh, for Christ's sake," Leamas snapped, and they walked on in silence for a while. . . .

In this scene Leamas represents the true spirit of technologism. His loyalty is simply to the job at hand, to good workmanship. Almost completely nonreflective, he finds satisfaction in immediate experience, with no vision at all of any large community good. He and the ideological Fiedler are a source of deep puzzlement and frustration to each other.

The irony, of course, is that neither would hesitate to use force to achieve his ends—Leamas because he seldom relies on intelligence, Fiedler because all totalitarian ideologies tend to maximize rather than to restrain power. Neither one of them would be capable of exercising the responsibility that minimizes force. "Power is the greatest crime," said William Faulkner, "mitigated only by responsibility." He echoed here Lord Action's famous aphorism, "Power tends to corrupt, and absolute power corrupts absolutely." William Fulbright's 1966 book on America, *The Arrogance of Power*, was one long reflection on that mindless irresponsibility by which force so easily takes the place of reason in the exercise of government power.[32]

If in an information society power resides in those who control information, then information can be used either to persuade or to coerce. It clearly can be wielded as a bludgeon, as a physical force that bypasses the freedom of persons, interferes in their private spheres without their consent, and reduces them to parts of the socio-technological machine. But those who control information can also use this storage bank of knowledge to expand the freedom and community of persons, because they believe such expansion to be both desirable and possible, whether in the realm of social morality, public order, or cultural endeavor. Whenever this takes place, there will also be a major effort to minimize the value of coercion and radically to narrow the field in which force can be legitimately employed.[33] In either case, however, the mechanisms of social engineering can never be morally neutral.

To some extent social engineering of this type is inevitable in our modern world, and illustrates well the remark of C. S. Lewis that all human power is in fact the power of some people over other people. The major ethical questions consequently become the following: Who shall own information? Who shall distribute it? To whom and on what terms? Shall there be the information rich and the information poor, classes of people who own and control information and classes of people who do not? Would not such a society be even more hostile to democratic values than one in which classes of people were divided into the commodity rich and the commodity poor?[34] Daniel Bell, for one, is clearly in favor of such a society. He envisions the inevitable growth of small groups of "knowledge elites," who produce and codify the information that makes the total system work. These elites, he believes, will be the true directors of future social change by instilling a greater and greater measure of rationality into the human enterprise.[35]

But here we must ask: At what price? Will those excluded from these elites begin to make life uncomfortable for those on the inside? Will their desperation be translated into violence, crime, and terrorism? If the future is to be built on finely tuned technologies of information control, then more and more coercion may be needed to protect the few against the violence of the many. One observer had drawn a startling analogy:

> Universal literacy, which began to spread in the United States and Britain in the second half of the nineteenth century, proved to be a great equalizer.... Instead of information being held in the relatively few hands of those who could read ... it was much more freely available. So dramatic are the changes that computers have brought to information handling that the inequalities of societies before universal literacy appear to be duplicated. Individual citizens compete unequally with private corporations and government agencies for electronically stored information. Their plight will be analogous to that of the illiterate working people of the early nineteenth century.[36]

—— Conclusion ——

My argument in these pages has been that political responsibility in our present age must be seen in the context of an information society that is both of human making and the result of God's providential design. The evolutionary system of Pierre Teilhard de Chardin characterizes that design as a divine programming by which the evolutionary process moves from nonlife to life to human life, and in which a higher degree of consciousness always corresponds experimentally to a more complex organic structure. This scientific knowledge of human origins and development, Teilhard believed, could provide a basis for confidence, even on the part of the nonreligious person, that the human enterprise has some hope of a successful outcome in the midst of entropic matter. Humankind is now in desperate need of such assurance, because the self-reflection by which these origins and development are known also reveals a human freedom responsible for deciding in the future how these dynamisms of life are to be oriented on planet earth.

There is thus at present a species anxiety pressuring humankind to make myriad prudential decisions in the public sphere in function of this new awareness of responsibility. At the same time, men and women have begun to abandon the image of the machine in their self-understanding and to replace it with the image of a biological organism. This has in large part been due to the discovery of the astonishing storage capacity of the DNA molecule, as well as to the realization that this phenomenon is being duplicated by a similar type of information storage at the human conscious level. This new capacity to store information of all types has been slowly transforming humanity into a cybernetic society, i.e. one preoccupied with the problem of controlling such information. Cybernetics is the science of such control, and its fundamental insight has been the closeness in which all levels of reality, including especially the human level, are tied together into one huge information system, one superorganism, with subsystems and lesser organisms linked together by common all-embracing laws, realized analogically in different ways at different levels of being.

In *The Control Revolution* James R. Beniger argues that all living systems must process matter and energy to maintain themselves counter to entropy. "Because control is necessary for such processing, and information . . . is necessary for control, both information processing and communication, insofar as they distinguish living systems from the inorganic universe, might be said to define life itself." By "control" Beniger means "purposive influence toward a predetermined goal," for which the feedback of information, continually comparing current states to future objectives, is essential. A society's ability to maintain control at all levels, from its interpersonal to its international relations, will thus be directly proportioned to its information technologies. The "control revolution," therefore, consists of all those rapid changes in the technologies and the economic arrangements by which information is collected, stored, processed, and communicated, and through which society influences human behavior. In Beniger's eyes, "the Control Revolution already appears to be as important to the history of this century as the Industrial Revolution was to the last."[37]

There is a negative religious assessment of this propensity for control in John Updike's novel *Roger's Version*. One of his characters, Dale Kohler, is a fundamentalist studying computer science. At one point he gazes at the patterns on a cathode-ray tube, hoping to find the fingerprints of God. Updike presents him almost as a caricature, utterly confident in his technological pursuit of scientific certainty about God. At one point Dale says to Roger: "What I'm coming to talk to you about is God as a *fact*, a fact about to burst upon us, right up out of nature." We've been "scraping away at physical reality all these centuries, and now the layer of the little left we don't understand is so fine God's face is staring right out at us." For Updike, on the other hand, as well as for Roger in the novel, the physical universe is utterly inhospitable to all our "anthropic" longings, and we have no recourse but to make our commitment to God in some other world. In another context Updike quotes his one-time spiritual mentor, Karl Barth: "You do not speak of God by speaking about man in a loud voice." For Roger, as for Updike himself, it would be unthinkable for God to have left vulgar fingerprints on His handiwork for all to see, much less to allow Himself to be intellectually trapped. But neither author nor character has very much to say to the millions who now register the full impact of scientific materialism, and who in desperation seek somewhere to turn for solace.

As much as Updike and Barth, Teilhard would have put his emphasis on an act of faith. But Teilhard's faith would have a human as well as a divine focus. Long before we became a "cybernetic society" he saw humanity as a great "thinking envelope" covering the surface of the earth, a noosphere, a system of human consciousness—in effect, an information system. And long before Updike, he located the contemporary crisis of that consciousness in a loss of nerve. Growing technological control, symbolized by the computer, appears to be either an invitation to self-destruction or a headlong return to the regimentation of the anthill. In this struggle between individual and collectivity, Teilhard wrote, there is no tangible evidence to produce on the side either of optimism or of pessimism. "Only, in support of hope, there are rational invitations to an act of faith."[38] The future of our cybernetic society is thus by definition open and indeterminate, characterized by process and change. The burden of responsibility in the public sphere is precisely the fact that human freedom can have no guarantees that its power over the total human system will not be exercised for ill.

It has been said that the essence of the technological mind is largely a refusal to believe on the basis of hope. Such belief will therefore always remain fragile and insecure. There will always be the suspicion that the values of individual persons, their desire for community, interpersonal creativity, and the preservation of the world of nature can no longer be fostered after so many centuries of growth. Here is where we must locate today the burden of political responsibility and power. For we live in a maximum-risk situation. On the one hand, the responsible use of freedom must focus on this new human capacity to control all governance decisions. On the other hand, from a religious point of view, relating such prudent decision-making to God's providential design must finally be the work of God's governance, not any human achievement. For power, as Karl Rahner has said, is something to be gradually modified and absorbed by love, like concupiscence and all its consequences. "Never did the might of the mighty bring them solely and clearly what they *planned*. The leader was always the follower as well, and his mightiest and best-planned deed was at the same time the most unforeseen. . . . He who is wise and loving knows this well."[39]

This is why the religious tradition has always insisted that there is divine decision-making in regard to the human as well as divine design in regard to the world of matter. Human dominion over the earth through science and technology, in other words, cannot be irrelevant to God's plan for the species. This is not to say that these human undertakings are themselves salvific or that they directly contribute to the kingdom of God. Nor is it to say that they can ever escape frustration and even subversion from the deeds of evil persons and the well-intentioned actions of good persons. It is simply to assert that they are human, and as such objects of a divine providential design whose source is love. This divine initiative proceeding from love, far from hurting the delicate functioning of human freedom, necessarily fosters the growth of human personality and, gradually in the course of time, the interrelationships of human community. But this meshing is as delicate as gossamer. It cannot be reduced to a mere intellectual problem. Ultimately it is an object not of probing curiosity but of reverence and adoration.

—— NOTES ——

1. Aquinas elaborates his teaching on divine providence by analogy to the virtue of prudence: *De veritate* q. 5, a. 1–2; *Summa Theologica* 1, q. 22, a. 103; 1–2, 57–58; 2–2, q. 47–51.

2. Robert Jay Lifton, *The Future of Immortality* (New York: Basic Books, 1987); Alvin Toffler, *Future Shock* (New York: Random House, 1970).

3. C. E. Black, *The Dynamics of Modernization* (New York: Harper Torchbook, 1967), 4; George Thompson, *The Foreseeable Future* (Cambridge: Cambridge Univ. Press, 1960), 1.

4. Erik H. Erikson, "Memorandum on Youth," in *Toward the Year 2000, Daedalus* 96 (1967): 864.

5. Lifton, *The Future of Immortality*, 25.

6. Jacques Monod, *Chance and Necessity* (New York: Knopf, 1971), 172–73.

7. Pierre Teilhard de Chardin, *The Phenomenon of Man* (New York: Harper & Row, 1965), 228–29, 231.

8. Ibid., 275–76.

9. These ideas are developed in many essays, e.g., *The Future of Man* (New York: Harper & Row, 1964), 47–52, 87–89, 103–23; *Science and Christ* (New York: Harper & Row, 1968), 92–97, 192–96; *Activation of Energy* (New York: Harcourt Brace Jovanovich, 1971), 329–37; *Man's Place in Nature* (New York: Harper & Row, 1966), 17–36.

10. *The Future of Man*, 199.

11. *The Phenomenon of Man*, 223, 233.

12. *The Future of Man*, 294.

13. Ibid., 275–76.

14. *Activation of Energy*, 73–74.

15. *The Phenomenon of Man*, 262. A more thorough development of this idea will be found in my *Teilhard de Chardin and the Mystery of Christ* (New York: Harper & Row, 1966), 46–55.

16. Pierre Teilhard de Chardin, *Human Energy* (New York: Harcourt Brace Jovanovich, 1970), 124.

17. H. Richard Niebuhr, *The Responsible Self* (New York: Harper & Row, 1963), 149–60.

18. Norbert Wiener, *Cybernetics*, 2nd ed. (New York: John Wiley, 1961).

19. See, e.g., Ilya Prigogine and Isabelle Stengers, *Order Out of Chaos* (New York: Bantam Books, 1984), esp. 177–209.

20. Wiener, *Cybernetics*, 11. See Robert Wright, *Three Scientists and Their Gods: Looking for Meaning in an Age of Information* (New York: Times Books, 1988), 83–110, 195–211. See also R. Wayne Kraft, *Symbols, Systems, Science and Survival* (New York: Vantage, 1975).

21. Norbert Wiener, *The Human Use of Human Beings* (New York: Doubleday Anchor Books, 1954), 95.

22. Kenneth E. Boulding, *The World as a Total System* (Beverly Hills: Sage Publications, 1985). On Boulding see the treatment by Wright, *Three Scientists*, 213–96.

23. Quoted from Wright, *Three Scientists*, 187–88.

24. Ibid., 263. See Daniel Bell, "The Social Framework of the Information Society," in *The Microelectronics Revolution*, ed. Tom Forester (Cambridge: MIT, 1981), 500–49.

25. Hans Jonas, *The Imperative of Responsibility: In Search of an Ethics for the Technological Age* (Chicago: Univ. of Chicago Press, 1984), 138.

26. Ibid., x.

27. Niebuhr, *The Responsible Self*, 87.

28. The First Vatican Council summarized this tradition in its classic formula, "by His providence God watches over and governs all the things that He made, reaching from end to end with might and disposing all things with gentleness (see Wis. 8:1). For 'all things are naked and open to His eyes' (Heb. 4:13), even those things that are going to occur by the free action of creatures" (DS 1784).

29. Boulding, *The World,* 28–30, 83–87.

30. See Prigogine and Stengers, *Order,* 167–76. The authors call this phenomenon a "singular moment" or a "bifurcation point."

31. Boulding, *The World,* 275. I am indebted to W. Norris Clarke, S.J., for the insight regarding the use of an information memory bank for moral decision-making in a cybernetic society.

32. See Karl Rahner, "The Theology of Power," in *Theological Investigations* 4 (Baltimore: Helicon, 1966), 391–409.

33. What Boulding calls "threat systems" can obviously be justified to some extent in any society. Law is often couched in terms of threat, especially criminal law. Most people pay taxes, e.g., because of threats if they refuse.

34. See the perceptive article by Victor Ferkiss, "Technology and the Future: Ethical Problems of the Decades Ahead," in *New Ethics for the Computer Age?* (Washington, D.C.: Brookings Institution, 1986), 41–53.

35. Bell, "Social Framework," 442–43.

36. Ian Reinecke, *Electronic Illusions* (New York: Penguin Books, 1984), 210–11; quoted by Ferkiss, "Technology," 45.

37. James R. Beniger, *The Control Revolution: Technological and Economic Origins of the Information Society* (Cambridge: Harvard Univ. Press, 1986), 7–10, vi.

38. *The Phenomenon of Man,* 233.

39. Rahner, "The Theology of Power," 406–7.

AFTERWORD AND RETROSPECTIVE

The Life and Writings of
Christopher F. Mooney, S.J.

────────────── ❖ ──────────────

Christopher Mooney, in his personality and in his writings, was clearly a man of great expectation, a theologian of great hope. As a colleague said of him after his death, Mooney sometimes had the sense that his strong optimism, his belief that reconciliation is woven into the order of things, was unwavering to a fault. With humor directed at himself, Mooney once recounted the story of a friend of his who felt obliged to tell him, "Remember Chris, behind every silver lining is a dark cloud." But his writings tell a deeper story, and those who knew him confirm it. Deep within Christopher Mooney's experience of the world was a paradoxical sense of the surge of life along with the inevitability of death, the movement in creation toward harmony but the wrenching conflicts within human social endeavors, the profound human need to sustain the drive of love toward immortality yet the pull of time toward diffusion and loss. His hope was forged out of this experience, and his expectation soared through it. With Gerard Manley Hopkins he could acknowledge both that "Sorrow's springs are the same," and that "for all this, nature is never spent; there lives the dearest freshness deep down things."[1]

Trained in classics, in European and American history, in philosophy and theology, and finally in law, Christopher Mooney formulated and sustained relentless questions about the religious meaning of seemingly secular life and reality.[2] Throughout his years of study (which did not end with the undertaking of professional responsibilities as a scholar and an educator), the questions did not change significantly, but they drew his attention to different spheres of human life and activity. The focus of this volume attests to Mooney's final (though longstanding) concern with what the sciences explore, while his earlier work moves from the more traditional terrain of theology to the relation of religion and law in

American society. In all of this, however, not only consistent questions but emerging normative commitments appear, so that what might in other hands be disparate investigations constitute in Christopher Mooney's work a recognizable and coherent whole.

It was Mooney who provided the first serious analysis of the writings of Teilhard de Chardin. His earliest book, *Teilhard de Chardin and the Mystery of Christ*, built upon the doctoral dissertation he had written for the Catholic University of Paris. Despite the suspicion that surrounded Teilhard's work at the time, Mooney discovered in it the brilliant and original insights that the rest of the intellectual world would later come to appreciate. And in Teilhard's thought, Mooney found a deep resonance with his own already forming convictions about the presence of God in the world. Teilhard wrote, "Nothing is profane to those who know how to see,"[3] and Christopher Mooney understood what he meant.

Teilhard's work was driven by his perception of the disjointedness between the sphere of the sacred and the sphere of the secular, particularly insofar as the latter was produced by modern science. Here began Mooney's lifelong scholarly interest in the dialogue between science and religion. Here, too, from the vantage point of Teilhard's theories, Mooney was able to find and to develop an innovative Christology, the data for which was drawn not only from the Christian Scriptures but from our knowledge of the cosmos and of the history of humanity in the world. Unlike others who interpreted Teilhard's theology as insensitive to suffering and to evil, Mooney took seriously the effort here to understand the "pain" of cosmic development and human survival in the light of salvation. No Christology would be adequate, in Teilhard's view, that did not address the threefold evil to be found in growth, in disorder and failure, and in the ultimate evil of death. The key is in the cross, which transforms the power of diminishment and extinction within the greater power of life—the cross in relation to which our task "is not to swoon in its shadow but to climb in its light."[4]

In the decade after the publication of *Teilhard de Chardin and the Mystery of Christ*, Mooney's energies were focused primarily in educational leadership. From 1965 to 1969 he served as chair of the Theology Department at Fordham University, and in 1969 became president of Woodstock College. This was a time of creative ferment in the Roman Catholic Church as well as startling changes in the social and political climate of the United States. In the aftermath of Vatican Council II, Catholic theologian and pastoral consciousness opened to markedly new concerns for the church's role in the world. Arguably for the first time, theological method took seriously the historical contexts of religious thought, and a new sense of urgency characterized a turn to the demands of social justice. Ecumenical overtures were begun with heretofore unheard of possibilities, and the role of theology in the American university took a quantum leap in its significance for Catholic higher education. At the heart of this ferment, Mooney was a national leader, as the conferences he organized and collections of essays he edited attest. Both inwardness and outwardness, the sacred and the secular, continued to preoccupy him in his work and in his writing; and the specific context of real peoples' lives and yearnings both motivated and shaped his developing thought.

In 1974 Woodstock College was closed by the Jesuit Order. This policy decision was in a profound way devastating to Mooney. It was a mistake, from his point of view, to eliminate the "oldest and best of the Jesuit theological schools in America."[5] He found himself struggling with judgments such as F. Scott Fitzgerald's, "Life is essentially a cheat, and its conditions are those of defeat."[6] Yet Mooney's own zest for life led him to press forward, first in the writing of *Man Without Tears* and then in the study of law. He described the chapters in *Man Without Tears* as "soundings for a Christian anthropology," but the book as a whole was more than this. It was his effort to make sense of central experiences in human life that constitute critical challenges to hope and to faith—experiences of conflict, of failure, of aging, of death. He wanted to inquire to what extent the second half of Fitzgerald's statement could be true without warranting the cynical and harsh premise of the first.

The themes struck in *Man Without Tears* are extensions of the ones identified in his first book, and they are to appear again and again throughout each of his works thereafter. Here the primary task of theology is construed as the illumination of the element of mystery, of transcendence, in human life; but already there is emerging a concern for the role of theology in clarifying the requirements of justice in human relations. Clues for a theological anthropology are sighted in the unfinished character of human beings, a theoretical harbinger of Mooney's later considerations of the inevitability of the sort of conflict in human affairs that is not always simply evil. The twofold trajectories of loss and gain, entropy and life, appear here briefly in Mooney's treatment of death, but they fairly cry out for the fuller analysis that comes only in his later study of biological evolution. Identification of the tension, indeed struggle, between the individual and the collectivity presages the social analysis that becomes so clear in subsequent works on religion and society. Human failure is real ("we fail because *we* fail"), but final victory is possible, and it is on the side of life. Here in this small volume, perhaps as clear as anywhere, there is the quiet refrain:"The challenge of death is a challenge to what I am doing with my life,"[7] and the promise of life is an ultimate "absolute nearness to absolute mystery."[8]

It is not sufficient, of course, to distill themes from Christopher Mooney's writings. In fact, it does a kind of violence to his own careful insistence that the large questions of life and the radical stretches of hope are to be rendered intelligible only by exploring them in the detailed contexts of social experience and scientific investigation. We have here no "cheap grace," no conclusions that can be torn from the fabric of human life and the world without trivialization or distortion. It was this conviction that led Mooney to embark on the study of American law and society. From the weavings of theological traditions he turned to the intricacies of the Constitution and the historically situated patterns of its interpretation. In order to do this with all seriousness, Mooney went to law school in 1974.

In a one-year program at Yale Law School, Mooney got a taste for the issue of jurisprudence. It was enough to persuade him to complete a J.D. later at the University of Pennsylvania. He never envisioned practicing law (though he was admitted to the Pennsylvania Bar in 1978), but immersion in legal studies, both as a student and then as a teacher, was his characteristic route to an understanding of religion and society. Along the way he produced four volumes on the questions he encountered.

The first question that intrigued Mooney was the influence of religion on American public life and the response of American law to this influence. In *Religion and the American Dream* he addressed what he called the public consequences of the fact that freedom in the United States has been experienced historically as freedom under God as well as freedom under law. The religious dimension of the national experience is profound, and against all predictions, it continues to be a significant factor in American public life. It undergirds concerns for justice as well as the direction of the pursuit of happiness. The law, for its part, aims simultaneously to protect freedom of religion and to keep the two institutions of church and state separate while functioning together in a culture that affects and is affected by both of them. In this volume and in the later works, *Public Virtue* and *Boundaries Dimly Perceived*, Mooney pursues the nature of the interaction between law and religion through judicial decisions and traditions of interpretation forged from the challenges of specific cases.

Commenting on issues such as school prayer, Mooney underscores changes in the religious beliefs and loyalties of American citizens over the years. Americans as a group, he argues, are simply not the same people religiously in the latter half of the twentieth century that they were in 1789. Hence, the religion clauses of the First Amendment have become more important, not less (for in the past the meshing of the civil and the religious raised fewer legal problems). Power relations have shifted, in large part for the better, restricting religious institutions in their direct influence on the law but at the same time freeing them for a more critical and prophetic role in relation to the law. What is often at stake is no less than the formation of a national conscience.

The problem associated with corporate conscience became a second major question for Mooney in his effort to understand the relationship between religion and society. These problems are sharply focused in *Inequality and the American Conscience*, Mooney's analysis of the law as it has related to policies of affirmative action. The Bakke case here serves as a microcosm of value conflicts in American society. The issues are racial discrimination and the fairness of its remedies. The conflict is between two different understandings of what is fair, what is just, when the claims of the individual compete with claims of the common good. At the heart of the conflict, Mooney argues, is the meaning and application of the principle of equality. Central to the American self-understanding, equality has nonetheless been honored more consistently in theory than in spheres of practice in American life. Affirmative action has as its rationale the promotion of racial equality (and, of course, in other cases gender equality), but the value of equality conflicts not only with some construals of individual rights and merit; it is rendered vulnerable when the complex consequences of racial classification are thought to be more injurious than beneficial to minorities.

Mooney himself comes down in favor of affirmative action as an instrument to achieve racial equality, with the major warrant lodged in present requirements ordered to future justice rather than in compensatory justice for past wrongs. His purpose, however, is less to advocate this position than to point to the role and power of the law as well as its dependence on the community of conscience that generates it. In the Bakke case and others that have followed, the Supreme Court has managed some compromise on both the social justice issue and the individual rights issue—a compromise that Mooney believes will hold only so long as the national conscience itself is not fully formed on the underlying moral issues.

But if a key question is the dependence of law on a community of conscience, then the role of religion gains some specificity. It is not that only or even primarily religious arguments are to be used in the public forum (though they have their place there); it is simply that religious understandings have been and remain significant in this nation for shaping an understanding of equality. Religion and culture have influenced one another, and the law is not indifferent to either. In the context of this case, then, Mooney searches again for religious meaning in secular experience, especially in the experience of the law. It is through law, he argues, that a nation implements its value judgments of how people are to live together in society. The laws of a culture aim to perpetuate a way of life and to promote the values of that way; hence, while law is not coextensive with morality, it is inextricably tied to moral consensus of some degree. In the United States, moral consensus (or lack thereof) is frequently religious in origin.

To note a religious dimension or grounding for values is by no means to render moral values immune from salutary critique. Hence, Mooney is not among those who wring their hands at either religious or moral pluralism. There have always been conflicts over moral values in this nation, and they have been adjudicated (well or badly) both in the political arena and in the courts. For Christopher Mooney these conflicts can be necessary to the process of community, whether in a nation or a smaller structure within a nation. The loss of an easy national belief in self-evident truths and inalienable rights makes the pursuit of happiness and the achievement of justice more difficult; but it can also reveal the unfinished character of humanity and heighten the responsibility for discernment and compromise. The issue ought always to be how to measure and judge which of many possible changes can be supported both by social coherence and individual freedom. And here Mooney's theological convictions tilt him in the direction of moral imperatives for better understandings of social equality and more just structures to implement these understandings.

If human relationships and society offer rich data for dicerning the presence of the sacred in all of reality, nonetheless toward the end of his life Mooney was drawn away from issues of religion and law back to his early interests in religion and science. This time, as with his legal studies, he took up the study of science in careful and disciplined detail. In 1989, he did what only the rare contemporary theologian has done; he undertook to learn whatever he could of the developments in modern physics and biology. This present volume represents his achievement of access to a common language with scientists and his insights to the time of his death on the potential dialogue between science and religion. His plans to pursue these studies and to refine these insights were cut short by a sudden illness and an unexpected ending of his life. Just before his death he was able to say, "It is as if God is saying to me, 'Your work is done. Come home—fast.'"

Mooney's turn to science and religion was both new and continuous with his lifelong intellectual and spiritual pursuits. Like Teilhard, he was fascinated with the cosmic dimensions of reality, from the smallest, the nearly infinitely minute, to the grandest, the nearly infinitely vast, reaches of the universe. Scientists were discovering and theorizing in ways that left him in awe and with a fueled curiosity. The questions of energy and entropy pressed him further than any earlier speculations he had made; the questions of life intrigued him in ways he could not ignore. Issues of social evolution, of self-interest and the common good, of conflict, of hope and of love, resurfaced for him at the various levels of reality. There could be, he wrote, no easy answers to the perennial human questions of suffering and of death. If pain and conflict are the result of biological inevitability, what is acceptable to the cosmos remains a problem and a mystery for humans. If in the quiet existence of the rest of nature new forms of life arise peacefully from the demise of old forms, humans are in some sense a misfit with their environment. Restlessness and depression, anguish in the face of death, suggest absurdity if read simply in the context of the universe.

Faith and theology were not for Mooney simply a *deus ex machina* to provide meaning where there otherwise was none. But in dialogue with the scientists and the social theorists, religion has something to say. Immanence and transcendence, dependence and an unlimited future, other-centered love which is also a finding of oneself, pain that has a revelatory word—all of this could not be imposed on understandings of reality, but it could make sense with them. That was the "sense" which interested and grasped Christopher Mooney. That was the meaning he wanted to explore in an ongoing dialogue.

We have, finally, a significant body of work, incomplete as in Mooney's view any work must be. Theology, law, and science were for him all entry points for seeing, for discovering the clues of divine presence and the guidelines for human activity. The clues gave Christopher Mooney courage, and the guidelines yielded moral imperatives. The motivation and the fruit of the work and the life were, then, these three—faith, hope, and yes, love.

MARGARET A. FARLEY
Yale University Divinity School

—— NOTES ——

1. Gerard Manley Hopkins, *The Poems of Gerard Manley Hopkins*, ed. W. H. Gardner and N. H. MacKenzie, 4th ed. rev. (New York: Oxford Univ. Press, 1970), 89, 66.

2. Mooney did his undergraduate work in classics and philosophy (1950), and an M.A. in history (1955), at Loyola University, Chicago; an S.T.D. in theology at Catholic University of Paris (1964); an M.S.L. in law at Yale University (1975); and a J.D. at the University of Pennsylvania (1978).

3. Pierre Teilhard de Chardin, *The Divine Milieu* (New York: Harper & Row, 1960), 38.

4. Teilhard de Chardin, cited in Christopher F. Mooney, *Teilhard de Chardin and the Mystery of Christ* (New York: Harper & Row, 1966), 119.

5. Christopher F. Mooney, *Man Without Tears: Soundings for a Christian Anthropology* (New York: Harper & Row, 1975), 9.

6. Ibid.

7. Ibid., p. 117.

8. Ibid., p. 110.

Works of
Christopher F. Mooney, S.J.

—— Books ——

Teilhard de Chardin and the Mystery of Christ. London and New York: Collins and
   Harper and Row, 1966. Also in Doubleday Image Books Edition, 1968.
   Spanish translation: *Teilhard de Chardin y el misterio de Christo.* Salamanca:
      Ediciones Sigueme, 1967.
   French translation: *Teilhard de Chardin et le mystère du Christ.* Paris: Aubier,
      1968.
The Presence and Absence of God. New York: Fordham Univ. Press, 1969. (Ed.)
Prayer: The Problem of Dialogue with God. New York: Paulist Press, 1969. (Ed.)
The Making of Man: Essays in the Christian Spirit. New York: Paulist Press, 1971.
Man Without Tears: Soundings for a Christian Anthropology. New York: Harper and
   Row, 1975.
Religion and the American Dream: The Search for Freedom Under God. Philadelphia:
   Westminster Press, 1977.
Inequality and the American Conscience: Justice Through the Judicial System. New York:
   Paulist Press, 1982.
Public Virtue: Law and the Social Character of Religion. Notre Dame, Ind.: Univ. of
   Notre Dame Press, 1986.
Boundaries Dimly Perceived: Law, Religion, Education, and the Common Good. Notre
   Dame, Ind.: Univ. of Notre Dame Press, 1990.
Theology and Scientific Knowledge: Changing Models of God's Presence in the World.
   Notre Dame, Ind.: Univ. of Notre Dame Press, 1995.

—— Chapters in Edited Works: ——

"Teilhard de Chardin on Freedom and Risk in Evolution." In *Freedom and Man*,
   edited by John Courtney Murray. New York: P. J. Kenedy, 1965, 87–104.
"Woman in Contemporary Theology." In *Woman in Modern Life*, edited by
   William C. Bier. New York: Fordham Univ. Press, 1968, 21–32.

"Man and His Future." In *Projections: Shaping an American Theology,* edited by Thomas O'Meara and Donald Weisser. New York: Doubleday, 1970, 18–40.

"The Role of Theology in the Education of Undergraduates." In *Catholic Colleges and the Secular Mystique,* edited by Eugene E. Grollmes. St. Louis: B. Herder, 1970, 88–103.

"Christology and the Contemporary American Experience." In *Proceedings of the Catholic Theological Society of America* 26 (1971): 38–55.

"Response to Jürgen Moltmann." In *Hope and the Future of Man,* edited by Ewert Cousins. Philadelphia: Fortress Press, 1972, 105–9.

"Christianity and the Change in Human Consciousness." In *Teilhard de Chardin: In Quest of the Perfection of Man,* edited by Geraldine O. Browning. Rutherford, N.J.: Fairleigh Dickenson Univ. Press, 1973, 143–61.

"Death and Human Expectation." In *Philosophical Aspects of Thanatology,* edited by Austin H. Kutscher and Florence M. Hetzler. Vol. 2. New York: Arno Press, 1978, 173–89.

"The Claim of the Church to be Guardian of a Universal Natural and Moral Law." In *True and False Universality of Christianity* (Concilium, 135), edited by Claude Geffré and Jean-Pierre Jossua. New York: Seabury Press, 1980, 23–32.

"Freedom and Pluralism in American Religious Commitment." In *Who Do People Say I Am?* edited by Francis A. Eigo. Philadelphia: Villanova Univ. Press, 1980, 147–74.

"Pierre Teilhard de Chardin." In *A Handbook of Christian Theologians,* edited by Martin E. Marty and Dean Pearman. Enlarged 2nd edition. Nashville: Abingdon Press, 1984, 503–18.

"Teilhard: Evolution and Creation." In *Evolution and Creation,* edited by Ernan McMullin. Notre Dame, Ind.: Univ. of Notre Dame Press, 1985, 290–302.

"Law: A Vocation to Justice and Love." In *The Professions in Ethical Context,* edited by Francis A. Eigo. Philadelphia: Villanova Univ. Press, 1986, 59–95.

"Pierre Teilhard de Chardin." In *Encyclopedia of Religion,* edited by Mircea Eliade, et al. Vol. 14. New York: Macmillan, 1987. 366–68.

"The Accommodation of Religious Conscience." In *Religion and Politics,* edited by W. Lawson Taitte. Austin, Tex.: Univ. of Texas Press, 1989, 75–109.

"Religious Freedom and the American Revolution." In *1789: The French Revolution and the Church* (Concilium, 201), edited by Claude Geffré and Jean-Pierre Jossua. Edinburgh: T. & T. Clark, 1989, 9–16.

"Moral Pluralism and the Political Activity of Religious Groups." In *Public Faith,* edited by W. Clark Gilpin. St. Louis: CBP Press, 1990, 27–46.

"Church-State Relations in the United States." In *New Dictionary of Catholic Social Thought,* edited by Judith A. Dwyer. Collegeville, Minn.: Liturgical Press, 1994, 171–75.

——— Articles ———

"College Theology and Liberal Education." *Thought* 34 (1959): 325–46.

"Social Consciousness and the College Student." *Catholic Mind* 58 (1960): 128–36.

"Theology and the Catholic College." *Religious Education* 56 (1961): 218–23.

"Ignation Spirituality and Modern Theology." *Downside Review* 80 (1962): 333–54.

"Blondel and Teilhard de Chardin." *Thought* 37 (1962): 543–62.

"Paul's Vision of the Church in Ephesians." *Scripture* 15 (1963): 33–43. Reprinted in: *The Life of the Church*, edited by Patrick J. Burns. Baltimore: Newman, 1964, 61–78. Also reprinted in: *Contemporary New Testament Studies*, edited by M. R. Ryan. Collegeville, Minn.: Liturgical Press, 1965, 407–16.

"The Body of Christ in the Writings of Teilhard de Chardin." *Theological Studies* 25 (1964): 576–610.

"Anxiety and Faith in Teilhard de Chardin." *Thought* 39 (1964): 510–30.

"Teilhard de Chardin and the Christological Problem." *Harvard Theological Review* 58 (1965): 91–126.

"Teilhard de Chardin on Suffering and Death." *Journal of Religion and Health* 5 (1965): 429–40. Reprinted in: *The Mystery of Suffering and Death*, edited by Michael J. Taylor. New York: Alba House, 1973, 57–70.

"Risk in Teilhard de Chardin." *Christianity and Crisis* 25 (1965): 172–75. Reprinted in: *Catholic Mind* 64 (1966): 34–39.

"The Spiritual Life as History." *The Way* 6 (1966): 26–34.

"Response to Paul Lehmann's 'The Tri-unity of God.'" *Union Quarterly Review* 21 (1966): 213–16.

"A Theologian's View of the Secular City." *Sociological Analysis* 27 (1966): 43–45.

"A Fresh Look at Man." *Saturday Review* (Feb. 26, 1966): 21–24.

"Union Theological and Fordham: A New Ecumenical Enterprise." *The Month*, New series 36 (1966): 29–33.

"Optimism and Christian Hope." *Pax Romana Journal*, Special Number, 2 (1967): 23–24.

"Agents, Objects and Witnesses." *The Critic* 25 (1967): 88–90.

"Teilhard de Chardin and Modern Philosophy." *Social Research* 34 (1967): 67–85.

"Teilhard de Chardin and Christian Spirituality." *Thought* 42 (1967): 383–402. Reprinted in: *Dimensions of the Future*, edited by M. Kessler and B. Brown. Washington: Corpus Books, 1968, 1–22. Also reprinted in: *Process Theology*, edited by Ewert Cousins. New York: Paulist Press, 1971, 299–320.

"Teilhard's Approach to Christology." *Theology Digest* 25 (1967): 18–25.

"The Bishops Return to School." *Jubilee* 25 (1968): 35–37.

"Teilhard on Man's Search for God." *Continuum* 5 (1968): 643–54.

"Vatican II and the Future of Theology." *Cross Currents* 19 (1969): 426–40.

"Death and the Phenomenon of Life." *America* (April 12, 1975): 276–79.

"Moral Consensus and Law." *Thought* 51 (1976): 231–54.

"The Legacy of Pierre Teilhard de Chardin." *Fairfield Now* 4 (1981): 13–16.

"Survival: Teilhard and an Unlimited Future." *Chicago Studies* 22 (1983): 207–20.

"Public Morality and Law." *The Journal of Law and Religion* 1 (1983): 45–58.

"The Christian Meaning of Israel." *Viewpoints* 12 (1983): 6–7.

"Education's Prism." *Cross Currents* 38 (1989): 395–412.

"Cybernation, Responsibility and Providential Design." *Theological Studies* 51 (1990): 286–309. Reprinted in: *Teilhard Studies Number 24*, edited by Arthur Fabel. Chambersburg, Pa.: Anima Books, 1991, 1–27.

"Theology and Science: A New Commitment to Dialogue." *Theological Studies* 52 (1991): 289–329. Condensed and reprinted in: *Selecciones de Teologia* 32 (1993): 305–26.

"Individual, Community and Cultural Change." *Thought* 67 (1992): 21–30.

"Theology and the Heisenberg Uncertainty Principle," *The Heythrop Journal* 34 (1993): 247–73, 373–86.

"The Anthropic Principle in Cosmology and Theology." *Horizons* 21 (1994): 105–29.

Index of Names

Anselm of Canterbury, 192 n. 138
Aquinas, Thomas. *See* Thomas Aquinas
Arbib, M. A., 38 n. 20
Aristotle, 1, 22, 90, 113 n. 33
Aspect, Alain, 115 n. 41
Augustine, 12, 102, 157, 172, 193, 208
Avery, Oswald, 126
Ayala, Francisco, 178 n. 9, 179 nn. 15, 17

Bacon, Francis, 210
Barbour, Ian, 17, 26, 38 n. 16, 39 n. 20,
    39 nn. 22, 26; 40 nn. 28–29, 34,
    36–37; 43 nn. 54, 64; 50; 68 n. 13;
    113 n. 26; 116 n. 51; 117 nn. 60, 63;
    118 nn. 71, 76; 178 n. 11
Barrow, John, 43 n. 62, 53, 67 n. 2, 69 nn.
    14, 19
Barth, Karl, 13, 14, 215
Bartholomew, D. J., 116 n. 51, 189 n. 110
Beadle, George, 126
Beatty, John, 179 n. 18
Bell, Daniel, 212, 217 n. 24, 218 n. 35
Bell, John, 94–96, 114 n. 40, 115 nn. 41,
    44–45
Beniger, James, 214, 218 n. 37
Bernstein, Jeremy, 114 n. 37, 115 nn.
    40, 44
Bethell, Tom, 180 n. 25
Bickerton, Derek, 182 n. 42
Bishop, Jerry, 178 n. 11
Black, C. E., 194, 216 n. 3

Blondel, Maurice, 190 n. 126
Boff, Leonardo, 41 n. 38
Bohm, David, 91–92, 95–96, 98, 114 n.
    35–37, 115 n. 43
Bohr, Niels, 8, 75–76, 81, 84, 86–90,
    93–96, 103, 112 n. 19, 113 nn. 29, 30
Bonhoeffer, Dietrich, 118 n. 75
Born, Max, 77–78, 81, 86, 103, 112 n. 23
Boulding, Kenneth, 206, 210, 217 n. 22,
    218 nn. 29, 31, 33
Bowler, Peter, 180 n. 26, 181 n. 28
Bronowski, Jacob, 3, 37 n. 3
Brown, Michael, 182 n. 41
Buckley, Michael, 37 n. 1
Bultmann, Rudolf, 14

Carr, Anne, 41 n. 38
Carr, Bernard, 67 n. 2
Carter, Brandon, 46, 67 n. 2
Casti, John, 67 n. 2, 112 n. 17, 113 n. 26,
    114 n. 38, 116 n. 55
Clark, R. W., 111 n. 6
Clarke, W. Norris, 218 n. 31
Coleman, Sidney, 69 n. 13
Compton, Arthur, 74, 117 n. 60
Copernicus, 12, 20
Coveney, Peter, 115–16 n. 57
Coyne, George, 37 n. 1
Crick, Francis, 121, 126, 155, 177 n. 3, 186
    n. 86
Cronin, Helena, 183 n. 56

Index of Subjects